John Barrow

Cook's Voyages of Discovery

John Barrow

Cook's Voyages of Discovery

ISBN/EAN: 9783744773294

Printed in Europe, USA, Canada, Australia, Japan

Cover: Foto ©Andreas Hilbeck / pixelio.de

More available books at **www.hansebooks.com**

COOK'S VOYAGES.

COOK'S

VOYAGES OF DISCOVERY

EDITED BY

JOHN BARROW, ESQ., F.R.S., F.S.A.

EDINBURGH: ADAM AND CHARLES BLACK

MDCCCLXXI.

PREFACE.

THE Editor of this little book is desirous of availing himself of the opportunity of expressing to the Right Honourable the Lords Commissioners of the Admiralty his thanks for the kind and most ready permission granted to him to inspect the documents in office relating to Cook's Voyages, as well as his Correspondence, and to make any extracts therefrom which he might think desirable. By this liberality he is enabled to present to the world many interesting letters not hitherto published, and which will be found to be remarkable for their perspicuity. His thanks are also due to Mr. Nelson Houghton, Keeper of the Records, for the facilities kindly afforded to him.

The Editor having had occasion repeatedly to refer to Captain Cook's Log Books, cannot forbear a passing tribute of admiration at the beautiful manner in which they have been kept, in his own handwriting (a *fac-simile* of which is annexed), amidst the multifarious duties, anxiety, and toil inseparable upon voyages of discovery in unknown seas,—equalled, perhaps—but not surpassed—by those of Sir Edward Parry, also in the Records of the Admiralty.

In one of Cook's Log Books is a circular chart of the southern hemisphere (showing the ship's track), upheld by two figures, with the appropriate motto—

"Ipsa subibo humeris ; nec me labor ipse gravabit."

TO
CAPTAIN PENNY,
OF THE

MERCANTILE MARINE, THE CRADLE OF CAPTAIN COOK,

THIS VOLUME IS INSCRIBED,

IN

GRATEFUL REMEMBRANCE OF HIS

ZEALOUS SERVICES IN THE ARCTIC SEAS IN 1850-51,

WHEN COMMANDING H.M. BRIGS "LADY FRANKLIN" AND "SOPHIA,"

EMPLOYED ON THE SEARCH FOR "SIR JOHN FRANKLIN," "CROZIER," AND "FITZJAMES,"

AND THE LOST CREWS OF H.M. SHIPS "EREBUS" AND "TERROR;"

AND IN ADMIRATION OF HIM AS ONE OF THE BRAVEST

AND MOST SKILFUL NAVIGATORS

OF THE PRESENT AGE.

J. B.

17 Hanover Terrace, Regent's Park,
   28th June 1860.

Sunday 7 at 9 AM spoke a Brig after another from London bound this Vessel that no acco.t had been received that we were lost. *

July 17th Friday 12th. Winds at S. up Channel at 1/2 past 3 [PM] Peverell Point. At 6 AM pa[st] of 4 or 5 Miles, at 10 Dungen[ess] Noon we were abreast of [?] Saturday 13th At 3 o'Clock . Soon after I landed in order t[o]

Liverpool bound to Porto & some time
the granades . . . . We learnt from
ved in England from us & that Wagers
. . . .

sh Gale with which we run briskly
sed the Bell of Portland & at 7
Beachy head at the distance
t the distance of 2 Miles & at

Anchor'd in the Downs &
air to London

Jam^s Cook

Life of Captain James Cook,

Born 27th October 1728; died 14th February 1779.
Aged 51.

WHEN we consider the career of this great navigator, and observe how from the humblest origin he rose, with gradual but certain steps, to become the greatest discoverer of modern times, we are lost in admiration of that character which enabled him to accomplish such great results.

It is almost difficult for us who live in the present day to realize that to Cook we owe the discovery of that great colony on the eastern coast of Australia, named by him New South Wales, and that it is not much beyond the space of a single human life since he drew the attention of the world to the great capabilities of that fifth continent, and the adjacent islands of the South Seas.

It is remarkable to think also that at that very spot where he landed to enjoy the chase of the kangaroo now rises the great city of Sydney, with its 53,000 inhabitants. The narrative of every traveller who, at the sacrifice of those comforts which are held most dear, goes forth to make discoveries for the benefit of his fellow-men, must be interesting, but how much more must this be the case when these discoveries are, as in the case of Cook, sealed by the life of the discoverer himself.

LIFE—(BY CAPTAIN KING, OF "THE RESOLUTION").

Captain James Cook was born near Whitby, in Yorkshire, in the year 1727; and, at an early age, was put apprentice to a shopkeeper in a neighbouring village. His natural inclination not having been consulted on this occasion, he soon quitted the counter from disgust, and bound himself for nine years to the master of a vessel in the coal trade. At the breaking out of the war in 1755, he entered into the King's service on board the Eagle, at that time commanded by Captain Hamer, and afterward by Sir Hugh Palliser, who soon discovered his merit, ar introduced him on the quarter-deck. In the year 1758 we find him master of "The Northumberland," the flag-ship of Lord Colville, who had then the command of the squadron stationed on the coast of America. It was here, as I have often heard him say, that, during a hard winter, he first read Euclid, and applied himself to the study of mathematics and astronomy, without any other assistance than what a few books and his own industry afforded him. At the same time that he thus found means to cultivate and improve his mind, and to supply the deficiencies of an early education, he was engaged in most of the busy and active scenes of the war in America. At the siege of Quebec, Sir Charles Saunders committed to his charge the execution of services of the first importance in the naval department. He piloted the boats to the attack of Montmorency; conducted the embarkation to the Heights of Abraham; examined the passage,

Life of Captain James Cook.

and laid buoys for the security of the large ships in proceeding up the river. The courage and address with which he acquitted himself in these services, gained him the warm friendship of Sir Charles Saunders and Lord Colville, who continued to patronise him during the rest of their lives with the greatest zeal and affection. At the conclusion of the war he was appointed, through the recommendation of Lord Colville and Sir Hugh Palliser, to survey the Gulf of St. Lawrence and the coasts of Newfoundland. In this employment he continued till the year 1767, when he was fixed on by Sir Edward Hawke, to command an expedition to the South Seas; for the purpose of observing the transit of Venus, and prosecuting discoveries in that part of the globe.

From this period, as his services are too well known to require a recital here, so his reputation has proportionably advanced to a height too great to be affected by my panegyric. Indeed, he appears to have been most eminently and peculiarly qualified for this species of enterprise. The earliest habits of his life, the course of his services, and the constant application of his mind, all conspired to fit him for it, and gave him a degree of professional knowledge which can fall to the lot of very few. The constitution of his body was robust, inured to labour, and capable of undergoing the severest hardships. His stomach bore, without difficulty, the coarsest and most ungrateful food. Indeed, temperance in him was scarcely a virtue; so great was the indifference with which he submitted to every kind of self-denial. The qualities of his mind were of the same hardy, vigorous kind with those of his body. His understanding was strong and perspicacious; his judgment, in whatever related to the services he was engaged in, quick and sure. His designs were bold and manly; and both in the conception, and in the mode of execution, bore evident marks of a great original genius. His courage was cool and determined, and accompanied with an admirable presence of mind in the moment of danger. His manners were plain and unaffected. His temper might perhaps have been justly blamed as subject to hastiness and passion, had not these been disarmed by a disposition the most benevolent and humane.

Such were the outlines of Captain Cook's character; but its most distinguishing feature was that unremitting perseverance in the pursuit of his object, which was not only superior to the opposition of dangers and the pressure of hardships, but even exempt from the want of ordinary relaxation. During the long and tedious voyages in which he was engaged, his eagerness and activity were never in the least abated. No incidental temptation could detain him for a moment; even those intervals of recreation, which sometimes unavoidably occurred, and were looked for by us with a longing, that persons who have experienced the fatigues of service will readily excuse, were submitted to by him with a certain impatience, whenever they could not be employed in making further provision for the more effectual prosecution of his designs.

It is not necessary here to enumerate the instances in which these qualities were displayed, during the great and important enterprises in which he was engaged. I shall content myself with stating the result of those services, under the two principal heads to which they may be referred, those of geography and navigation, placing each in a separate and distinct point of view. Perhaps no science ever received greater additions from the labour of a single man than geography has done from those of

Captain Cook. In his first voyage to the South Seas, he discovered the Society Islands; determined the insularity of New Zealand; discovered the straits which separate the two islands, and are called after his name; and made a complete survey of both. He afterward explored the eastern coast of New Holland, hitherto unknown; an extent of twenty-seven degrees of latitude, or upwards of two thousand miles. In his second expedition he resolved the great problem of a southern continent; having traversed that hemisphere between the latitudes of 40° and 70°, in such a manner as not to leave a possibility of its existence, unless near the pole, and out of the reach of navigation. During this voyage he discovered New Caledonia, the largest island in the Southern Pacific except New Zealand; the island of Georgia; and an unknown coast which he named Sandwich Land, the Thule of the southern hemisphere; and having twice visited the tropical seas, he settled the situations of the old, and made several new discoveries.

But the third voyage which he made is distinguished above all the rest by the extent and importance of its discoveries. Besides several smaller islands in the Southern Pacific, he discovered, to the north of the equinoctial line, the group called the Sandwich Islands; which, from their situation and productions, bid fairer for becoming an object of consequence, in the system of European navigation, than any other discovery in the South Sea. He afterward explored what had hitherto remained unknown of the western coast of America, from the latitude of 43° to 70° north, containing an extent of three thousand five hundred miles; ascertained the proximity of the two great continents of Asia and America; passed the straits between them, and surveyed the coast, on each side, to such a height of northern latitude as to demonstrate the impracticability of a passage in that hemisphere, from the Atlantic into the Pacific Ocean, either by an eastern or a western course. In short, if we except the Sea of Amur, and the Japanese Archipelago, he completed the hydrography of the habitable globe.

As a navigator, his services were not perhaps less splendid; certainly not less important and meritorious. The method which he discovered, and so successfully pursued, of preserving the health of seamen, forms a new era in navigation, and will transmit his name to future ages amongst the friends and benefactors of mankind. Those who are conversant in naval history need not be told at how dear a rate the advantages which have been sought through the medium of long voyages at sea have always been purchased. That dreadful disorder which is peculiar to this service, and whose ravages have marked the tracks of discoverers with circumstances almost too shocking to relate, must, without exercising an unwarrantable tyranny over the lives of our seamen, have proved an insuperable obstacle to the prosecution of such enterprises. It was reserved for Captain Cook to shew the world, by repeated trials, that voyages might be protracted to the unusual length of three or even four years, in unknown regions, and under every change and rigour of climate, not only without affecting the health, but even without diminishing the probability of life in the smallest degree. The method he pursued has been fully explained by himself in a paper which was read before the Royal Society, in the year 1776, on which occasion Sir Godfrey Copley's gold medal was adjudged to him.

With respect to his professional abilities, I shall leave them to the judgment of those who are best acquainted with the nature of the services in which he was engaged. They will readily acknowledge, that to have conducted three expeditions of so much danger and difficulty, of so unusual a length, and in such a variety of situation, with uniform and invariable success, must have required not only a thorough and accurate knowledge of his business, but a powerful and comprehensive genius, fruitful in resources, and equally ready in the application of whatever the higher and inferior calls of the service required.

Having given the most faithful account I have been able to collect, both from my own observation, and the relations of others, *of the death* of my ever-honoured friend, and also of his character and services, I shall now leave his memory to the gratitude and admiration of posterity; accepting, with a melancholy satisfaction, the honour, which the loss of him hath procured me, of seeing my name joined with his; and of testifying that affection and respect for his memory, which, whilst he lived, it was no less my inclination, than my constant study to shew him. JAMES KING,

(Captain H. M. Sloop Resolution.)

THE complement of "The Endeavour," in which Cook made his first voyage, consisted of eighty-four persons. She was victualled for eighteen months, and carried ten carriage and twelve swivel guns, with abundance of ammunition: and all manner of stores were taken on board. The following were the principal officers :—

"ENDEAVOUR," BARQUE.*

James Cook, appointed Lieutenant-Commander, 25th May 1768.
Zachary Hicks, lieutenant.
John Gore.
Robert Molineux, master, died 15th April 1771; succeeded by Richard Pickersgill.
Charles Clerke, mate.
John Gathray, boatswain, died 4th February 1771; succeeded by Samuel Evans.
Stephen Forward, gunner.
John Satterley, carpenter, died 12th February 1771; succeeded by George Nowell.
William B. Munkhouse, surgeon, died 5th November 1770; succeeded by William Perry.
Richard Orton, clerk.

They were accompanied by Mr. Charles Green, the coadjutor of Dr. Bradley, the astronomer royal, who was nominated to assist in conducting the astronomical part of the undertaking; and by Joseph, afterwards Sir Joseph, Banks, the President of the Royal Society, a friend of science who possessed, at an early period of life, an opulent fortune, and being zealous to apply it

---

* Records, Admiralty, Whitehall.

to the best ends, embarked on this tedious and hazardous enterprise, animated by the wish of improving himself, and enlarging the bounds of knowledge. He took two draughtsmen with him, and had likewise a secretary and four servants in his retinue.

Dr. Solander, an ingenious and learned Swede, who had been appointed one of the librarians in the British Museum, and who was particularly skilled as a disciple of Linnæus, and distinguished in his knowledge of natural history, likewise joined the expedition. Possessed of the enthusiasm with which Linnæus inspired his disciples, he braved danger in the prosecution of his favourite studies, and being a man of erudition and capacity, he added no small éclat to the voyage in which he had embarked.

Though the principal intention of this expedition was to observe the transit of Venus, it was thought proper to make it comprehend other objects as well. Captain Cook was therefore directed, after he had accomplished his main business, to proceed in making further discoveries in the South Seas, which now began to be explored with uncommon resolution.

First Voyage of Discovery Round the World

IN H. M. BARQUE "ENDEAVOUR," 370 TONS, COMPLEMENT 84.

YEARS 1768, 1769, 1770, and 1771.

CHAPTER I.

Passage to Tahiti and the Society Islands.

HAVING received my commission, which was dated the 25th of May 1768, I went on board on the 27th, hoisted the pennant, and took charge of the ship, which then lay in the basin in Deptford

Yard. She was fitted for sea with all expedition; and stores and provisions being taken on board, sailed down the river on the 30th of July, and on the 13th of August anchored in Plymouth Sound.

While we lay here waiting for a wind, the articles of war and the Act of Parliament were read to the ship's company, who were paid two months' wages in advance, and told that they were to expect no additional pay for the performance of the voyage.

On Friday, the 26th of August, the wind becoming fair, we got under sail, and put to sea. On the 31st, we saw several of the birds which the sailors call Mother Carey's Chickens, and which they suppose to be the forerunners of a storm; and on the next day we had a very hard gale, which brought us under our courses, washed overboard a small boat belonging to the boatswain, and drowned three or four dozen of our poultry, which we regretted still more.

On Friday, the 2d of September, we saw land between Cape Finisterre and Cape Ortegal, on the coast of Gallicia, in Spain; and on the 5th, by an observation of the sun and moon, we found the latitude of Cape Finisterre to be 42° 53' north, and its longitude 8° 46' west, our first meridian being always supposed to pass through Greenwich; variation of the needle 21° 4' west.

MADEIRA.

On the 12th, we discovered the islands of Porto Santo and Madeira, and on the next day anchored in Funchal road, and moored with the stream anchor; but, in the night, the bend of the hawser of the stream-anchor slipped, owing to the negligence of the person who had been employed to make it fast. In the morning the anchor was heaved up into the boat, and carried out to the southward; but in heaving it again, Mr. Weir, the master's mate, was carried overboard by the buoy-rope, and went to the bottom with the anchor; the people in the ship saw the accident, and got the anchor up with all possible expedition; it was, however, too late; the body came up entangled in the buoy-rope, but it was dead.

When the island of Madeira is first approached from the sea, it has a very beautiful appearance, the sides of the hills being entirely covered with vines almost as high as the eye can distinguish; and the vines are green when every kind of herbage, except where they shade the ground, and here and there by the sides of a rill, is entirely burnt up, which was the case at this time.

The only article of trade in this island is wine; and the manner in which it is made is so simple, that it might have been used by Noah, who is said to have planted the first vineyard after the flood. The grapes are put into a square wooden vessel, the dimensions of which are proportioned to the size of the vineyard to which it belongs; the servants then, having taken off their stockings and jackets, get into it, and with their feet and elbows press out as much of the juice as they can: the stalks are afterwards collected, and being tied together with a rope, are put under a square piece of wood, which is pressed down upon them by a lever with a stone tied to the end of it. The inhabitants have made so little improvement in knowledge or art, that they have but very lately brought all the fruit of a vineyard to be of one sort, by engrafting their vines: there seems to be in mind, as there is in matter, a kind of *vis inertiæ*, which resists the first impulse to change. He who proposes to assist the artificer or the husbandman by a new application of the principles of philosophy, or the powers of mechanism, will find, that his having hitherto done without them will be a stronger motive for continuing to do without them still than any advantage, however manifest and considerable, for adopting the improvement. Wherever there is ignorance there is prejudice; and the common people of all nations are, with respect to improvements, like the parish poor of England with respect to a maintenance, for whom the law must not only make a provision, but compel them to accept it, or else they will be still found begging in the streets. It was, therefore, with great difficulty that the people of Maderia were persuaded to engraft their vines; and some of them still obstinately refuse to adopt the practice, though a whole vintage is very often spoiled by the number of bad grapes which are mixed in the vat.

The town of Funchal derives its name from *Funcho*, the Portuguese name for fennel, which grows in great plenty upon the neighbouring rocks. It is situated in the bottom of a bay, and though the houses of the principal inhabitants are large, those of the common people are small; the streets narrow, and worse paved than any I ever saw. The churches are loaded with ornaments, among which are many pictures, and images of favourite saints; but the pictures are in general wretchedly painted, and the saints are dressed in laced clothes. Some of the convents are in a better taste, especially that of the Franciscans, which is plain, simple, and neat in the highest degree.

We visited the good fathers of this convent on a Thursday evening, just before supper-time, and they received us with great politeness: "We will not ask you," said they, "to sup with us, because we are not prepared; but if you will come to-morrow, though it is a fast with us, we will have a turkey roasted for

The town of Funchal, Madeira, p. 14.

you." This invitation, which shewed a liberality of sentiment not to have been expected in a convent of Portuguese friars at this place, gratified us much, though it was not in our power to accept it.

We visited also a convent of nuns, dedicated to *Santa Clara*, and the ladies did us the honour to express a particular pleasure in seeing us there: they had heard that there were great philosophers among us, and not at all knowing what were the objects of philosophical knowledge, they asked us several questions that were absurd and extravagant in the highest degree. One was, when it would thunder; and another, whether a spring of fresh water was to be found anywhere within the walls of their convent, of which it seems they were in great want. It will naturally be supposed that our answers to such questions were neither satisfactory to the ladies, nor, in their estimation, honourable to us; yet their disappointment did not in the least lessen their civility, and they talked, without ceasing, during the whole of our visit, which lasted about half an hour.

On Friday the 23d we saw the Peak of Teneriffe, determined by Dr. Heberden to be 15,396 feet, which is but 148 yards less than three miles, reckoning the mile at 1760 yards.* Its appearance at sunset was very striking; when the sun was below the horizon, and the rest of the island appeared of a deep black, the mountain still reflected his rays, and glowed with a warmth of colour which no painting can express.

As several articles of our stock and provisions began to fall short, I determined to put into Rio de Janeiro, rather than at any port in Brazil or Falkland's Islands, knowing that it could better

---

* The correct height, as now determined by Professor Charles Piazzi Smyth of Edinburgh, in his interesting work on Teneriffe, is 12,200 feet.—ED.

supply us with what we wanted, and making no doubt but that we should be well received.*

We stood off and on along the shore till the 12th of November, and at nine the next morning made sail for the harbour of Rio de Janeiro.

Rio de Janeiro, or the river of Januarius, was probably so called from its having been discovered on the feast-day of that saint; and the town, which is the capital of the Portuguese dominions in America, derives its name from the river, which, indeed, is rather an arm of the sea, for it did not appear to receive any considerable stream of fresh water: it stands on a plain, close to the shore, on the west side of the bay, at the foot of several high mountains which rise behind it. It is neither ill designed nor ill built: the houses, in general, are of stone, and two stories high, every house having, after the manner of the Portuguese, a little balcony before its windows, and a lattice of wood before the balcony. I computed its circuit to be about three miles; for it appears to be equal in size to the largest country towns in England, Bristol and Liverpool not excepted: the streets are straight, and of a convenient breadth, intersecting each other at right angles; the greater part, however, lie in a line with the citadel called St. Sebastian, which stands on the top of a hill that commands the town.

While we lay here, one of the churches was rebuilding; and to defray the expense, the parish to which it belonged had leave to beg in procession through the whole city once a week, by which very considerable sums were collected. At this ceremony, which was performed by night, all the boys of a certain age were

* In this he was greatly disappointed, as he received shocking usage from the Viceroy.—ED.

obliged to assist, the sons of gentlemen not being excused. Each of these boys was dressed in a black cassock, with a short red cloak hanging about as low as the waist, and carried in his hand a pole about six or seven feet long, at the end of which was tied a lantern: the number of lanterns was generally above two hundred, and the light they gave was so great, that the people who saw it from the cabin windows thought the town had been on fire.

The inhabitants, however, may pay their devotions at the shrine of any saint in the calendar, without waiting till there is a procession; for before almost every house there is a little cupboard, furnished with a glass window, in which one of these tutelary powers is waiting to be gracious.

The humility and submission of the inhabitants to the military is such, that I was told that if any of them should neglect to take off his hat upon meeting an officer, he would immediately be knocked down. This haughty severity renders the people extremely civil to any stranger who has the appearance of a gentleman. But the subordination of the officers themselves to the viceroy is enforced with circumstances equally mortifying, for they are obliged to attend in his hall three times every day to ask his commands; the answer constantly is, "There is nothing new." I have been told that this servile attendance is exacted to prevent their going into the country; and if so, it effectually answers the purpose.

The country, at a small distance round the town, which is all that any of us saw, is beautiful in the highest degree; the wildest spots being varied with a greater luxuriance of flowers, both as to number and beauty, than the best gardens in England.

Upon the trees and bushes sat an almost endless variety of

birds, especially small ones, many of them covered with the most elegant plumage, among which were the humming-bird. Of insects, too, there was a great variety, and some of them very beautiful.

The riches of the place consist chiefly in the gold mines, which we supposed to lie far up the country, though we could never learn where, or at what distance. The jewels found are diamonds, topazes of several kinds, and amethysts.

Though the climate is hot, the situation is certainly wholesome; while we stayed here the thermometer never rose higher than 83 degrees. We had frequent rains, and once a very hard gale of wind. So that, upon the whole, Rio de Janeiro is a very good place for ships to put in at that want refreshment.

We did not get under sail till the 7th of December, when we stood out to sea.

Rio Janeiro to Terra del Fuego.

Nothing remarkable happened till the 11th of January, when, having passed Falkland's islands, we discovered the coast of Terra del Fuego.

Having continued to range the coast, on the 14th we entered the straight of Le Maire; but the tide turning against us drove us out with great violence, and raised such a sea that the waves had exactly the same appearance as they would have had if they had broke over a ledge of rocks; and when the ship was in this torrent she frequently pitched so that the bowsprit was under water. It will probably be thought strange that where weeds, which grow at the bottom of the sea, appear above the surface, there should be a great depth of water; but the weeds which grow upon rocky ground in these countries, and which always distinguish it from sand and oose, are of an enormous size. The leaves are four feet long, and some of the stalks, though not thicker than a man's thumb, above one hundred and twenty. Banks and Solander examined some of them, over which we sounded and had fourteen fathom, which is eighty-four feet; and, as they made a very acute angle with the bottom, they were thought to be at least one half longer. Upon the report of the master I stood in with the ship, but not trusting implicitly to his intelligence I continued to sound, and found but four fathom upon the first ledge that I went over; concluding, therefore, that I could not anchor here without risk, I determined to seek some port in the strait, where I might get on board such wood and water as we wanted.

This I found at two o'clock on the 15th, when we anchored in the bay of Good Success, and after dinner I went on shore, accompanied by Banks and Solander, to look for a watering-place, and speak to the Indians, several of whom had come in sight. We landed on the starboard side of the bay near some rocks, which made smooth water and good landing; thirty or forty of them soon made their appearance, and three of them accompanied us back to the ship. When they came on board, one of them, whom we took to be a priest, performed much the same ceremonies which M. Bougainville describes, and supposes to be an exorcism. When he was introduced into a new part of the ship, or when any thing that he had not seen before caught his attention, he shouted with all his force for some minutes, without directing his voice either to us or his companions. They ate some bread and some beef, but not apparently with much pleasure, though such part of what was given them as they did not eat they took away with them; but they would not swallow a drop either of wine or spirits; they put the glass to their lips, but, having tasted the liquor, they returned it, with strong expressions of disgust.

Curiosity seems to be one of the few passions which distinguish men from brutes; and of this our guests appeared to have very little. They went from one part of the ship to another, and looked at the vast variety of new objects that every moment presented themselves, without any expression either of wonder or pleasure; for the vociferation of our exorcist seemed to be neither.

TERRIBLE EFFECT OF EXTREME COLD WHEN JOINED WITH FATIGUE.

On the 16th, early in the morning, Banks and Solander, with their attendants, servants, and two seamen, accompanied by Monkhouse the surgeon and Green the astronomer, set out from the ship, with a view to penetrate as far as they could into the country, and return at night. The hills, when viewed at a distance, seemed to be partly a wood, partly a plain, and above them a bare rock. Banks hoped to get through the wood, and made no doubt that, beyond it, he should find, in a country which no botanist had ever yet visited, alpine plants which would abundantly compensate his labour. They entered the wood at a small sandy beach, a little to the westward of the watering-place, and continued to ascend the hill, through the pathless wilderness, till three o'clock. Soon after they reached what they had taken for a plain; but, to their great disappointment, found it a swamp, covered with low bushes of birch, about three feet high, interwoven with each other, and so stubborn that they could not be bent out of the way; it was therefore necessary to lift the leg over them, which at every step was buried, ankle deep, in the soil. To aggravate the pain and difficulty of such travelling, the weather, which had hitherto been very fine (much like one of our bright days in May), became gloomy and cold, with sudden blasts of a most piercing wind, accompanied with snow. They pushed forward, however, in good spirits, hoping the worst of the way was past, and that the bare rock which they had seen from the tops of the lower hills was not more than a mile before them; but when they had got about two-thirds over this woody swamp, Buchan, one of Banks's draughtsmen, was unhappily seized with a fit. This made it necessary for the whole company to halt, and as it was impossible that he should go any further, a fire was kindled, and those who were most fatigued were left behind to take care of him, whilst Banks, Solander, and the others, went on to botanize at the summit.

The cold was now become more severe, and the snow-blasts more frequent; the day also was so far spent, that it was found impossible to get back to the ship before the next morning; but to pass the night upon such a mountain, in such a climate, was not only comfortless, but dreadful.

By an arrangement the whole company assembled at an appointed rendezvous, and, though pinched with cold, were in health and spirits, Buchan himself having recovered his strength in a much greater degree than could have been expected. It was now near eight o'clock in the evening, but still good daylight, and they set forward for the nearest valley, Banks himself undertaking to bring up the rear, and see that no straggler was left behind, a caution afterwards found to be by no means superfluous. Solander, who had more than once crossed the mountains which divide Sweden from Norway, well knew that extreme cold, especially when joined with fatigue, produces a torpor and sleepiness that are almost irresistible, conjured the company to keep moving, whatever pain it might cost them, and whatever relief they might be promised by an inclination to rest, enforcing his warning by these words :—

"WHOEVER SITS DOWN WILL SLEEP; AND WHOEVER SLEEPS WILL WAKE NO MORE."

Thus, at once admonished and alarmed, they set forward; but while they were still upon the naked rock, and before they had got among the bushes, the cold became suddenly so intense, as to produce the effects that had been most dreaded. Solander himself was the first to succumb to its influence, finding the inclination, against which he had warned others, irresistible; and he insisted upon being suffered to lie down. Banks entreated and remonstrated in vain: down he lay upon the ground, though it was covered with snow; and it was with great difficulty that his friend kept him from sleeping. One of the black servants also began to linger, having suffered from the cold in the same manner, and when he was told that if he did not go on he would in a short time be frozen to death, he answered, that he desired nothing but to lie down and die: the doctor did not so explicitly renounce his life; he said he was willing to go on, but that he must first take some sleep, though he had before told the company "that to sleep was to perish." There being no remedy, they were both suffered to sit down, and in a few minutes they fell into a profound sleep; soon after, some of those people who had been sent forward returned with the welcome news that a fire was kindled about a quarter of a mile farther on the way. Banks then endeavoured to wake Solander, and happily succeeded; but, though he had not slept five minutes, he had almost lost the use of his limbs, and the muscles were so shrunk that his shoes fell from his feet. As no attempts to relieve the poor black servant were successful, he was necessarily left to his fate, with another black servant and a seaman to look after him. Another fall of snow now came on, and continued incessantly for two hours, so that all hope of seeing those left behind again alive was given up; but about twelve o'clock, to the great joy of those at the fire, a shouting was heard at some distance, which proceeded from the seaman and the other two, who had just strength enough left to stagger along, and call out for assistance. The black servant was upon his legs, but not able to put one before the other; his companion was lying upon the ground, insensible as a stone. All hands were now called from the fire, and an attempt was made to carry them to it; but this, notwithstanding the united efforts of the whole company, was found to be impossible. They were, therefore, reduced to the sad necessity of again leaving the unhappy wretches to their fate, having first made them a bed of boughs from the trees, and spread a covering of the same kind over them to a considerable height.

When the morning dawned, they saw nothing round them, as far as the eye could reach, but snow, which seemed to lie as thick upon the trees as upon the ground; and the blasts returned so frequently, and with such violence, that they found it impossible for them to set out; how long this might last they knew not, and they had but too much reason to apprehend that it would confine them in that desolate forest till they perished with hunger and cold. After having suffered the misery and terror of this situation till six o'clock in the morning, they conceived some hope of deliverance by discovering the place of the sun through the clouds, which were become thinner, and began to break away.

Their first care was to see whether the poor wretches whom they had been obliged to leave among the bushes were yet alive; three of the company were dispatched for that purpose, and very soon afterwards returned with the melancholy news that they were dead.*

Those who were left alive were now pressed by the calls of hunger, to which, after long fasting, every consideration of future good or evil immediately gives way. Before they set forward, therefore, it was unanimously agreed that they should eat a vulture which they happened to shoot; the bird was accordingly skinned, and it being thought best to divide it before it was fit to be eaten, it was cut into ten portions, and every man cooked his own as he thought fit. After this repast, which furnished each of them with about three mouthfuls, they prepared to set out; but it was ten o'clock before the snow was sufficiently gone off to render a march practicable. After a walk of about three hours, they were very agreeably surprised to find themselves upon the beach, and much nearer to the ship than they had any reason to expect.† When they came on board, they congratulated each other upon their safety with a joy that no man can feel who has not been exposed to equal

---

* Could the two poor fellows of Franklin's ships, found by M'Clintock's expedition under a quantity of clothing in the boat on King William's Island, have been left there (with their guns loaded and cocked), under somewhat similar circumstances?—by no means improbable.

† On more than one occasion, parties employed on the recent expeditions in search of Franklin, in the Arctic Seas, have been placed in a similar position, but happily no life was ever lost. Sir R. M'Clure was himself in great peril, when he ascertained the junction of the Pacific Ocean with the Atlantic, through the waters of Barrow Straits. It was on a sledge journey when "every now and then one of their party would experience a severe fall into some deep cleft, or over some huge hummock, and then, thoroughly jaded, they would sit down and feel inclined to

danger; and as I had suffered great anxiety at their not returning in the evening of the day on which they set out, I was not wholly without my share.

On the 20th, Banks and Solander went on shore to visit an Indian town, which some of the people had reported to lie about two miles up the country. When they got within a small distance, two of the people came out to meet them, with such state as they could assume. When they joined them, they began to halloo as they had done on board the ship, without addressing themselves either to the strangers or their companions; and having continued this strange vociferation for some time, they conducted them to the town. It was situated on a dry knoll, or small hill, covered with wood, none of which seemed to have been cleared away, and consisted of about twelve or fourteen hovels, of the most rude and inartificial structure that can be imagined. They were nothing more than a few poles set up so as to incline towards each other, and meet at the top, forming a kind of a cone, like some of our bee-hives: on the weather-side they were covered with a few boughs and a little grass, and on the lee-side about one-eighth of the circle was left open, both for a door and a fire-place; and of this kind were the huts that had been seen in St. Vincent's bay, in one of which the embers of a fire were still remaining. Furniture they had none; a little grass, which lay round the inside of the hovel, served both for

drop off into a sleep from which they never would have awakened in this world. Captain M'Clure, however, was aware of this danger; and his voice aroused them to exertion."—*Capt. Sherard Osborn's narrative of M'Clure's Voyage.*

On another occasion a man named Whitefield was very nearly lost, having strayed from the ship, and was found "stiff and rigid as a corpse."

Dr. M'Cormack also had a very narrow escape. He passed a whole day and night without food or shelter, beyond what the snow drift afforded, about seven miles from his ship, in a dense fog and snow storm.

chairs and beds; and of all the utensils which necessity and ingenuity have concurred to produce among other savage nations, they saw only a basket to carry in the hand, a satchel to hang at the back, and the bladder of some beast to hold water, which the natives drink through a hole that is made near the top for that purpose. The only clothing they had was scarcely sufficient to prevent their perishing with cold in the summer of this country, much less in the extreme severity of winter.

We saw no appearance of their having any food but shell-fish; for though seals were frequently seen near the shore, they seemed to have no implements for taking them. The shell-fish is collected by the women, whose business it seems to be to attend at low water, with a basket in one hand, and a stick, pointed and barbed, in the other, and a satchel at their backs. They loosen the limpets and other fish that adhere to the rocks with the stick, and put them into the basket, which, when full, they empty into the satchel.

The only things that we found among them, in which there was the least appearance of neatness or ingenuity, were their weapons, which consisted of a bow and arrows. The bow was not inelegantly made, and the arrows were the neatest that we had ever seen: they were of wood, polished to the highest degree; and the point, which was of glass or flint, and barbed, was formed and fitted with wonderful dexterity. We saw also some pieces of glass and flint among them unwrought, besides rings, buttons, cloth, and canvass, with other European commodities; they must, therefore, sometimes travel to the northward, for it is many years since any ship has been so far south as this part of Terra del Fuego. We observed, also, that they shewed no surprise at our fire-arms, with the use of which they appeared to be well acquainted; for they made signs to Mr. Banks to shoot a seal which followed the boat, as they were going on shore from the ship.

M. de Bougainville, who, in January 1768, just one year before us, had been on shore upon this coast in latitude 53° 40′ 41″, had, among other things, given glass to the people whom he found here; for he says, that a boy about twelve years old took it into his head to eat some of it. By this unhappy accident he died in great misery; but the endeavours of the good father, the French *aumonier*, were more successful than those of the surgeon; for though the surgeon could not save his life, the charitable priest found means to steal a Christian baptism upon him so secretly that none of his pagan relations knew anything of the matter.

Upon the whole, these people appear to be the most destitute and forlorn, as well as the most stupid, of all human beings; the outcasts of nature, who spent their lives in wandering about the dreary wastes, where two of our people perished with cold in the midst of summer; with no dwelling but a wretched hovel of sticks and grass, which would not only admit the wind, but the snow and the rain; almost naked; and destitute of every convenience that is furnished by the rudest art, having no implement even to dress their food: yet they were content.* They seemed to have no wish for anything more than they possessed, nor did anything that we offered them appear acceptable but beads, as an ornamental superfluity of life. What bodily pain they might suffer from the severities of their winter we could

* Mr. Parker Snow, in his deeply interesting narrative of a "Two Years' Cruize off Terra del Fuego," etc., describes the natives of the present day as "perfectly nude, wild and shaggy in appearance, with long spears in their hands" —"they were indeed, in appearance, like so many fiendish imps."

not know; but it is certain that they suffered nothing from the want of the innumerable articles which we consider not as the luxuries and conveniences only but the necessaries of life: as their desires are few, they probably enjoy them all; and how much they may be gainers by an exemption from the care, labour, and solicitude, which arise from a perpetual and unsuccessful effort to gratify that infinite variety of desires which the refinements of artificial life have produced among us, is not very easy to determine: possibly this may counterbalance all the real disadvantages of their situation in comparison with ours, and make the scales by which good and evil are distributed to man hang even between us.

On the 26th January we took our departure from Cape Horn, and by the first of March we were in latitude 38° 44' S., and longitude 110° 33' W., both by observation and by the log. This agreement, after a run of 660 leagues, was thought to be very extraordinary; and is a demonstration, that after we left the land of Cape Horn we had no current that affected the ship. It renders it also highly probable that we had been near no land of any considerable extent; for currents are always found when land is not remote, and sometimes, particularly on the east side of the continent in the North Sea, when land has been distant 100 leagues.

On Tuesday the 4th of April, about ten o'clock in the morning, Banks' servant, Briscoe, discovered land, bearing south, at the distance of about three or four leagues. I immediately hauled up for it, and found it to be an island of an oval form, with a lagoon in the middle, which occupied much the larger part of it; the border of land which circumscribes the lagoon is in many places very low and narrow, particularly on the south side, where it consists principally of a beach or reef of rocks. We saw several of the natives upon the shore, and counted four and twenty. They appeared to be tall, and to have heads remarkably large; perhaps they had something wound round them which we could not distinguish; they were of a copper colour, and had long black hair. Their habitations were under some clumps of palm-nut trees, which at a distance appeared like high

Polynesian Island—Lagoon shaped, and composed of Coral.

ground; and to us, who for a long time had seen nothing but water and sky, except the dreary hills of Terra del Fuego, these groves seemed a terrestrial Paradise. To this spot we gave the name of Lagoon Island.

About one o'clock we made sail to the westward, and about half an hour after three we saw land again to the N.W. We got up with it at sunset, and it proved to be a low woody island, of a circular form, and not much above a mile in compass. We called it Thrumb Cap.

We went on with a fine trade-wind and pleasant weather, and on the 5th, about three in the afternoon, we discovered land to the westward. It proved to be a low island of much greater extent than either of those that we had seen before, being about ten or twelve leagues in compass. Several of us remained at the mast-head the whole evening, admiring its extraordinary figure; it was shaped exactly like a bow, the arc and cord of which were land, and the space between them water; the cord was a flat beach, without any signs of vegetation, having nothing upon it but heaps of sea-weed, which lay in different ridges, as higher or lower tides had left them. We sailed a-breast of the low beach or bow-string, within less than a league of the shore, till sunset, and we then judged ourselves to be half way between the two horns. Here we brought too and sounded, but found no bottom with one hundred and thirty fathoms; and, as it is dark almost instantly after sunset in these latitudes, we suddenly lost sight of the land, and making sail again, before the line was well hauled in, we steered by the sound of the breakers, which were distinctly heard till we got clear of the coast. We knew this island to be inhabited, by smoke which we saw in different parts of it, and we gave it the name of Bow Island.

On the next day, Thursday the 6th, about noon, we saw land again to the westward, and came up with it about three. It appeared to be two islands, or rather groups of islands, extending from N.W. by N., to S.E. by S., about nine leagues. To these islands we gave the name of the Groups.

On the 7th, about half an hour after six in the morning, being just at daybreak, we discovered another island to the northward, which we judged to be about four miles in circumference. The land lay very low, and there was a piece of water in the middle of it; there seemed to be some wood upon it, and it looked green and pleasant; but we saw neither cocoa-trees nor inhabitants: it abounded, however, with birds, and we, therefore, gave it the name of Bird Island.

On the 8th, about two o'clock in the afternoon, we saw land to the northward, and about sunset came abreast of it, at about the distance of two leagues. It appeared to be a double range of low woody islands joined together by reefs, so as to form one island, in the form of an ellipsis or oval, with a lake in the middle of it. The small islands and reefs that circumscribe the lake have the appearance of a chain, and we therefore gave it the name of Chain Island.

On the 10th, having had a tempestuous night with thunder and rain, the weather was hazy till about nine o'clock in the morning, when it cleared up, and we saw the island to which Captain Wallis, who first discovered it, gave the name of Osnaburgh Island. It is a high round island, not above a league in circuit; in some parts it is covered with trees, and in others a naked rock. In this direction it looked like a high-crowned hat; but when it bears north, the top of it has more the appearance of the roof of a house.

TAHITI OR OTAHEITE.

About one o'clock, on Monday the 10th of April, some of the people who were looking out for the island to which we were bound, said they saw land a-head, in that part of the horizon where it was expected to appear; but it was so faint that whether there was land in sight or not remained a matter of dispute till sunset. The next morning, however, at six o'clock, we were convinced that those who said they had discovered land were not mistaken; it appeared to be very high and mountainous, extending from W. by S. ½ S. to W. by N. ½ N., and we knew it to be the same that Captain Wallis had called King George III.'s Island. We were delayed in our approach to it by light airs and calms, so that in the morning of the 12th we were but little nearer than we had been the night before; but about seven a breeze sprang up, and before eleven several canoes were seen making towards the ship: there were but few of them, however, that would come near; and the people in those that did could not be persuaded to come on board. In every canoe there were young plantains, and branches of a tree which the Indians call *E'Midho:* these, as we afterwards learnt, were brought as tokens of peace and amity; and the people in one of the canoes handed them up the ship's side, making signals at the same time with great earnestness, which we did not immediately understand; at length we guessed that they wished these symbols should be placed in some conspicuous part of the ship; we, therefore, immediately stuck them among the rigging, at which they expressed the greatest satisfaction. We then purchased their cargoes, consisting of cocoa-nuts and various kinds of fruit, which after our long voyage were very acceptable.

We stood on with an easy sail all night, with soundings from twenty-two fathom to twelve, and about seven o'clock in the morning we came to an anchor in thirteen fathom, in Portroyal Bay, called by the natives *Matavai*. We were immediately surrounded by the natives in their canoes, who gave us cocoa-nuts, fruit resembling apples, bread-fruit, and some small fishes, in exchange for beads and other trifles. They had with them a pig, which they would not part with for anything but a hatchet, and therefore we refused to purchase it; because if we gave them a hatchet for a pig now, we knew they would never afterwards sell one for less, and we could not afford to buy as many as it was probable we should want at that price. The bread-fruit grows on a tree that is about the size of a middling oak; its leaves are frequently a foot and a half long, of an oblong shape, deeply sinuated like those of the fig-tree, which they resemble in consistence and colour, and in the exuding of a white milky juice upon being broken. The fruit is about the size and shape of a child's head, and the surface is reticulated, not much unlike a truffle: it is covered with a thin skin, and has a core about as big as the handle of a small knife: the eatable part lies between the skin and the core: it is as white as snow, and somewhat of the consistence of new bread: it must be roasted before it is eaten, being first divided into three or four parts: its taste is insipid, with a slight sweetness, somewhat resembling that of the crumb of wheaten bread mixed with a Jerusalem artichoke.

Bread Fruit.

Among others who came off to the ship was an elderly man, whose name, as we learnt afterwards, was Owhaw, and who was immediately known to Mr. Gore, and several others who had been here with Captain Wallis. As I was informed that he had been very useful to them, I took him on board the ship with some others, and was particularly attentive to gratify him, as I hoped he might also be useful to us.

As soon as the ship was properly secured, I went on shore with a party of men under arms. We were received from the boat by some hundreds of the inhabitants, whose looks at least gave us welcome, though they were struck with such awe, that the first who approached us crouched so low that he almost crept upon his hands and knees. It is remarkable that he, like the people in the canoes, presented to us the same symbol of peace that is known to have been in use among the ancient and mighty nations of the northern hemisphere, the green branch of a tree. We received it with looks and gestures of kindness and satisfaction; and observing that each of them held one in his hand, we immediately gathered every one a bough, and carried it in our hands in the same manner.

Our circuit was not less than four or five miles, through groves of trees, which were loaded with cocoa-nuts and breadfruit, and afforded the most grateful shade. Under these trees were the habitations of the people, most of them being only a roof without walls, and the whole scene realised the poetical fables of Arcadia. We remarked, however, not without some regret, that in all our walk we had seen only two hogs, and not a single fowl.

In the morning, before we could leave the ship, several canoes came about us, most of them from the westward, and two of them were filled with people, who, by their dress and deportment, appeared to be of a superior rank: two of these came on board, and each singled out his friend; one of them, whose name we found to be Matahah, fixed upon Mr. Banks, and the other upon me: this ceremony consisted in taking off great part of their clothes and putting them upon us. In return for this, we presented each of them with a hatchet and some beads. Soon after, they made signs for us to go with them to the places where they lived, pointing to the S.W.; and as I was desirous of finding a more commodious harbour, and making farther trial of the disposition of the people, I consented.

I ordered out two boats, and after rowing about a league, they made signs that we should go on shore, and gave us to understand that this was the place of their residence. We accordingly landed, among several hundreds of the natives, who conducted us into a house of much greater length than any we had seen. When we entered, we saw a middle-aged man, whose name was afterwards discovered to be Tootahah: mats were immediately spread, and we were desired to sit down over against him. Soon after we were seated, he ordered a cock and hen to be brought out, which he presented to Mr. Banks and me: we accepted the present; and in a short time each of us received a piece of cloth, perfumed after their manner, by no means disagreeably, which they took great pains to make us remark. The piece presented to Mr. Banks was eleven yards long and two wide; in return for which, he gave a laced silk neckcloth, which he happened to have on, and a linen pocket-handkerchief: Tootahah immediately dressed himself in this new finery, with an air of perfect complacency and satisfaction.

On taking leave of our friendly chief, we directed our course along the shore. When we had walked about a mile, we met, at the head of a great number of people, another chief, whose name was Tubourai Tamaide, with whom we were also to ratify a treaty of peace, with the ceremony of which we were now become better acquainted. Having received the branch which he presented to us, and given another in return, we laid our hands upon our left breasts, and pronounced the word *Taio*, which we supposed to signify friend; the chief then gave us to understand, that if we chose to eat, he had victuals ready for us. We accepted his offer, and dined very heartily upon fish, bread-fruit, cocoa-nuts, and plantains, dressed after their manner: they ate some of their fish raw; and raw fish was offered to us, but we declined that part of the entertainment.

During this visit a wife of our noble host, whose name was Tomio, did Mr. Banks the honour to place herself upon the same mat, close by him. Tomio was not in the first bloom of her youth, nor did she appear to have been ever remarkable for her beauty; he did not, therefore, I believe, pay her the most flattering attention: it happened, too, as a farther mortification to this lady, that seeing a very pretty girl among the crowd, he, not adverting to the dignity of his companion, beckoned her to come to him: the girl, after some entreaty, complied, and sat down on the other side of him: he loaded her with beads, and every showy trifle that would please her: his princess, though she was somewhat mortified at the preference that was given to her rival, did not discontinue her civilities, but still assiduously supplied him with the milk of the cocoa-nut, and such other dainties as were in her reach. This scene might possibly have become more curious and interesting, if it had not been suddenly interrupted by an interlude of a more serious kind. Just at this time, Dr. Solander and Mr. Monkhouse complained that their pockets had been picked. Dr. Solander had lost an opera-glass in a shagreen case, and Mr. Monkhouse his snuff-box. This incident unfortunately put an end to the good-humour of the company. Complaint of the injury was made to the chief; and to give it weight, Mr. Banks started up, and hastily struck the butt end of his firelock upon the ground: this action, and the noise that accompanied it, struck the whole assembly with a panic; and every one of the natives ran out of the house with the utmost precipitation, except the chief, three women, and two or three others, who appeared by their dress to be of a superior rank.

As in my excursion to the westward, I had not found any more convenient harbour than that in which we lay, I determined to go on shore, and fix upon some spot, commanded by the ship's guns, where I might throw up a small fort for our defence, and prepare for making our astronomical observation. I therefore took a party of men, and landed without delay, accompanied by Banks, Solander, and the astronomer, Green. We soon fixed upon a part of the sandy beach, on the N.E. point of the bay, which was in every respect convenient for our purpose, and not near any habitation of the natives. Having marked out the ground that we intended to occupy, a small tent belonging to Mr. Banks was set up, which had been brought on shore for that purpose. By this time a great number of the people had gathered about us; but, as it appeared, only to look on, there not being a single weapon of any kind among them. I intimated, however, that none of them were to come within the line I had drawn, except one who appeared to be a chief, and Owhaw. To these two persons I addressed myself by signs, and endeavoured to make them understand that we wanted the ground which we had marked out to sleep upon for a certain number of nights, and that then we should go away. Whether I was understood I cannot certainly determine; but the people behaved with a deference and respect that at once pleased and surprised us. They sat down peaceably without the circle, and looked on without giving us any interruption till we had done, which was upwards of two hours. As we had seen no poultry, and but two hogs, in our walk when we were last on shore at this place, we suspected that, upon our arrival, they had been driven further up the country; and the rather, as Owhaw was very importunate with us, by signs, not to go into the woods, which, however, and partly for these reasons, we were determined to do. Having, therefore, appointed the thirteen marines and a petty officer to guard the tent, we set out, and a great number of the natives joined our party. As we were crossing a little river that lay in our way, we saw some ducks, and Mr. Banks, as soon as he had got over, fired at them, and happened to kill three at one shot: this struck them with the utmost terror, so that most of them fell suddenly to the ground, as if they also had been shot at the same discharge. It was not long, however, before they recovered from their fright, and we continued our route, but we had not gone far before we were alarmed by the report of two pieces, which were fired by the guard at the tent. We had then straggled a little distance from each other, but Owhaw immediately called us together, and, by waving his hand, sent away every Indian who followed us except three, each of whom, as a pledge of peace on their part, and an entreaty that there might be peace on ours, hastily broke a branch from the trees, and came to us with it in their hands. As we had too much reason to fear that some mischief had happened, we hasted back to the tent, which was not distant above half a mile, and when we came up, we found it entirely deserted, except by our own people.

It appeared that one of the Indians, who remained about the tent after we left it, had watched his opportunity, and, taking the sentry unawares, had snatched away his musket. Upon this, the petty officer, a midshipman, who commanded the party, perhaps from a sudden fear of farther violence, perhaps from the natural petulance of power newly acquired, and perhaps from a brutality in his nature, ordered the marines to fire. The men, with as little consideration or humanity as the officer, immediately discharged their pieces among the thickest of the flying crowd, consisting of more than a hundred; and observing that the thief did not fall, pursued him, and shot him dead. We afterwards learnt that none of the others were either killed or wounded.

Owhaw, who had never left us, observing that we were now totally deserted, got together a few of those who had fled, though not without some difficulty, and ranged them about us. We endeavoured to justify our people as well as we could, and to convince the Indians that, if they did no wrong to us, we should do no wrong to them. They went away without any appearance of distrust or resentment; and having struck our tent, we returned to the ship, but by no means satisfied with the transactions of the day.

On the 18th, at daybreak, I went on shore, with as many people as could possibly be spared from the ship, and began to erect our fort. While some were employed in throwing up intrenchments, others were busy in cutting pickets and fascines, which the natives, who soon gathered round us as they had been used to do, were so far from hindering, that many of them voluntarily assisted us, bringing the pickets and fascines from the wood where they had been cut, with great alacrity. We had, indeed, been so scrupulous of invading their property, that we purchased every stake which was used upon this occasion, and cut down no tree till we had first obtained their consent.

Our residence on shore would by no means have been disagreeable, if we had not been incessantly tormented by the flies, which, among other mischief, made it almost impossible for Parkinson, Mr. Banks's natural history painter, to work; for they not only covered his subject so as that no part of its surface could be seen, but even ate the colour off the paper as fast as he could lay it on. We had recourse to mosquito-nets and fly-traps, which, though they made the inconvenience tolerable, were very far from removing it.

On the 22d, Tootahah gave us a specimen of the music of this country: four persons performed upon flutes, which had only two stops, and therefore could not sound more than four notes, by half tones: they were sounded like our German flutes, except that the performer, instead of applying it to his mouth, blew into it with one nostril, while he stopped the other with his thumb: to these instruments four other persons sung, and kept very good time; but only one tune was played during the whole concert.

I must bear my testimony, that the people of this country, of all ranks, men and women, are the arrantest thieves upon the face of the earth. The very day after we arrived here, when they came on board us, the chiefs were employed in stealing what they could in the cabin, and their dependents were no less industrious in other parts of the ship; they snatched up everything that it was possible for them to secrete till they got on shore, even to the glass ports, two of which they carried off undetected. It may also be observed that these people have a knowledge of right and wrong from the mere dictates of natural conscience; and involuntarily condemn themselves when they do that to others which they would condemn others for doing to them. We must, indeed, estimate the virtue of these people by the only standard of morality, the conformity of their conduct to what in their opinion is right; but we must not hastily conclude that theft is a testimony of the same depravity in them that it is in us, in the instances in which our people were sufferers by their dishonesty; for their temptation was such as to surmount what would be considered as a proof of uncommon integrity among those who have more knowledge, better principles, and stronger motives to resist the temptations of illicit advantage : an Indian among penny knives and beads, or even nails and broken glass, is in the same state of trial with the meanest servant in Europe among unlocked coffers of jewels and gold.

Their tears, indeed, like those of children, were always ready to express any passion that was strongly excited, and like those of children they also appeared to be forgotten as soon as shed ; of which the following, among many others, is a remarkable instance :—Very early in the morning of the 28th, even before it was day, a great number of them came down to the fort, and Terapo being observed among the women on the outside of the gate, Mr. Banks went out and brought her in ; he saw that the tears then stood in her eyes, and as soon as she entered they began to flow in great abundance : he inquired earnestly the cause, but instead of answering she took from under her garment a shark's tooth, and struck it six or seven times into her head with great force ; a profusion of blood followed, and she talked loud, but in a most melancholy tone, for some minutes, without at all regarding his inquiries, which he repeated with still more impatience and concern, while the other Indians, to his great surprise, talked and laughed, without taking the least notice of her distress. But her own behaviour was still more extraordinary. As soon as the bleeding was over, she looked up with a smile, and began to collect some small pieces of cloth, which during her bleeding she had thrown down to catch the blood ; as soon as she had picked them all up, she carried them out of the tent, and threw them into the sea, carefully dispersing them abroad, as if she wished to prevent the sight of them from reviving the remembrance of what she had done. She then plunged into the river, and after having washed her whole body returned to the tents with the same gaiety and cheerfulness as if nothing had happened.

It is not, indeed, strange, that the sorrows of these artless people should be transient, any more than that their passions should be suddenly and strongly expressed: what they feel they have never been taught either to disguise or suppress, and having no habits of thinking which perpetually recall the past and anticipate the future, they are affected by all the changes of the passing hour, and reflect the colour of the time, however frequently it may vary; they have no project which is to be pursued from day to day, the subject of unremitted anxiety and solicitude, that first rushes into their mind when they awake in the morning, and is last dismissed when they sleep at night. Yet if we admit that they are upon the whole happier than we, we must admit that the child is happier than the man, and that we are losers by the perfection of our nature, the increase of our knowledge, and the enlargement of our views.

Queen Oberea.

The attention of all was now diverted from every other object, and wholly engaged in considering a person who had made so distinguished a figure in the accounts that had been given of this island by its first discoverers; and we soon learnt that her name was Oberea. She seemed to be about forty years of age, and was not only tall but of a large make; her skin was white, and there was an uncommon intelligence and sensibility in her eyes; she appeared to have been handsome when she was young, but at this time little more than memorials of her beauty were left.

As soon as her quality was known, an offer was made to conduct her to the ship. Of this she readily accepted, and came on board with two men and several women, who seemed to be all of her family: I received her with such marks of distinction as I thought would gratify her most, and was not sparing of my presents, among which this august personage seemed particularly delighted with a child's doll. After some time spent on board, I attended her back to the shore; and as soon as we landed, she presented me with a hog and several bunches of plantains, which she caused to be carried from her canoes up to the fort in a kind of procession, of which she and myself brought up the rear. In our way to the fort we met Tootahah, who, though not king, appeared to be at this time invested with the sovereign authority; he seemed not to be well pleased with the distinction that was shown to the lady, and became so jealous when she produced her doll, that to propitiate him it was thought proper to compliment him with another. At this time he thought fit to prefer a doll to a hatchet; but this preference arose only from a childish jealousy, which could not be soothed but by a gift of exactly the same kind with that which had been presented to Oberea; for dolls in a very short time were universally considered as trifles of no value.

In the afternoon of Monday the 1st of May, we set up the observatory, and took the astronomical quadrant, with some other instruments, on shore, for the first time. The next morning, about nine o'clock, I went on shore with Mr. Green to fix the quadrant in a situation for use, when to our inexpressible surprise and concern it was not to be found. It had been deposited in the tent which was reserved for my use, where, as I passed the night on board, nobody slept; it had never been taken out of the packing-case, which was eighteen inches square, and the whole was of considerable weight; a sentinel had been posted the whole night within five yards of the tent door, and none of the other instruments were missing. Mr. Banks, who upon such occasions declined neither labour nor risk, and who had more influence over the Indians than any of us, determined to go in search of it into the woods. He set out, accompanied by a midshipman and Mr. Green, and as he was crossing the river he was met by Tubourai Tamaide, who immediately made the figure of a triangle with three bits of straw upon his hand. By this he knew that the Indians were the thieves; and that, although they had opened the case, they were not disposed to part with the contents. No time was therefore to be lost, and he made Tubourai Tamaide understand, that he must instantly go with him to the place whither the quadrant had been carried; he consented, and they set out together to the eastward, the chief inquiring at every house which they passed after the thief by name: the people readily told him which way he was gone, and how long it was since he had been there: the hope which this gave them that they should overtake him, supported them under their fatigue, and they pressed forward, sometimes walking, sometimes running, though the weather was intolerably hot; when they had climbed a hill at the distance of about four miles, their conductor shewed them a point full three miles farther, and gave them to understand that they were not to expect the instrument till they had got thither. Here they paused; they had no arms except a pair of pistols, which Mr. Banks always carried in his pocket; they were going to a place that was at least seven miles distant from the fort, where the Indians might be less submissive than at home, and to take from them what they had ventured their lives to get, and what, notwithstanding our conjectures, they appeared desirous to keep: these were discouraging circumstances, and their situation would become more critical at every step. They determined, however, not to relinquish their enterprise, nor to pursue it without taking the best measures for their security that were in their power. It was therefore determined that Banks and Green should go on, and that the midshipman should return to me, and desire that I would send a party of men after them, acquainting me, at the same time, that it was impossible they should return till it was dark. Upon receiving this message I set out with such a party as I thought sufficient for the occasion; leaving orders, both at the ship and at the fort that no canoe should be suffered to go out of the bay, but that none of the natives should be seized or detained.

In the meantime Banks and Green pursued their journey under the auspices of Tubourai Tamaide, and in the very spot which he had specified they met one of his own people with part of the quadrant in his hand. At this most welcome sight they stopped, and a great number of Indians immediately came up, some of whom pressing rather rudely upon them, Mr. Banks thought it necessary to shew one of his pistols, the sight of which reduced them instantly to order: as the crowd that gathered round them was every moment increasing, he marked out a circle in the grass, and they ranged themselves on the outside of it to the number of several hundreds, with great quietness and decorum. Into the middle of this circle the box, which was now arrived, was ordered to be brought, with several reading-glasses, and other small matters, which in their hurry they had put into a pistol-case that Mr. Banks knew to be his property, it having been some time before stolen from the tents with a horse-pistol in it, which he immediately demanded, and which was also restored.

On the 10th, I put some seeds of melons and other plants into a spot of ground which had been turned up for the purpose; they had all been sealed up by the person of whom they were bought, in small bottles with rosin; but none of them came up except mustard; even the cucumbers and melons failed, and Mr. Banks is of opinion that they were spoiled by the total exclusion of fresh air.

This day we learnt the Indian name of the island, which is Otaheite, and by that name I shall hereafter distinguish it.

Wonderful Feats in Swimming.

As we were returning to the ship, from another visit to Tootahah, who had removed to a place called Atahourou, we were entertained with a sight that in some measure compensated for the fatigue and disappointment which that visit had occasioned. In our way we came to one of the few places where access to the island is not guarded by a reef, and, consequently, a high surf breaks upon the shore; a more dreadful one, indeed, I had seldom seen; it was impossible for any European boat to have lived in it; and if the best swimmer in Europe had, by any accident, been exposed to its fury, I am confident that he would not have been able to preserve himself from drowning, especially as the shore was covered with pebbles and large stones; yet, in the midst of these breakers, were ten or twelve Indians swimming for their amusement: whenever a surf broke near them, they dived under it, and, to all appearance with infinite facility, rose again on the other side. This diversion was greatly improved by the stern of an old canoe, which they happened to find upon the spot: they took this before them, and swam out with it as far as the outermost breach, then two or three of them getting into it, and turning the square end to the breaking wave, were driven in towards the shore with incredible rapidity, sometimes almost to the beach; but generally the wave broke over them before they got half way, in which case they dived, and rose on the other side with the canoe in their hands: they then swam out with it again, and were again driven back, just as our holiday youth climb the hill in Greenwich Park for the pleasure of rolling down it. At this wonderful scene we stood gazing for more than half an hour, during which time none of the swimmers attempted to come on shore, but seemed to enjoy their sport in the highest degree.

Upon this occasion it may be observed, that human nature is endued with powers which are only accidentally exerted to the utmost; and that all men are capable of what no man attains, except he is stimulated to the effort by some uncommon circumstances or situation. These Indians effected what to us appeared to be supernatural, merely by the application of such powers as they possessed in common with us, and all other men who have no particular infirmity or defect. The truth of the observation is also manifest from more familiar instances. The rope-dancer and balance-master owe their art, not to any peculiar liberality of nature, but to an accidental improvement of her common gifts; and though equal diligence and application would not always produce equal excellence in these, any more than in other arts, yet there is no doubt but that a certain degree of proficiency in them might be universally attained. Another proof of the existence of abilities in mankind, that are almost universally dormant, is furnished by the attainments of blind men. It cannot be supposed that the loss of one sense, like the amputation of a branch from a tree, gives new vigour to those that remain. Every man's hearing and touch, therefore, are capable of the nice distinctions which astonish us in those that have lost their sight, and if they do not give the same intelligence to the mind, it is merely because the same intelligence is not required of them: he that can see may do from choice what the blind do by necessity, and by the same diligent attention to the other senses may receive the same notices from them; let it, therefore, be remembered, as an encouragement to persevering diligence, and a principle of general use to mankind, that he who does all he can will ever effect much more than is generally thought to be possible.

THE TRANSIT OF VENUS.

In consequence of some hints which had been given me by Lord Morton, I determined to send out two parties to observe the transit from other situations; hoping, that if we should fail at Otaheite, they might have better success.

At daybreak of June 3, they got up, and had the satisfaction to see the sun rise without a cloud, and to make a most successful observation of the first internal contact of the planet with the sun.

The observation was made with equal success by the persons whom I had sent to the eastward; and at the fort, there not being a cloud in the sky from the rising to the setting of the sun, the whole passage of the planet Venus over the sun's disk was observed with great advantage by Green, Solander, and myself: Green's telescope and mine were of the same magnifying power, but that of Solander was greater. We all saw an atmosphere or dusky cloud round the body of the planet, which very much disturbed the times of contact, especially of the internal ones; and we differed from each other in our accounts of the times of the contacts much more than might have been expected. According to Mr. Green,

	H.	M.	S.	
The first external contact, or first appearance of Venus on the sun, was	9	25	42	Morning.
The first internal contact, or total emersion, was	9	44	4	
The second internal contact, or beginning of the emersion	3	14	8	Afternoon.
The second external contact, or total emersion	3	32	10	

The latitude of the observatory was found to be 17° 29' 15", and the longitude 149° 32' 30" W. of Greenwich.

FUNEREAL RITES AND SUPERSTITIONS.

About this time the death of an old woman of some rank, gave us an opportunity to see how they disposed of the body, and confirmed us in our opinion that these people, contrary to the present custom of all other nations now known, never bury their dead. In the middle of a small square, neatly railed in with bamboo, the awning of a canoe was raised upon two posts, and under this the body was deposited upon a frame covered with fine cloth, and near it was placed bread-fruit, fish, and other provisions: we suppose that the food was placed there for the spirit of the deceased, and consequently, that these Indians had some confused notion of a separate state; but upon our applying for further information to Tubourai Tamaide, he told us that the food was placed there as an offering to their gods. They do not, however, suppose that the gods eat, any more than the Jews suppose that Jehovah could dwell in a house: the offering is made here upon the same principle as the temple was built at Jerusalem, as an expression of reverence and gratitude, and a solicitation of the more immediate presence of the Deity. In the front of the area was a kind of stile, where the relations of the deceased stood, to pay the tribute of their sorrow; and under the awning were innumerable small pieces of cloth, on which the tears and blood of the mourners had been shed; for in their paroxysms of grief it is a universal custom to wound themselves with the shark's tooth. Within a few yards two occasional houses were set up, in one of which some relations of the deceased constantly resided, and in the other the chief mourner, who is always a man, and who keeps there a very singular dress in which a ceremony is performed. Near the place where the dead are thus set up to rot, the bones are afterwards buried.

What can have introduced among these people the custom of exposing their dead above ground till the flesh is consumed by putrefaction, and then burying the bones, it is, perhaps, impossible to guess; but it is remarkable, that Ælian and Apollonius Rhodius impute a similar practice to the ancient inhabitants of Colchis, a country near Pontus, in Asia, now called Mingrelia; except that among them this manner of disposing of the dead did not extend to both sexes: the women they buried; but the men they wrapped in a hide, and hung up in the air by a chain. This practice among the Colchians is referred to a religious cause. The principal objects of their worship were the earth and the air; and it is supposed that, in consequence of some superstitious notion, they devoted their dead to both. Whether the natives of Otaheite had any notion of the same kind, we were never able certainly to determine; but we soon discovered, that the repositories of their dead were also places of worship.

Upon this occasion it may be observed, that nothing can be

more absurd than the notion that the happiness or misery of a future life depends, in any degree, upon the disposition of the body when the state of probation is past; yet that nothing is more general than a solicitude about it. However cheap we may hold any funeral rites which custom has not familiarised, or superstition rendered sacred, most men gravely deliberate how to prevent their body from being broken by the mattock and devoured by the worm, when it is no longer capable of sensation; and purchase a place for it in holy ground, when they believe the lot of its future existence to be irrevocably determined. So strong is the association of pleasing or painful ideas with certain opinions and actions which affect us while we live, that we involuntarily act as if it was equally certain that they would affect us in the same manner when we are dead, though this is an opinion that nobody will maintain. Thus it happens, that the desire of preserving from reproach even the name that we leave behind us, or of procuring it honour, is one of the most powerful principles of action, among the inhabitants of the most speculative and enlightened nations. Posthumous reputation, upon every principle, must be acknowledged to have no influence upon the dead; yet the desire of obtaining and securing it, no force of reason, no habits of thinking, can subdue, except in those whom habitual baseness and guilt have rendered indifferent to honour and shame while they lived. This, indeed, seems to be among the happy imperfections of our nature, upon which the general good of society in a certain measure depends; for as some crimes are supposed to be prevented by hanging the body of the criminal in chains after he is dead, so in consequence of the same association of ideas, much good is procured to society, and much evil prevented, by a desire of preventing disgrace or procuring honour to a name, when nothing but a name remains.

Perhaps no better use can be made of reading an account of manners altogether new, by which the follies and absurdities of mankind are taken out of that particular connection in which habit has reconciled them to us, than to consider in how many instances they are essentially the same. When an honest devotee of the church of Rome reads, that there are Indians on the banks of the Ganges who believe that they shall secure the happiness of a future state by dying with a cow's tail in their hands, he laughs at their folly and superstition; and if these Indians were to be told, that there are people upon the continent of Europe, who imagine that they shall derive the same advantage from dying with the slipper of St. Francis upon their foot, they would laugh in their turn. But if, when the Indian heard the account of the Catholic, and the Catholic that of the Indian, each was to reflect, that there was no difference between the absurdity of the slipper and of the tail, but that the veil of prejudice and custom, which covered it in their own case, was withdrawn in the other, they would turn their knowledge to a profitable purpose.

On Monday the 26th of June, I set out in the pinnace, accompanied by Mr. Banks, to make the circuit of the island, with a view to sketch out the coast and harbours. At the district called Paparra, which belonged to our friends Oamo and Oberea, we walked out to a point, upon which we had seen, at a distance, trees that are here called *Etoa*, which generally distinguish the places where these people bury the bones of their dead. Their name for such burying-grounds, which are also places of worship, is Morai. We were soon struck with the sight of an enormous pile, which we were told was the morai of Oamo and Oberea, and the principal piece of Indian architecture in the island. It was a pile of stone-work, raised pyramidically upon an oblong base, or square, two hundred and sixty-seven feet long, and eighty-seven wide. It was built like the small pyramidal mounts upon which we sometimes fix the pillar of a sun-dial, where each side is a flight of steps; the steps, however, at the sides, were broader than those at the ends, so that it terminated not in a square of the same figure with the base, but in a ridge, like the roof of a house. There were eleven of these steps, each of which was four feet high, so that the height of the pile was forty-four feet: each step was formed of one course of white coral stone, which was neatly squared and polished; the rest of the mass, for there was no hollow within, consisted of round pebbles, which, from the regularity of their figure, seemed to have been wrought. Some of the coral stones were very large; we measured one of them, and found it three feet and a half by two feet and a half. The foundation was of rock stones, which were also squared; and one of them measured four feet seven inches by two feet four. Such a structure, raised without the assistance of iron tools to shape the stones, or mortar to join them, struck us with astonishment: it seemed to be as compact and firm as it could have been made by any workman in Europe, except that the steps, which range along its greatest length, are not perfectly straight, but sink in a kind of hollow in the middle, so that the whole surface, from end to end, is not a right line, but a curve. On Saturday July the 1st, we got back to our fort at Matavai, having found the circuit of the island, including both peninsulas, to be about thirty leagues.

Mr. Banks employed himself in planting a great quantity of the seeds of water-melons, oranges, lemons, limes, and other plants and trees which he had collected at Rio de Janeiro. For these he prepared ground on each side of the fort, with as many varieties of soil as he could choose. He also gave liberally of these seeds to the Indians, and planted many of them in the woods : some of the melon seeds having been planted soon after our arrival, the natives shewed him several of the plants, which appeared to be in the most flourishing condition, and were continually asking him for more.

Among the natives who were almost constantly with us was Tupia, whose name has been often mentioned in this narrative. He had been the first minister of Oberea, when she was in the height of her power; he was also the chief Tahowa or priest of the island, consequently well acquainted with the religion of the country, as well with respect to its ceremonies as principles. He had also great experience and knowledge in navigation, and was particularly acquainted with the number and situation of the neighbouring islands. This man had often expressed a desire to go with us, and he now came on board, with a boy about thirteen years of age, his servant, and urged us to let him proceed with us on our voyage. To have such a person on board was certainly desirable, for many reasons ; by learning his language, and teaching him ours, we should be able to acquire a much better knowledge of the customs, policy, and religion of the people, than our short stay among them could give us ; I therefore gladly agreed to receive them on board. As we were prevented from sailing to-day, by having found it necessary to make new stocks to our small and best bower anchors, the old ones having been totally destroyed by the worms, Tupia said he would go once more on shore, and make a signal for the boat to fetch him off in the evening. He went accordingly, and took with him a miniature picture of Mr. Banks, to show his friends, and several little things to give them as parting presents.

On the morning of Thursday the 13th of July, the ship was very early crowded with our friends, and surrounded by a multitude of canoes, which were filled with the natives of an inferior class. Between eleven and twelve we weighed anchor, and as soon as the ship was under sail, the Indians on board took their leaves, and wept, with a decent and silent sorrow, in which there was something very striking and tender: the people in the canoes, on the contrary, seemed to vie with each other in the loudness of their lamentations, which we considered rather as affectation than grief. Tupia sustained himself in this scene with a firmness and resolution truly admirable: he wept, indeed, but the effort that he made to conceal his tears concurred with them to do him honour. He sent his last present, a shirt, to Potomai, and then went with Mr. Banks to the mast-head, waving to the canoes as long as they continued in sight.

Thus we took leave of Otaheite, and its inhabitants, after a stay of just three months; for much the greater part of the time we lived together in the most cordial friendship, and a perpetual reciprocation of good offices. The accidental differences which now and then happened could not be more sincerely regretted on their part than they were on ours: the principal causes were such as necessarily resulted from our situation and circumstances, in conjunction with the infirmities of human nature, from our not being able perfectly to understand each other, and from the disposition of the inhabitants to theft, which we could not at all times bear with or prevent. They had not, however, except in one instance, been attended with any fatal consequence; and to that accident were owing the measures that I took to prevent others of the same kind.

The produce of this island is bread-fruit, cocoa-nuts, bananas, of thirteen sorts, the best we had ever eaten; plantains; a fruit not unlike an apple, which, when ripe, is very pleasant; sweet potatoes, yams, cocoas; a fruit known here by the name of *Jambu*, and reckoned most delicious; sugar-cane, which the inhabitants eat raw; a fruit that grows in a pod, like that of a large kidney-bean, which, when it is roasted, eats very much like a chestnut, by the natives called *Ahee;* a tree called *Wharra*, called in the East Indies *Pandanes*, which produces fruit something like the pine-apple; a shrub called *Nono;* a species of fern, of which the root is eaten, and sometimes the leaves; but the fruits of the Nono, the fern, and the Theve, are eaten only by the inferior people, and in times of scarcity. All these, which serve the inhabitants for food, the earth produces spontaneously, or with so little culture, that they seem to be exempted from the first general curse, that "man should eat his bread in the sweat of his face."

Of tame animals they have only hogs, dogs, and poultry; neither is there a wild animal in the island, except ducks, pigeons, paroquets, with a few other birds, and rats, there being no other quadruped, nor any serpent. But the sea supplies them with great variety of most excellent fish, to eat which is their chief luxury, and to catch it their principal labour.

As to the people they are of the largest size of Europeans. The men are tall, strong, well-limbed, and finely shaped. The tallest that we saw was a man upon a neighbouring island, called Huaheine, who measured six feet three inches and a half. The women of the superior rank are also in general above our middle stature, but those of the inferior class are rather below it, and some of them are very small. Their natural complexion is that kind of clear olive, or *brunette,* which many people in Europe prefer to the finest white and red. In those that are exposed to the wind and sun, it is considerably deepened, but in others that live under shelter, especially the superior class of women, it continues of its native hue, and the skin is most delicately smooth and soft: they have no tint in their cheeks which we distinguish by the name of colour. The shape of the face is comely, the cheek-bones are not high, neither are the eyes hollow, nor the brow prominent: the only feature that does not correspond with our ideas of beauty is the nose, which, in general, is somewhat flat; but their eyes, especially those of the women, are full of expression, sometimes sparkling with fire, and sometimes melting with softness; their teeth also are, almost without exception, most beautifully even and white, and their breath perfectly without taint.

In their dispositions, also, they seemed to be brave, open, and candid, without either suspicion or treachery, cruelty or revenge; so that we placed the same confidence in them as in our best friends, many of us, particularly Mr. Banks, sleeping frequently in their houses in the woods, without a companion, and consequently wholly in their power. They were, however, all thieves; and when that is allowed, they need not much fear a competition with the people of any other nation upon earth.

They have a custom of staining their bodies, nearly in the same manner as is practised in many other parts of the world, which they call *Tattowing*. They prick the skin, so as just not to fetch blood, with a small instrument, something in the form of a hoe. The operation is painful, and it is some days before the wounds are healed. It is performed upon the youth of both sexes when they are about twelve or fourteen years of age, on several parts of the body, and in various figures, according to the fancy of the parent, or perhaps the rank of the party.

The houses, or rather dwellings, of these people have been occasionally mentioned before: they are all built in the wood between the sea and the mountains, and no more ground is cleared for each house than just sufficient to prevent the dropping of the branches from rotting the thatch with which they are covered; from the house, therefore, the inhabitant steps immediately under the shade, which is the most delightful that can be imagined. It consists of groves of bread-fruit and cocoa-nuts, without underwood, which are intersected in all directions by the paths that lead from one house to the other. Nothing can be more grateful than this shade in so warm a climate, nor anything more beautiful than these walks. As there is no underwood, the shade cools without impeding the air; and the houses, having no walls, receive the gale from whatever point it blows.

Of the many vegetables that have been mentioned already as serving them for food, the principal is the bread-fruit, to procure which costs them no trouble or labour but climbing a tree: the tree which produces it does not indeed shoot up spontaneously; but if a man plants ten of them in his lifetime, which he may do in about an hour, he will as completely fulfil his duty to his own and future generations as the natives of our less temperate climate can do by ploughing in the cold of winter, and reaping in the summer's heat, as often as these seasons return; even if, after he has procured bread for his present household, he should convert a surplus into money, and lay it

First Voyage.

up for his children. It is true, indeed, that the bread-fruit is not always in season; but cocoa-nuts, bananas, plantains, and a great variety of other fruits supply the deficiency.

It may well be supposed that cookery is but little studied by these people as an art; and indeed they have but two ways of applying fire to dress their food,—broiling and baking. Of the bread-fruit they also make three dishes, by putting either water or the milk of the cocoa-nut to it, then beating it to a paste with a stone pestle, and afterwards mixing it with ripe plantains, bananas, or the sour paste which they call *Mahie*.

Salt-water is the universal sauce, no meal being eaten without it: those who live near the sea have it fetched as it is wanted; those who live at some distance keep it in large bamboos, which are set up in their houses for use. They make another of the kernels of cocoa-nuts, which being fermented till they dissolve into a paste somewhat resembling butter, are beaten up with salt-water. The flavour of this is very strong, and was, when we first tasted it, exceedingly nauseous.

For drink, they have in general nothing but water, or the juice of the cocoa-nut; the art of producing liquors that intoxicate by fermentation, being happily unknown among them; neither have they any narcotic which they chew, as the natives of some other countries do opium, betel-root, and tobacco. Some of them drank freely of our liquors, and in a few instances became very drunk; but the persons to whom this happened were so far from desiring to repeat the debauch, that they would never touch any of our liquors afterwards. We were, however, informed, that they became drunk by drinking a juice that is expressed from the leaves of a plant which they call *Ava Ava*. This plant was not in season when we were there, so that we saw no instances of its effects; and as they considered drunkenness as a disgrace, they probably would have concealed from us any instances which might have happened during our stay. This vice is almost peculiar to the chiefs and considerable persons, who vie with each other in drinking the greatest number of draughts, each draught being about a pint. They keep this intoxicating juice with great care from their women.

Table they have none; but their apparatus for eating is set out with great neatness, though the articles are too simple and too few to allow anything for show; and they commonly eat alone; but when a stranger happens to visit them he sometimes makes a second in their mess. Of the meal of one of their principal people I shall give a particular description. He sits down under the shade of the next tree, or on the shady side of his house, and a large quantity of leaves, either of the breadfruit or banana, are neatly spread before him upon the ground as a table-cloth; a basket is then set by him that contains his provision, which, if fish or flesh, is ready dressed, and wrapped up in leaves, and two cocoa-nut shells, one full of salt water and the other of fresh: his attendants, who are not few, seat themselves round him, and when all is ready he begins by washing his hands and his mouth thoroughly with the fresh water, and this he repeats almost continually throughout the whole meal; he then takes part of his provision out of the basket, which generally consists of a small fish or two, two or three bread-fruits, fourteen or fifteen ripe bananas, or six or seven apples; he first takes half a bread-fruit, peels off the rind, and takes out the core with his nails; of this he puts as much into his mouth as it can hold, and while he chews it takes the fish out of the leaves, and breaks one of them into the salt water, placing the other, and what remains of the bread-fruit, upon the leaves that have been spread before him. When this is done, he takes up a small piece of the fish that has been broken into the salt water with all the fingers of one hand, and sucks it into his mouth, so as to get with it as much of the salt water as possible : in the same manner he takes the rest by different morsels, and between each, at least very frequently, takes a small sup of the salt water either out of the cocoa-nut shell or the palm of his hand : in the meantime one of his attendants has prepared a young cocoa-nut, by pealing off the outer rind with his teeth, an operation which to a European appears very surprising ; but it depends so much upon sleight that many of us were able to do it before we left the island, and some that could scarcely crack a filbert : the master, when he chooses to drink, takes the cocoa-nut thus prepared, and boring a hole through the shell with his finger, or breaking it with a stone, he sucks out the liquor. When he has eaten his bread-fruit and fish he begins with his plantains, one of which makes but a mouthful, though it be as big as a black-pudding ; if, instead of plantains, he has apples, he never tastes them till they have been pared ; to do this a shell is picked up from the ground, where they are always in plenty, and tossed to him by an attendant : he immediately begins to cut or scrape off the rind, but so awkwardly that great part of the fruit is wasted. If, instead of fish, he has flesh, he must have some succedaneum for a knife to divide it ; and for this purpose a piece of bamboo is tossed to him, of which he makes the necessary implement by splitting it transversely with his nail. While all this has been doing, some of his attendants have been employed in beating bread-fruit with a stone pestle upon a block of wood ; by being beaten in this manner, and sprinkled from time to time with water, it is reduced to the consistence of a soft paste, and is then put into a vessel somewhat like a butcher's tray, and either made up alone, or mixed with banana or mahie, according to the taste of the master, by pouring water upon it by degrees and squeezing it often through the hand : under this operation it acquires the consistence of a thick custard, and a large cocoa-nut shell full of it being set before him, he sips it as we should do a jelly if we had no spoon to take it from the glass : the meal is then finished by again washing his hands and his mouth. After which the cocoa-nut shells are cleaned, and everything that is left is replaced in the basket.

The quantity of food which these people eat at a meal is prodigious : I have seen one man devour two or three fishes as big as a perch ; three bread-fruits, each bigger than two fists ; fourteen or fifteen plantains or bananas, each of them six or seven inches long, and four or five round ; and near a quart of the pounded bread-fruit, which is as substantial as the thickest unbaked custard. This is so extraordinary that I scarcely expect to be believed ; and I would not have related it upon my own single testimony ; but Mr. Banks, Dr. Solander, and most of the other gentlemen, have had ocular demonstration of its truth, and know that I mentioned them upon the occasion.

It is very wonderful that these people, who are remarkably fond of society, and particularly that of their women, should exclude its pleasures from the table, where, among all other nations, whether civil or savage, they have been principally enjoyed. How a meal, which everywhere else brings families and friends together, came to separate them here, we often inquired, but could never learn. They ate alone, they said, because it was right; but why it was right to eat alone they never attempted to tell us: such, however, was the force of habit, that they expressed the strongest dislike, and even disgust, at our eating in society, especially with our women, and of the same victuals. At first, we thought this strange singularity arose from some superstitious opinion; but they constantly affirmed the contrary. We observed also some caprices in the custom, for which we could as little account as for the custom itself. We could never prevail with any of the women to partake of the victuals at our table when we were dining in company; yet they would go, five or six together, into the servants' apartments, and there eat very heartily of whatever they could find; nor were they in the least disconcerted if we came in while they were doing it. When any of us have been alone with a woman, she has sometimes eaten in our company; but then she has expressed the greatest unwillingness that it should be known, and always extorted the strongest promises of secrecy.

Among themselves even two brothers and two sisters have each their separate baskets with provision and the apparatus of their meal.

But I must not conclude my account of the domestic life of these people without mentioning their personal cleanliness. If that which lessens the good of life and increases the evil is vice, surely cleanliness is a virtue: the want of it tends to destroy both beauty and health, and mingles disgust with our best pleasures.

After parting with our friends, we made an easy sail, with gentle breezes and clear weather, for four of the neighbouring islands, which Tupia distinguished by the names of Huaheine, Ulietea, Otaha, and Bolabola (Borabora).

While we were about these, we expended very little of the

ship's provisions, and were very plentifully supplied with hogs, fowls, plantains, and yams, which we hoped would have been of great use to us in our course to the southward; but the hogs would not eat European grain of any kind, pulse, or bread-dust, so that we could not preserve them alive; and the fowls were all very soon seized with a disease that affected the head so, that they continued to hold it down between their legs till they died: much dependence, therefore, must not be placed in live stock taken on board at these places, at least not till a discovery is made of some food that the hogs will eat, and some remedy for the disease of the poultry. Having been necessarily detained at Ulietea so long, by the carpenters, in stopping our leak, we determined to give up our design of going on shore at Bolabola, especially as it appeared to be difficult of access.

To these islands, as they lie contiguous to each other, I gave the names of Society Islands, but did not think it proper to distinguish them separately by any other names than those by which they were known to the natives. They are situated between the latitude of 16° 10′ and 16° 55′ S., and between the longitude of 150° 57′ and 152° W. from the meridian of Greenwich.

CHAPTER II.

New Zealand.

WE sailed from the Society Islands on the 15th of August 1769, and on Friday the 25th we celebrated the anniversary of our leaving England, by taking a Cheshire cheese from a locker, where it had been carefully treasured up for this occasion, and tapping a cask of porter, which proved to be very good, and in excellent order.

On the 1st of September, being in the latitude of 40° 22′ S., and longitude 147° 29′ W., and there not being any signs of land, with a heavy sea from the westward, and strong gales, I wore, and stood back to the northward, fearing that we might receive such damage in our sails and rigging, as would hinder the prosecution of the voyage. On the next day, there being strong gales to the westward, I brought to, with the ship's head to the northward; but in the morning of the 3d, the wind being more moderate, we loosened the reef of the mainsail, set the topsails, and plied to the westward.

On the 24th, being in latitude 33° 18′, longitude 162° 51′, we observed a small piece of sea-weed, and a piece of wood covered with barnacles. On the 27th, we saw a seal asleep upon the water, and several bunches of sea-weed. The next day we saw more sea-weed in bunches, and on the 29th, a bird, which we thought a land bird; it somewhat resembled a snipe, but had a short bill. On the 1st of October we saw birds innumerable, and another seal asleep upon the water; it is a general opinion, that seals never go out of soundings, or far from land, but those that we saw in these seas prove the contrary. Rock-weed is, however, a certain indication that land is not far distant. The next day, it being calm, we hoisted out the boat, to try whether there was a current, but found none. Our latitude was 37° 10′, longitude 172° 54′ W. On the 3d, being in latitude 36° 56′, longitude 173° 27′, we took up more sea-weed, and another piece of wood covered with barnacles. The next day, we saw two more seals, and a brown bird, about as big as a raven, with some white feathers under the wing. Mr. Gore told us that birds of this kind were seen in great numbers about Falkland's Islands, and our people gave them the name of Port Egmont hens.

On the 5th, we thought the water changed colour, but, upon casting the lead, had no ground with one hundred and eighty fathom. In the evening of this day, the variation was 12° 50′ E., and, while we were going nine leagues, it increased to 14° 2′. On the next day, Friday, October the 6th, we saw land from the mast-head, bearing W. by N., and stood directly for it; in the evening, it could just be discerned from the deck, and appeared large. The variation this day was, by azimuth and amplitude, 15° 4½′ E., and by observation made of the sun and moon, the longitude of the ship appeared to be 180° 55′ W., and by the medium of this and subsequent observations, there appeared to be an error in the ship's account of longitude during her run from Otaheite of 3° 16′, she being so much to the westward of the longitude resulting from the log. At midnight, I brought to and sounded, but had no ground with one hundred and seventy fathom.

On the 7th it fell calm, we therefore approached the land

slowly, and in the afternoon, when a breeze sprung up, we were still distant seven or eight leagues. It appeared still larger as it was more distinctly seen, with four or five ranges of hills, rising one over the other, and a chain of mountains above all, which appeared to be of an enormous height. This land became the subject of much eager conversation; but the general opinion seemed to be that we had found

THE TERRA AUSTRALIS INCOGNITA.

About five o'clock, we saw the opening of a bay, which seemed to run pretty far inland, upon which we hauled our wind and stood in for it: we also saw smoke ascending from different places on shore. When night came on, however, we kept plying off and on till day-light, when we found ourselves to the leeward of the bay, the wind being at north: we could now perceive that the hills were clothed with wood, and that some of the trees in the valleys were very large. By noon we fetched in with the south-west point; but not being able to weather it, tacked and stood off: at this time we saw several canoes standing across the bay, which, in a little time, made to shore, without seeming to take the least notice of the ship; we also saw some houses, which appeared to be small, but neat; and near one of them a considerable number of the people collected together, who were sitting upon the beach, and who, we thought, were the same that we had seen in the canoes. Upon a small peninsula, at the north-east head, we could plainly perceive a pretty high and regular paling, which enclosed the whole top of a hill; this was also the subject of much speculation, some supposing it to be a park of deer, others an enclosure for oxen and sheep. About four o'clock in the afternoon, we anchored on the north-west side of the bay, before the entrance of a small river, in ten fathom water, with a fine sandy bottom, and at about half a league from the shore. The sides of the bay are white cliffs of a great height; the middle is low land, with hills gradually rising behind, one towering above another, and terminating in the chain of mountains which appeared to be far inland.

In the evening I went on shore, accompanied by Mr. Banks and Dr. Solander, with the pinnace and yawl, and a party of men. We landed abreast of the ship, on the east side of the river, which was here about forty yards broad; but seeing some natives on the west side whom I wished to speak with, and finding the river not fordable, I ordered the yawl in to carry us over, and left the pinnace at the entrance. When we came near the place where the people were assembled, they all ran away; however, we landed, and leaving four boys to take care of the yawl, we walked up to some huts which were about two or three hundred yards from the water-side. When we had got some distance from the boat, four men, armed with long lances, rushed out of the woods, and running up to attack the boat, would certainly have cut her off, if the people in the pinnace had not discovered them, and called to the boys to drop down the stream: the boys instantly obeyed, but being closely pursued by the Indians, the cockswain of the pinnace, who had the charge of the boats, fired a musket over their heads; at this they stopped and looked round them, but in a few minutes renewed the pursuit, brandishing their lances in a threatening manner: the cockswain then fired a second musket over their heads, but of this they took no notice; and one of them lifting up his spear to dart it at the boat, another piece was fired, which shot him dead. When he fell, the other three stood motionless for some minutes, as if petrified with astonishment; as soon as they recovered, they went back, dragging after them the dead body, which, however, they soon left, that it might not encumber their flight. At the report of the first musket, we drew together, having straggled to a little distance from each other, and made the best of our way back to the boat; and crossing the river, we soon saw the Indian lying dead upon the ground. Upon examining the body, we found that he had been shot through the heart: he was a man of the middle size and stature; his complexion was brown, but not very dark, and one side of his face was tatooed in spiral lines of a very regular figure: he was covered with a fine cloth, of a manufacture altogether new to us, and it was tied on exactly according to the representation in Valentyn's Account of Abel Tasman's Voyage, vol. iii., part 2, page 50: his hair also was tied in a knot on the top of his head, but had no feather in it. We returned immediately to the ship, where we could hear the people on shore talking with great earnestness, and in a very loud tone, probably about what had happened, and what should be done.

In the morning, we saw several of the natives where they had been seen the night before, and some walking with a quick pace towards the place where we had landed, most of them unarmed; but three or four with long pikes in their hands. As I was desirous to establish an intercourse with them, I ordered three boats to be manned with seamen and marines, and proceeded towards the shore, accompanied by Mr. Banks, Dr. Solander, the other gentlemen, and Tupia; about fifty of them seemed to wait for our landing, on the opposite side of the river, which we thought a sign of fear, and seated themselves upon the ground: at first, therefore, myself, with only Mr. Banks, Dr. Solander, and Tupia, landed from the little boat, and advanced towards them; but we had not proceeded many paces before they all started up, and every man produced either a long pike, or a small weapon of green talc, extremely well polished, about a foot long, and thick enough to weigh four or five pounds: Tupia called to them in the language of Otaheite; but they answered only by flourishing their weapons, and making signs to us to depart; a musket was then fired wide of them, and the ball struck the water, the river being still between us; they saw the effect, and desisted from their threats: but we thought it prudent to retreat till the marines could be landed. This was soon done; and they marched, with a jack carried before them, to a little bank, about fifty yards from the water-side; here they were drawn up, and I again advanced with Mr. Banks and Dr. Solander; Tupia, Mr. Green, and Mr. Monkhouse, being with us. Tupia was again directed to speak to them, and it was with great pleasure that we perceived he was perfectly understood, he and the natives speaking only different dialects of the same language. He told them that we wanted provision and water, and would give them iron in exchange, the properties of which he explained as well as he was able. They were willing to trade, and desired that we would come over to them for that purpose: to this we consented, provided that they would lay by their arms; which, however, they could by no means be persuaded to do. During this conversation Tupia warned us to be upon our guard, for that they were not our friends: we then pressed them in our turn to come over to us; and at last one of them stripped himself, and swam over without his arms: he was almost immediately followed by two more, and soon after by most of the rest, to the number of twenty or thirty; but these brought their arms with them. We made them all presents of iron and beads; but they seemed to set little value upon either, particularly the iron, not having the least idea of its use; so that we got nothing in return but a few feathers: they offered, indeed, to exchange their arms for ours, and when we refused, made many attempts to snatch them out of our hands. As soon as they came over, Tupia repeated his declaration, that they were not our friends, and again warned us to be upon our guard; their attempts to snatch our weapons, therefore, did not succeed; and we gave them to understand by Tupia, that we should be obliged to kill them if they offered any farther violence. In a few minutes, however, Mr. Green happening to turn about, one of them snatched away his hanger, and retiring to a little distance, waved it round his head, with a shout of exultation: the rest now began to be extremely insolent, and we saw more coming to join them from the opposite side of the river. It was therefore become necessary to repress them, and Mr. Banks fired at the man who had taken the hanger, with small shot, at the distance of about fifteen yards: when the shot struck him, he ceased his cry; but instead of returning the hanger, continued to flourish it over his head, at the same time slowly retreating to a greater distance. Mr. Monkhouse seeing this, fired at him with ball, and he instantly dropped. Upon this the main body, who had retired to a rock in the middle of the river upon the first discharge, began to return; two that were near to the man who had been killed, ran up to the body, one seized his weapon of green talc, and the other endeavoured to secure the hanger, which Mr. Monkhouse had but just time to prevent. As all that had retired to the rock were now advancing, three of us discharged our pieces, loaded only with small shot, upon which they swam back for the shore; and we perceived, upon their landing, that two or three of them were wounded. They retired slowly up the country, and we re-embarked in our boats.

As we had unhappily experienced, that nothing was to be done with these people at this place; and finding the water in the river to be salt, I proceeded in the boats round the head of the bay in search of fresh water, and with a design, if possible, to surprise some of the natives, and take them on board, where, by kind treatment and presents, I might obtain their friendship, and by their means establish an amicable correspondence with their countrymen.

To my great regret, I found no place where I could land, a dangerous surf everywhere beating upon the shore; but I saw two canoes coming in from the sea, one under sail, and the other worked with paddles. I thought this a favourable opportunity to get some of the people into my possession without mischief, as those in the canoe were probably fishermen, and without arms, and I had three boats full of men. I therefore disposed the boats so as most effectually to intercept them in their way to the shore; the people in the canoe that was paddled perceived us so soon, that, by making to the nearest land with their utmost strength, they escaped us; the other sailed on till she was in the midst of us without discerning what we were; but the moment she discovered us, the people on board struck their sail, and took to their paddles, which they plied so briskly that she out-ran the boat. They were, however, within hearing, and Tupia called out to them to come alongside, and promised for us that they should come to no hurt: they chose, however, rather to trust to their paddles than our promises, and continued to make from us with all their power. I then ordered a musket to be fired over their heads, as the least exceptionable expedient to accomplish my design, hoping it would either make them surrender, or leap into the water. Upon the discharge of the piece, they ceased paddling; and all of them, being seven in number, began to strip, as we imagined, to jump overboard; but it happened otherwise. They immediately formed a resolution not to fly, but to fight; and when the boat came up, they began the attack with their paddles, and with stones and other offensive weapons that were in the boat, so vigorously that we were obliged to fire upon them in our own defence; four were unhappily killed, and the other three, who were boys, the eldest about nineteen, and the youngest about eleven, instantly leaped into the water; the eldest swam with great vigour, and resisted the attempts of our people to take him into the boat by every effort that he could make: he was, however, at last overpowered, and the other two were taken up with less difficulty. I am conscious that the feeling of every reader of humanity will censure me for having fired upon these unhappy people, and it is impossible that, upon a calm review, I should approve it myself. They certainly did not deserve death for not choosing to confide in my promises; or not consenting to come on board my boat, even if they had apprehended no danger; but the nature of my service required me to obtain a knowledge of their country, which I could no otherwise effect than by forcing my way into it in a hostile manner, or gaining admission through the confidence and good-will of the people. I had already tried the power of presents without effect; and I was now prompted, by my desire to avoid further hostilities, to get some of them on board, as the only method left of convincing them that we intended them no harm, and had it in our power to contribute to their gratification and convenience. Thus far my intentions certainly were not criminal; and though in the contest, which I had not the least reason to expect, our victory might have been complete without so great an expense of life; yet in such situations, when the command to fire has been given, no man can restrain its excess, or prescribe its effect.

As soon as the poor wretches whom we had taken out of the water were in the boat, they squatted down, expecting no doubt instantly to be put to death; we made haste to convince them of the contrary, by every method in our power; we furnished them with clothes, and gave them every other testimony of kindness that could remove their fears and engage their good-will. Those who are acquainted with human nature will not wonder that the sudden joy of these young savages at being unexpectedly delivered from the fear of death, and kindly treated by those whom they supposed would have been their instant executioners, surmounted their concern for the friends they had lost, and was strongly expressed in their countenances and behaviour. Before we reached the ship, their suspicions and fears being wholly removed, they appeared to be not only reconciled to their situation, but in high spirits, and upon being offered some bread when they came on board, they devoured it with a voracious appetite. They answered and asked many questions with great appearance of pleasure and curiosity; and when our dinner came they expressed an inclination to taste everything that they saw; they seemed best pleased with the salt pork, though we had other provisions upon the table. At sunset they ate another meal with great eagerness, each devouring a large quantity of bread, and drinking above a quart of water. We then made them beds upon the lockers, and they went to sleep with great seeming content. In the night, however, the tumult of their minds having subsided, and given way to reflection, they sighed often and loud. Tupia, who was always upon the watch to comfort them, got up, and by soothing and encouragement made them not only easy but cheerful; their cheerfulness was encouraged so that they sung a song with a degree of taste that surprised us: the tune was solemn and slow, like those of our Psalms, containing many notes and semitones. Their countenances were intelligent and expressive, and the middlemost, who seemed to be about fifteen, had an openness in his aspect, and an ease in his deportment, which were very striking: we found that the two eldest were brothers, and that their names were Taahourange and Koikerange; the name of the youngest was Maragovete. As we were returning to the ship, after having taken these boys into the boat, we picked up a large piece of pumice-stone floating upon the water; a sure sign that there either is, or has been, a volcano in this neighbourhood.

In the morning they all seemed to be cheerful, and ate another enormous meal; after this we dressed them, and adorned them with bracelets, anklets, and necklaces, after their own fashion, and the boat being hoisted out, they were told that we were going to set them ashore; this produced a transport of joy; but upon perceiving that we made towards our first landing-place near the river, their countenances changed, and they entreated with great earnestness that they might not be set ashore at that place, because they said it was inhabited by their enemies, who would kill them and eat them. This was a great disappointment to me, because I hoped the report and appearance of the boys would procure a favourable reception for ourselves. I had already sent an officer on shore with the marines and a party of men to cut wood, and I was determined to land near the place;

not, however, to abandon the boys, if, when we got on shore, they should be unwilling to leave us; but to send a boat with them in the evening to that part of the bay to which they pointed, and which they called their home. Mr. Banks, Dr. Solander, and Tupia, were with me, and upon our landing with the boys, and crossing the river, they seemed at first to be unwilling to leave us; but at length they suddenly changed their mind, and, though not without a manifest struggle and some tears, they took their leave; when they were gone we proceeded along a swamp, with a design to shoot some ducks, of which we saw great plenty, and four of the marines attended us, walking abreast of us upon a bank that overlooked the country. After we had advanced about a mile, these men called out to us and told us that a large body of the Indians was in sight, and advancing at a great rate. Upon receiving this intelligence we drew together, and resolved to make the best of our way to the boats; we had scarcely begun to put this into execution, when the three Indian boys started suddenly from some bushes, where they had concealed themselves, and again claimed our protection; we readily received them, and repairing to the beach as the clearest place, we walked briskly towards the boats. The Indians were in two bodies; one ran along the bank which had been quitted by the marines, the other fetched a compass by the swamp, so that we could not see them: when they perceived that we had formed into one body they slackened their pace, but still followed us in a gentle walk; that they slackened their pace, was for us, as well as for them, a fortunate circumstance; for when we came to the side of the river, where we expected to find the boats that were to carry us over to the wooders, we found the pinnace at least a mile from her station, having been sent to pick up a bird which had been shot by the officer on shore, and the little boat was obliged to make three trips before we could all get over to the rest of the party. As soon as we were drawn up on the other side, the Indians came down, not in a body as we expected, but by two or three at a time, all armed, and in a short time their number increased to about two hundred: as we now despaired of making peace with them, seeing that the dread of our small arms did not keep them at a distance, and that the ship was too far off to reach the place with a shot, we resolved to re-embark, lest our stay should embroil us in another quarrel, and cost more of the Indians their lives. We, therefore, advanced towards the pinnace, which was now returning, when one of the boys suddenly cried out that his uncle was among the people who had marched down to us, and desired us to stay and talk with them; we complied, and a parley immediately commenced between them and Tupia, during which the boys held up everything we had given them as tokens of our kindness and liberality; but neither would either of the boys swim over to them, or any of them to the boys. The body of the man who had been killed the day before still lay exposed upon the beach; the boys seeing it lie very near us, went up to it, and covered it with some of the clothes that we had given them; and soon after a single man, unarmed, who proved to be the uncle of Maragovete, the youngest of the boys, swam over to us, bringing in his hand a green branch, which we supposed, as well here as at Otaheite, to be an emblem of peace. We received his branch by the hands of Tupia, to whom he gave it, and made him many presents; we also invited him to go on board the ship, but he declined it; we therefore left him, and expected that his nephew and the two other young Indians would have stayed with him, but to our great surprise, they chose rather to go with us. As soon as we had retired he went and gathered another green branch, and with this in his hand, he approached the dead body which the youth had covered with part of his clothes, walking sideways, with many ceremonies, and then throwing it towards him. When this was done, he returned to his companions, who had sat down upon the sand to observe the issue of his negotiation: they immediately gathered round him, and continued in a body above an hour, without seeming to take any farther notice of us. We were more curious than they, and observing them with our glasses from on board the ship, we saw some of them cross the river upon a kind of raft, or catamarine, and four of them carry off the dead body which had been covered by the boy, and over which his uncle had performed the ceremony of the branch, upon a kind of bier, between four men; the other body was still suffered to remain where it had been first left.

After dinner I directed Tupia to ask the boys if they had now any objection to going ashore where we had left their uncle, the body having been carried off, which we understood was a ratification of peace; they said they had not; and the boat being ordered, they went into it with great alacrity: when the boat, in which I had sent two midshipmen, came to land, they went willingly ashore; but soon after she put off they returned to the rocks, and wading into the water, earnestly entreated to be taken on board again; but the people in the boat having positive orders to leave them could not comply. We were very attentive to what happened on shore, and keeping a constant watch with our glasses, we saw a man pass the river upon another raft, and fetch them to a place where forty or fifty of the natives were assembled, who closed round them, and continued in the same place till sunset: upon looking again, when we saw them in motion, we could plainly distinguish our three prisoners, who separated themselves from the rest, came down to the beach, and having waved their hands three times towards the ship, ran nimbly back and joined their companions, who walked leisurely away towards that part which the boys had pointed to as their dwelling-place; we had therefore the greatest reason to believe that no mischief would happen to them, especially as we perceived that they went off in the clothes we had given them.

After it was dark loud voices were heard on shore in the bottom of the bay as usual, of which we could never learn the meaning. The next morning, at six o'clock, we weighed, and stood away from this unfortunate and inhospitable place, to which I gave the name of

POVERTY BAY.

When these people had recovered from the first impressions of fear, which, notwithstanding their resolution in coming on board, had manifestly thrown them into some confusion, we inquired after our poor boys. The man who first came on board immediately answered, that they were unhurt, and at home; adding, that they had been induced to venture on board by the account which they had given him of the kindness with which they had been treated, and the wonders which were contained in the ship. While they were on board they shewed every sign of friendship, and invited us very cordially to go back to our old bay, or to a small cove which they pointed out, that was not quite so far off; but I chose rather to prosecute my discoveries than go back, having reason to hope that I should find a better harbour than any I had yet seen.

About an hour before sun-set, the canoes put off from the ship with the few paddles they had reserved, which were scarcely sufficient to set them on shore ; but, by some means or other, three of their people were left behind. As soon as we discovered it, we hailed them, but not one of them would return to take them on board. This greatly surprised us ; but we were surprised still more to observe that the deserted Indians did not seem at all uneasy at their situation, but entertained us with dancing and singing after their manner, ate their suppers, and went quietly to bed.

A light breeze springing up soon after it was dark, we steered along the shore under an easy sail till midnight, and then brought to ; soon after which it fell calm. We were now some leagues distant from the place where the canoes had left us ; and at day-break, when the Indians perceived it, they were seized with consternation and terror, and lamented their situation in loud complaints, with gestures of despair, and many tears. Tupia, with great difficulty, pacified them ; and about seven o'clock in the morning, a light breeze springing up, we continued to stand south-west along the shore. Fortunately for our poor Indians, two canoes came off about this time, and made towards the ship ; they stopped, however, at a little distance, and seemed unwilling to trust themselves nearer. Our Indians were greatly agitated in this state of uncertainty, and urged their fellows to come alongside of the ship, both by their voice and gestures, with the utmost eagerness and impatience. Tupia interpreted what they said, and we were much surprised to find that, among other arguments, they assured the people in the canoes, that

We did not eat men.

We now began seriously to believe that this horrid custom prevailed among them; for what the boys had said we considered as a mere hyperbolical expression of their fear. An old man came on board, who seemed to be a chief, from the finery of his garment and the superiority of his weapon, which was a Patoo-patoo made of bone that, as he said, had belonged to a whale. He stayed on board but a short time; and when he went away, he took with him our guests, very much to the satisfaction both of them and us.

At the time when we sailed, we were abreast of a point from which the land trends S.S.W., and which, on account of its figure, I called Cape Table; and a small island, which was the southernmost land in sight, I named the Island of Portland, from its very great resemblance to Portland, in the English Channel.

Having got round Portland, we hauled in for the land N.W., having a gentle breeze at N.E., which about five o'clock died away, and obliged us to anchor.

About five o'clock in the morning of the 13th October, a breeze springing up northerly, we weighed, and steered in for the land. The shore here forms a large bay, of which Portland is the north-east point, and the bay, that runs behind Cape Table, an arm. This arm I had a great inclination to examine.

Being abreast of the point, several fishing boats came off to us, and sold us some stinking fish; it was the best they had, and we were willing to trade with them upon any terms; these people behaved very well, and we should have parted good friends if it had not been for a large canoe, with two-and-twenty armed men on board, which came boldly up alongside of the ship. We soon saw that this boat had nothing for traffic, yet we gave them two or three pieces of cloth, an article which they seemed very fond of. I observed that one man had a black skin thrown over him, somewhat resembling that of a bear, and being desirous to know what animal was its first owner, I offered him for it a piece of red baize, and he seemed greatly pleased with the bargain, immediately pulling off the skin, and holding it up in the boat; he would not, however, part with it till he had the cloth in his possession, and as there could be no transfer of property, if with equal caution I had insisted upon the same condition, I ordered the cloth to be handed down to him, upon which, with amazing coolness, instead of sending up the skin, he began to pack up both that and the baize, which he had received as the purchase of it, in a basket, without paying the least regard to my demand or remonstrances, and soon after, with the fishing-boats, put off from the ship; when they were at some distance, they drew together, and after a short consultation returned; the fishermen offered more fish, which, though good for nothing, was purchased, and trade was again renewed. Among others who were placed over the ship's side to hand up what we bought, was little Tayeto, Tupia's boy; and one of the Indians, watching his opportunity, suddenly seized him, and dragged him down into the canoe; two of them held him down in the forepart of it, and the others, with great activity, paddled her off, the rest of the canoes following as fast as they could; upon this the marines, who were under arms upon deck, were ordered to fire. The shot was directed to that part of the canoe which was farthest from the boy, and rather wide of her, being willing rather to miss the rowers than to hurt him; it happened, however, that one man dropped, upon which the others quitted their hold of the boy, who instantly leaped into the water, and swam towards the ship; the large canoe immediately pulled round and followed him, but

Effect of a little consternation at Kidnapper's Cape, p. 83.

some muskets and a great gun being fired at her, she desisted from the pursuit. The ship being brought to, a boat was lowered, and the poor boy taken up unhurt, though so terrified, that for a time he seemed to be deprived of his senses.

To the cape off which this unhappy transaction happened, I gave the name of

CAPE KIDNAPPERS.

It lies in latitude 39° 43', and longitude 182° 24' W., and is rendered remarkable by two white rocks like haystacks, and the high white cliffs on each side. It lies S.W. by W. distant thirteen leagues from the isle of Portland; and between them is the bay of which it is the south point, and which, in honour of Sir Edward Hawke, then First Lord of the Admiralty, I called Hawke's Bay.

As soon as Tayeto recovered from his fright, he brought a fish to Tupia, and told him that he intended it as an offering to his Eatua, or god, in gratitude for his escape; Tupia commended his piety, and ordered him to throw the fish into the sea, which was accordingly done.*

I passed a remarkable headland, which I called Gable-End-Foreland, from the very great likeness of the white cliff at the point to the gable-end of a house: it is not more remarkable for its figure, than for a rock which rises like a spire at a little distance.

I made sail in shore, in order to look into two bays, which appeared about two leagues to the northward of the Foreland;

---

* How true are Pope's beautiful lines in the opening of his "Universal Prayer,"—

> "Father of all! in every age,
> In every clime adored,
> By saint, by savage, and by sage,
> Jehovah, Jove, or Lord!"

the southernmost I could not fetch, but I anchored in the other about eleven o'clock. Into this bay, which is called by the natives Tolago, we were invited by the people on board many canoes, who pointed to a place where they said there was plenty of fresh water: I did not find so good a shelter from the sea as I expected; but the natives who came about us, appearing to be of a friendly disposition, I was determined to try whether I could not get some knowledge of the country here before I proceeded farther to the northward.

On landing we were received with great expressions of friendship by the natives, who behaved with a scrupulous attention not to give offence. In particular, they took care not to appear in great bodies: one family, or the inhabitants of two or three houses only, were generally placed together, to the number of fifteen or twenty, consisting of men, women, and children. These little companies sat upon the ground, not advancing towards us, but inviting us to them, by a kind of beckon, moving one hand towards the breast. We made them several little presents; and in our walk round the bay found two small streams of fresh water. This convenience, and the friendly behaviour of the people, determined me to stay at least a day, that I might fill some of my empty casks, and give Mr. Banks an opportunity of examining the natural produce of the country.

These fair appearances encouraged Mr. Banks and Dr. Solander to range the bay with very little precaution, where they found many plants, and shot some birds of exquisite beauty. In their walk, they visited several houses of the natives, and saw something of their manner of life; for they shewed, without any reserve, everything which they desired to see. They were sometimes found at their meals, which the approach of the strangers never interrupted. Their food at this season consisted of fish, with which, instead of bread, they eat the root of a kind of fern, very like that which grows upon our commons in England. These roots they scorch over the fire, and then beat with a stick, till the bark and dry outside fall off; what remains is a soft substance, somewhat clammy and sweet, not unpleasing to the taste, but mixed with three or four times its quantity of strings and fibres, which are very disagreeable; these were swallowed by some, but spit out by the far greater number, who had baskets under them to receive the rejected part of what had been chewed, which had an appearance very like that of tobacco in the same state.

The women were plain, and made themselves more so by painting their faces with red ochre and oil, which, being generally fresh and wet upon their cheeks and foreheads, was easily transferred to the noses of those who thought fit to salute them; and that they were not wholly averse to such familiarity, the noses of several of our people strongly testified. In personal delicacy they were not equal to our friends at Otaheite, for the coldness of the climate did not invite them so often to bathe; but we saw among them one instance of cleanliness in which they exceeded them, and of which, perhaps, there is no example in any other Indian nation. Every house, or every little cluster of three or four houses, was furnished with a privy, so that the ground was everywhere clean. The offals of their food, and other litter, were also piled up in regular dunghills, which probably they made use of at a proper time for manure.

In this decent article of civil economy they were beforehand with one of the most considerable nations of Europe; for I am credibly informed, that, till the year 1760, there was no such thing as a privy in Madrid, the metropolis of Spain, though it is plentifully supplied with water. Before that time it was the universal practice to throw the ordure out of the windows, during the night, into the street, where numbers of men were employed to remove it, with shovels, from the upper parts of the city to the lower, where it lay till it was dry, and was then carried away in carts, and deposited without the gates. His present Catholic Majesty, having determined to free his capital from so gross a nuisance, ordered, by proclamation, that the proprietors of every house should build a privy, and that sinks, drains, and common sewers should be made at the public expense. The Spaniards, though long accustomed to an arbitrary government, resented this proclamation with great spirit, as an infringement of the common rights of mankind, and made a vigorous struggle against its being carried into execution. Every class devised some objection against it, but the physicians bid the fairest to interest the king in the preservation of the ancient privileges of his people; for they remonstrated, that if the filth was not, as usual, thrown into the streets, a fatal sickness would probably ensue, because the putrescent particles of the air, which such filth attracted, would then be imbibed by the human body. But this expedient, with every other that could be thought of, proved unsuccessful; and the popular discontent then ran so high, that it was very near producing an insurrection; his majesty, however, at length prevailed, and Madrid is now as clean as most of the considerable cities in Europe.

On Monday the 30th October, having made sail again to the northward for about ten hours, with a light breeze, I hauled round a small island which lay east one mile from the north-east point of the land; from this place I found the land trend away N.W. by W. and W.N.W. as far as I could see. This point being the easternmost land on the whole coast, I gave it the name of East Cape, and I called the island that lies off it East Island; it is of a small circuit, high and round, and appears white and barren. At six in the evening, being four leagues to the westward of East Cape, we passed a bay which was first discovered by Lieutenant Hicks, and which, therefore, I called Hicks's Bay. At eight in the evening, being eight leagues to the westward of the Cape, and three or four miles from the shore, I shortened sail and brought to for the night, having at this time a fresh gale at S.S.E. and squally; but it soon became moderate, and at two in the morning we made sail again to the S.W. as the land now trended; and at eight o'clock in the morning saw land, which made like an island, bearing west, the south-westernmost part of the main bearing south-west; and about nine no less than five canoes came off, in which were more than forty men, all armed with their country pikes and battle-axes, shouting, and threatening an attack; this gave us great uneasiness, and was, indeed, what we did not expect, for we hoped that the report both of our power and clemency had spread to a greater extent. When one of these canoes had almost reached the ship, another of an immense size, the largest we had yet seen, crowded with people, who were also armed, put off from the shore, and came up at a great rate; as it approached it received signals from the canoe that was nearest to the ship, and we could see that it had sixteen paddles on a side, beside people that sat, and others that stood in a row from stem to stern, being in all about sixty men: as they made directly to the ship, we were desirous of preventing an attack, by showing what we could do, and, therefore, fired a gun, loaded with grape-shot, a-head of them: this made them stop, but not retreat; a round-shot was then fired over them, and upon seeing it fall they seized their paddles and made towards the shore with such precipitation that they seemed scarcely to allow themselves time to breathe. In the evening three or four more canoes came off unarmed, but they would not venture within a musket-shot of the vessel. The cape off which we had been threatened with hostilities I called, from the hasty retreat of the enemy, Cape Runaway.

On the 1st of November we saw a large opening or inlet, for which we bore up; we had now forty-one fathom water, which gradually decreased to nine, at which time we were one mile and a half distant from a high towered rock which lay near the south point of the inlet: this rock and the northernmost of the Court of Aldermen being in one, bearing S. 61 E.

We anchored in seven fathom, a little within the south entrance of the bay: to this place we were accompanied by several canoes and people like those we had seen last, and for some time they behaved very civilly. While they were hovering about us, a bird was shot from the ship as it was swimming upon the water; at this they shewed less surprise than we expected, and taking up the bird, they tied it to a fishing line that was towing astern; as an acknowledgment for this favour, we gave them a piece of cloth; but notwithstanding this effect of our fire-arms, and this interchange of civilities, as soon as it grew dark, they sung their war-song, and attempted to tow away the buoy of the anchor. Two or three muskets were then fired over them, but this seemed rather to make them angry than afraid, and they went away, threatening that to-morrow they would return with more force, and be the death of us all; at the same time sending off a boat, which they told us was going to another part of the bay for assistance.

As I intended to continue in this place five or six days, in order to make an observation of the transit of Mercury, it was absolutely necessary, in order to prevent future mischief, to shew these people that we were not to be treated ill with impunity; some small shot were fired at the canoe of a thief, and a musket-ball through the bottom of his boat; upon this it was paddled to about a hundred yards' distance, and to our great surprise the people in the other canoes took not the least notice of their wounded companion, though he bled very much, but returned to the ship, and continued to trade with the most perfect indifference and unconcern. They sold us many more of their weapons, without making any other attempt to defraud us for a considerable time; at last, however, one of them thought fit to paddle away with two different pieces of cloth which had been given for the same weapon: when he had got about a hundred yards' distance, and thought himself secure of his prize, a musket was fired after him, which fortunately struck the boat just at the water's edge, and made two holes in her side; this only incited them to ply their paddles with greater activity, and the rest of the canoes also made off with the utmost expedition. As the last proof of our superiority, therefore, we fired a round shot over them, and not a boat stopped till they got on shore.

On the 9th, after an early breakfast, I went ashore, with Mr. Green and proper instruments, to observe the transit of Mercury, Mr. Banks and Dr. Solander being of the party; the weather had for some time been very thick, with much rain, but this day was so favourable that not a cloud intervened during the whole transit. The observation of the ingress was made by Mr. Green alone.

while I was employed in taking the sun's altitude to ascertain the time. It came on at 7^h 20' 58" apparent time: according to Mr. Green's observation, the internal contact was at 12^h 8' 58", the external at 12^h 9' 55" P.M. And according to mine, the internal contact was at 12^h 8' 54", and the external 12^h 9' 48"; the latitude of the place of observation was 36° 48' $5\frac{1}{4}$". The latitude observed at noon was 36° 48' 28". The mean of this and yesterday's observation gives 36° 48' $5\frac{1}{2}$" S. the latitude of the place of observation.

MERCURY BAY.

On the 15th I sailed out of the bay, to which I gave the name of Mercury Bay, on account of the observation which we had made there of the transit of that planet over the sun. Passing Point Mercury, two canoes, in which there might be about sixty men, came near enough to make themselves heard, they sung their war-song; but seeing that we took little notice of it, they threw a few stones at us, and then rowed off towards the shore. We hoped that we had now done with them, but in a short time they returned, as if with a fixed resolution to provoke us into a battle, animating themselves by their song as they had done before. Tupia, without any directions from us, went to the poop, and began to expostulate: he told them, that we had weapons which would destroy them in a moment; and that, if they ventured to attack us, we should be obliged to use them. Upon this, they flourished their weapons, and cried out in their language—

"Come on shore, and we will kill you all!"

On the 29th, I bore up for a bay which lies to the westward of Cape Bret. The natives, to the number of near four hundred, crowded upon us in their canoes, and some of them were admitted on board: to one, who seemed to be a chief, I gave a piece of broad-cloth, and distributed some trifling presents among the rest. I perceived that some of these people had been about the ship when she was off at sea, and that they knew the power of our fire-arms, for the very sight of a gun threw them into manifest confusion. We observed that the canoes which were about the ship did not follow us upon our leaving her, which we thought a good sign; but we had no sooner landed than they crowded to different parts of the island and came on shore. We were in a little cove, and in a few minutes were surrounded by two or three hundred people, some rushing from behind the heads of the cove, and others appearing on the tops of the hills: they were all armed, but they came on in so confused and straggling a manner that we scarcely suspected they meant us any harm, and we were determined that hostilities should not begin on our part. We marched towards them, and then drew a line upon the sand between them and us, which we gave them to understand they were not to pass. At first they continued quiet, but their weapons were held ready to strike, and they seemed to be rather irresolute than peaceable. While we remained in this state of suspense, another party of Indians came up, and now growing more bold as their number increased, they began the dance and song, which are their preludes to a battle; still, however, they delayed the attack, but a party ran to each of our boats, and attempted to draw them on shore: this seemed to be the signal, for the people about us at the same time began to press in upon our line. Our situation was now become too critical for us to remain longer inactive; I therefore discharged my musket, which was loaded with small-shot, at one of the forwardest, and Mr. Banks and two of the men fired immediately afterwards. This made them fall back in some confusion; but one of the chiefs, who was at the distance of about twenty yards, rallied them, and running forward, waving his patoo-patoo, and calling loudly to his companions, led them to the charge. Dr. Solander, whose piece was not yet discharged, fired at this champion, who stopped short upon feeling the shot, and then ran away with the rest; they did not, however, disperse, but got together upon a rising ground, and seemed only to want some leader of resolution to renew their attack. As they were now beyond the reach of small-shot, we fired with ball; but as none of the shots took effect, they continued in a body, and in this situation we remained about a quarter of an hour. In the meantime the ship, from whence a much greater number of Indians were seen than could be discovered in our situation, brought her broadside to bear, and entirely dispersed them by firing a few shot over their heads. In this skirmish only two of the Indians were hurt with the small-shot, and not a single life was lost, which would not have been the case if I had not restrained the men, who, either from fear or the love of mischief, showed as much impatience to destroy them as a sportsman to kill his game.

At four o'clock in the morning of the 5th of December, we weighed, with a light breeze; but it being variable, with frequent calms, we made little way. We kept turning out of the bay till the afternoon, and about ten o'clock we were suddenly becalmed, so that the ship would neither wear nor stay; and the tide or current setting strong, she drove towards land so fast that, before any measures could be taken for her security, she was within a cable's length of the breakers. We had thirteen fathom water, but the ground was so foul that we did not dare to drop our anchor; the pinnace, therefore, was immediately hoisted out to take the ship in tow, and the men, sensible of their danger, exerting themselves to the utmost, and a faint breeze springing up off the land, we perceived, with unspeakable joy, that she made head-way, after having been so near the shore that Tupia, who was not sensible of our hair's-breadth escape, was at this very time conversing with the people upon the beach, whose voices were distinctly heard, notwithstanding the roar of the breakers. We now thought all danger was over, but about an hour afterwards, just as the man in the chains had cried "seventeeen fathom," the ship struck. The shock threw us all into the utmost consternation; Mr. Banks, who had undressed himself, and was stepping into bed, ran hastily up to the deck, and the man in the chains called out "five fathom;" by this time, the rock on which we had struck being to windward, the ship went off without having received the least damage, and the water very soon deepened to twenty fathom.

This bay I named the Bay of Islands, from the great number of islands which line its shores, and from several harbours equally safe and commodious, where there is room and depth for any number of shipping.

About the middle of January 1770, I stood for an inlet which runs in S.W.; and got within the entrance which may be known by a reef of rocks, stretching from the north-west point, and some rocky islands which lie off the south-east point. At nine o'clock, there being little wind, and what there was being variable, we were carried by the tide or current within two cables' length of the north-west shore, where we had fifty-four fathom water, but by the help of our boats we got clear. Just at this time we saw a sea-lion rise twice near the shore, the head of which exactly resembled that of the male which has been described in the Account of Lord Anson's Voyage. We also saw some of the natives in a canoe cross the bay, and a village situated upon the point of an island which lies seven or eight miles within the entrance.

I went in the pinnace with Banks, Solander, Tupia, and some others, into a cove, about two miles distant from that in which the ship lay; in our way we saw something floating upon the water, which we took for a dead seal, but upon rowing up to it, found it to be the body of a woman, which, to all appearance, had been dead some days. We proceeded to our cove, where we went on shore, and found a small family of Indians, who appeared to be greatly terrified at our approach, and all ran away except one. A conversation between this person and Tupia soon brought back the rest, except an old man and a child, who still kept aloof, but stood peeping at us from the woods. Of these people, our curiosity naturally led us to inquire after the body of the woman, which we had seen floating upon the water; and they acquainted us, by Tupia, that she was a relation, who had died a natural death; and that, according to their custom, they had tied a stone to the body, and thrown it into the sea, which stone, they supposed, had by some accident been disengaged.

HORRORS OF CANNIBALISM.

This family, when we came on shore, was employed in dressing some provisions; the body of a dog was at this time buried in their oven, and many provision-baskets stood near it. Having cast our eyes carelessly into one of these, as we passed it, we saw two bones pretty cleanly picked, which did not seem to be the bones of a dog, and which, upon a nearer examination, we discovered to be those of a human body. At this sight we were struck with horror, though it was only a confirmation of what we had heard many times since we arrived upon this coast. As we could have no doubt but the bones were human, neither could we have any doubt but that the flesh which covered them had been eaten. They were found in a provision-basket; the flesh that remained appeared manifestly to have been dressed by fire; and in the gristles at the end were the marks of the teeth which had gnawed them; to put an end, however, to conjecture, founded upon circumstances and appearances, we directed Tupia to ask what bones they were; and the Indians, without the least hesitation, answered, the bones of a man; they were then asked what had become of the flesh, and they replied that they had eaten it. But, said Tupia, why did you not eat the body of the woman which we saw floating upon the water? The woman, said they, died of disease; besides, she was our relation, and we eat only the bodies of our enemies, who are killed in battle. Upon inquiry who the man was whose bones we had found, they told us, that about five days before, a boat belonging to their enemies came into the bay, with many persons on board, and that this man was of the seven whom they had killed. Though stronger evidence of this horrid practice prevailing among the inhabitants of this coast will scarcely be required, we have still stronger to give. One of us asked if they had any human bones with the flesh remaining upon them, and upon their answering us that all had been eaten, we affected to disbelieve that the bones were human, and said that they were the bones of a dog; upon which one of the Indians, with some eagerness, took hold of his own fore-arm, and thrusting it towards us, said, that the bone which Mr. Banks held in his hand had belonged to that part of the human body; at the same time, to convince us that the flesh had been eaten, he took hold of his own arm with his teeth, and made show of eating; he also bit and gnawed the bone which Mr. Banks had taken, drawing it through his mouth, and showing, by signs, that it had afforded a delicious repast; the bone was then returned to Mr. Banks, and he brought it away with him. Among the persons of this family, there was a woman who had her arms, legs, and thighs, frightfully cut in several places; and we were told that she had inflicted the wounds upon herself, in token of her grief for the loss of her husband, who had been lately killed and eaten by their enemies, who had come from some place to the eastward, towards which the Indians pointed.

The ship lay at the distance of somewhat less than a quarter of a mile from the shore, and in the morning we were awakened by the singing of the birds: the number was incredible, and they seemed to strain their throats in emulation of each other. This wild melody was infinitely superior to any that we had ever heard of the same kind; it seemed to be like small bells, most exquisitely tuned, and perhaps the distance, and the water between, might be no small advantage to the sound. Upon inquiry, we were informed that the birds here always began to sing about two hours after midnight, and continuing their music till sunrise, were, like our nightingales, silent the rest of the day In the forenoon, a small canoe came off from the Indian village to the ship, and among those that were in it was the old man who had first come on board at our arrival in the bay. As soon as it came alongside, Tupia renewed the conversation that had passed the day before concerning their practice of eating human flesh, during which they repeated what they had told us already. But, said Tupia, where are the heads? do you eat them too? Of the heads, said the old man, we eat only the brains, and the next time I come I will bring some of them to convince you that what we have told you is truth. After some further conversation between these people and Tupia, they told him that they expected their enemies to come very shortly to revenge the death of the seven men whom they had killed and eaten.

The 23d I employed in carrying on a survey of the place; and upon one of the islands where I landed, I saw many houses which seemed to have been long deserted, and no appearance of any inhabitant. On the 24th, we went to visit friends at the Hippah or village on the point of the island near the ship's station, who had come off to us on our first arrival in the bay. They received us with the utmost confidence and civility, showing us every part of their habitations, which were commodious and neat. The island or rock on which this town is situated is divided from the main by a breach or fissure, so narrow that a man might almost leap from one to the other: the sides of it are everywhere so steep as to render the artificial fortification of these people almost unnecessary; there was, however, one slight palisade, and one small fighting-stage, towards that part of the rock where access was least difficult.

The people here brought us out several human bones, the flesh of which they had eaten, and offered them for sale; for the curiosity of those among us, who had purchased them as memorials of the horrid practice which many, notwithstanding the reports of travellers, have professed not to believe, had rendered them a kind of article of trade. In one part of this village we observed, not without some surprise, a cross exactly like that of a crucifix; it was adorned with feathers, and, upon our inquiring for what purpose it had been set up, we were told that it was a monument for a man who was dead. We had before understood that their dead were not buried, but thrown into the sea; but to our inquiry how the body of the man had been disposed of, to whose memory this cross had been erected, they refused to answer.

TAKING POSSESSION OF NEW ZEALAND.

The carpenter having prepared two posts to be left as memorials of our having visited this place, 1 ordered them to be inscribed with the ship's name, and the year and month: one of them I set up at the watering-place, hoisting the Union flag upon the top of it; and the other I carried over to the island that lies nearest to the sea, called by the natives Motuara. I went first to the village or hippah, accompanied by Mr. Monkhouse and Tupia, where I met with our old man, and told him and several others, by means of Tupia, that we were come to set up a mark upon the island, in order to show to any other ship which should happen to come thither, that we had been there before. To this they readily consented, and promised that they never would pull it down: I then gave something to every one present; and to the old man I gave a silver threepence, dated 1736, and some spike-nails, with the king's broad arrow cut deep upon them; things which I thought most likely to remain long among them: I then took the post to the highest part of the island, and after fixing it firmly in the ground, I hoisted upon it the Union flag, and honoured this inlet with the name of Queen Charlotte's Sound; at the same time taking formal possession of this and the adjacent country in the name and for the use of his Majesty King George the Third. We then drank a bottle of wine to her Majesty's health, and gave the bottle to the old man who attended us up the hill, and who was mightily delighted with his present.

New Zealand was first discovered by Abel Jansen Tasman, a Dutch navigator, on the 13th of December, in the year 1642. He traversed the eastern coast from latitude 34° to 43°, and entered the strait which divides the two islands, and in the chart is called Cook's Strait; but, being attacked by the natives soon after he came to an anchor, in the place to which he gave the name of Murderer's Bay, he never went on shore. He gave the country the name of Staaten Land, or the land of the States, in honour of the states-general, and it is now generally distinguished in our maps and charts by the name of New Zealand. As the whole of this country, except that part of the coast which was seen by Tasman from on board his ship, has from his time, to the voyage of the "Endeavour," remained altogether unknown, it has by many been supposed to be part of a southern continent. It is, however, now known to consist of two large islands, divided from each other by a strait or passage, which is about four or five leagues broad.

Among the vegetable productions of this country, the trees claim a principal place; for here are forests of vast extent, full of the straightest, the cleanest, and the largest timber trees that we had ever seen : their size, their grain, and apparent durability, render them fit for any kind of building, and indeed for every other purpose except masts, for which they are too hard and too heavy.

But among all the trees, shrubs, and plants of this country, there is not one that produces fruit, except a berry, which has neither sweetness nor flavour, and which none but the boys took pains to gather, should be honoured with that appellation.

There is, however, a plant (the New Zealand flax) that serves the inhabitants instead of hemp and flax, which excels all that are put to the same purposes in other countries. Of the leaves, with very little preparation, they make all their common apparel; and of these they make also their strings, lines, and cordage for every purpose, which are so much stronger than anything we can make with hemp, that they will not bear a comparison. From the same plant, by another preparation, they draw long slender fibres which shine like silk, and are as white as snow: of these, which are also surprisingly strong, the finer clothes are made ; and of the leaves, without any other preparation than splitting them into proper breadths, and tying the strips together, they make their fishing-nets ; some of which, as I have before remarked, are of an enormous size. A plant which, with such advantage, might be applied to so many useful and important purposes, would certainly be a great acquisition to England.

If the settling of this country should ever be thought an object worthy the attention of Great Britain, the best place for establishing a colony would be either on the banks of the Thames, or in the country bordering upon the Bay of Islands. In either place there would be the advantage of an excellent harbour; and, by means of the river, settlements might be extended, and a communication established with the inland parts of the country : vessels might be built of the fine timber which abounds in these parts, at very little trouble and expense, fit for such a navigation as would answer the purpose.

The stature of the men in general is equal to the largest of those in Europe : they are stout, well-limbed, and fleshy ; but not fat, like the lazy and luxurious inhabitants of the islands in the South Seas : they are also exceedingly vigorous and active;

and have an adroitness and manual dexterity in an uncommon degree, which are discovered in whatever they do. I have seen the strokes of fifteen paddles on a side in one of their canoes made with incredible quickness, and yet with such minute exactness of time, that all the rowers seemed to be actuated by one common soul. The dispositions both of the men and women seemed to be mild and gentle: they treat each other with the tenderest affection, but are implacable towards their enemies, to whom they never give quarter. It may, perhaps, at first seem strange, that where there is so little to be got by victory, there should so often be war; and that every little district of a country inhabited by people so mild and placid, should be at enmity with all the rest. But possibly more is to be gained by victory among these people than at first appears, and they may be prompted to mutual hostilities by motives which no degree of friendship or affection is able to resist. Their principal food is fish, which can only be procured upon the sea-coast; and there in sufficient quantities only at certain times: the tribes, therefore, who live inland, if any such there are, and even those upon the coast, must be frequently in danger of perishing by famine. Their country produces neither sheep nor goats, nor hogs, nor cattle: tame fowls they have none, nor any art by which those that are wild can be caught in sufficient plenty to serve as provision. If there are any whose situation cuts them off from a supply of fish, the only succedaneum of all other animal food, except dogs, they have nothing to support life but the vegetables that have already been mentioned, of which the chief are fernroot, yams, clams, and potatoes; when by any accident these fail, the distress must be dreadful; and even among the inhabitants of the coast, many tribes must frequently be reduced to nearly the same situation, either by the failure of their plantations, or the deficiency of their dry stock, during the season when but few fish are to be caught. These considerations will enable us to account, not only for the perpetual danger in which the people who inhabit this country appear to live, by the care which they take to fortify every village, but for the horrid practice of eating those who are killed in battle; for the hunger of him who is pressed by famine to fight will absorb every feeling and every sentiment which would restrain him from allaying it with the body of his adversary. It may, however, be remarked, that if this account of the origin of so horrid a practice is true, the mischief does by no means end with the necessity that produced it; after the practice has been once begun on one side by hunger, it will naturally be adopted on the other by revenge. Nor is this all; for though it may be pretended by some who wish to appear speculative and philosophical, that whether the dead body of an enemy be eaten or buried is in itself a matter perfectly indifferent; and that prejudice and habit only make us shudder at the violation of custom in one instance, and blush at it in the other: yet leaving this as a point of doubtful disputation, to be discussed at leisure, it may safely be affirmed that the practice of eating human flesh, whatever it may be in itself, is relatively, and in its consequences, most pernicious; tending manifestly to eradicate a principle which is the chief security of human life, and more frequently restrains the hand of murder than the sense of duty, or even the fear of punishment.

Among those who are accustomed to eat the dead, death must have lost much of its horror; and where there is little horror at the sight of death, there will not be much repugnance to kill. A sense of duty, and fear of punishment, may be more easily surmounted than the feelings of nature, or those which have been ingrafted upon nature by early prejudice and uninterrupted custom. The horror of the murderer arises less from the guilt of the fact than its natural effect; and he who has familiarised the effect will consequently lose much of the horror. By our laws, and our religion, murder and theft incur the same punishment, both in this world and the next; yet, of the multitude who would deliberately steal, there are but very few who would deliberately kill, even to procure much greater advantage. But there is the strongest reason to believe, that those who have been so accustomed to prepare a human body for a meal, that they can with as little feeling cut up a dead man as our cookmaids divide a dead rabbit for a fricassee, would feel as little horror in committing a murder as in picking a pocket, and consequently would take away life with as little compunction as property; so that men, under these circumstances, would be made murderers by the slight temptations that now make them thieves. If any man doubts whether this reasoning is conclusive, let him ask himself, whether in his own opinion he should not be safer with a man in whom the horror of destroying life is strong, whether in consequence of natural instinct unsubdued, or of early prejudice, which has nearly an equal influence, than in the power of a man who, under any temptation to murder him, would be restrained only by considerations of interest; for to these all motives of mere duty may be reduced, as they must terminate either in hope of good or fear of evil. The situation and circumstances, however, of these poor people, as well as their temper, are favourable to those who shall settle as a colony among them. Their situation sets them in need of protection, and their temper renders it easy to attach them by kindness;

and whatever may be said in favour of a savage life among people who live in luxurious idleness upon the bounty of nature, civilization would certainly be a blessing to those whom her parsimony scarcely furnishes with the bread of life, and who are perpetually destroying each other by violence as the only alternative of perishing by hunger.

But these people, from whatever cause, being inured to war, and by habit considering every stranger as an enemy, were always disposed to attack us when they were not intimidated by our manifest superiority. At first, they had no notion of any superiority but numbers; and when this was on their side, they considered all our expressions of kindness as the artifices of fear and cunning, to circumvent them and preserve ourselves; but when they were once convinced of our power, after having provoked us to the use of our firearms, though loaded only with small-shot, and of our clemency, by our forbearing to make use of weapons so dreadful except in our defence, they became at once friendly, and even affectionate, placing in us the most unbounded confidence, and doing everything which could incite us to put equal confidence in them. It is also remarkable, that when an intercourse was once established between us, they were very rarely detected in any act of dishonesty. Before, indeed, and while they considered us as enemies, who came upon their coast only to make an advantage of them, they did not scruple by any means to make any advantage of us; and would, therefore, when they had received the price of anything they had offered to sell, pack up both the purchase and the purchase-money with all possible composure, as so much lawful plunder from people who had no view but to plunder them.

The bodies of both sexes are marked with the black stains

called Amoco, by the same method that is used at Otaheite, and called Tattowing; but the men are more marked, and the women less. The women in general stain no part of their bodies but the lips, though sometimes they are marked with small black patches on other parts: the men, on the contrary, seem to add something every year to the ornaments of the last, so that some of them, who appeared to be of an advanced age, were almost covered from head to foot. Besides the Amoco, they have marks impressed by a method unknown to us, of a very extraordinary kind: they are furrows of about a line deep, and a line broad, such as appear upon the bark of a tree which has been cut through after a year's growth; the edges of these furrows are afterwards indented by the same method, and being perfectly black, they make a most frightful appearance. But though we could not but be disgusted with the horrid deformity which these stains and furrows produced in the "human face divine," we could not but admire the dexterity and art with which they were impressed.

New Zealand Chief.

Water is their universal and only liquor, as far as we could discover; and if they have really no means of intoxication, they are, in this particular, happy beyond any other people that we have yet seen or heard of.

As there is, perhaps, no source of disease, either critical or chronic, but intemperance and inactivity, it cannot be thought strange that these people enjoy perfect and uninterrupted health.

A proof of this is the great number of old men that we saw, many of whom, by the loss of their hair and teeth, appeared to be very ancient, yet none of them were decrepit; and though not equal to the young in muscular strength, were not a whit behind them in cheerfulness and vivacity.

I think it appears to demonstration that the language of New Zealand and Otaheite is radically the same. The language of the northern and southern parts of New Zealand differs chiefly in the pronunciation, as the same English word is pronounced *gate* in Middlesex, and *geäte* in Yorkshire. I must also observe, that it is the genius of the language, especially in the southern parts, to put some article before a noun, as we do *the* or *a;* the articles used here were generally *ke* or *ko;* it is also common here to add the word *öeia* after another word as an iteration, especially if it is an answer to a question; as we say, *yes, indeed, to be sure, really, certainly:* this sometimes led our gentlemen into the formation of words of an enormous length, judging by the ear only, without being able to refer each sound into its signification. An example will make this perfectly understood.

In the Bay of Islands there is a remarkable one, called by the natives Matuaro. One of our gentlemen having asked a native the name of it, he answered, with the particle, *Kematuaro;* the gentleman hearing the sound imperfectly, repeated his question, and the Indian repeating his answer, added *öeia,* which made the word *Kematuaroöeia;* and thus it happened that in the log-book I found *Matuaro* transformed into *Cumettiwarrowöia:* and the same transformation by the same means might happen to an English word. Suppose a native of New

Zealand at Hackney church, to inquire, "What village is this?" the answer would be, "It is Hackney;" suppose the question to be repeated with an air of doubt and uncertainty, the answer might be, "It is Hackney indeed;" and the New Zealander, if he had the use of letters, would probably record, for the information of his countrymen, that during his residence among us he had visited a village called "Ityshakneeindede."

But supposing these islands, and those in the South Seas, to have been peopled originally from the same country, it will perhaps for ever remain a doubt what country that is : we were, however, unanimously of opinion that the people did not come from America, which lies to the eastward; and except there should appear to be a continent to the southward, in a moderate latitude, it will follow that they came from the westward.

Thus far our navigation has certainly been unfavourable to the notion of a southern continent, for it has swept away at least three-fourths of the positions upon which it has been founded. The principal navigators whose authority has been urged on this occasion, are Tasman, Juan Fernandez, Hermite, the commander of a Dutch squadron, Quiros, and Roggewein; and the track of the "Endeavour" has demonstrated that the land seen by these persons, and supposed to be part of a continent, is not so; it has also totally subverted the theoretical arguments which have been brought to prove that the existence of a southern continent is necessary to preserve an equilibrium between the two hemispheres; for upon this principle what we have already proved to be water, would render the southern hemisphere too light.

CHAPTER III.

Discovery of New South Wales.

HAVING sailed from Cape Farewell—New Zealand—on the 31st of March 1770, we steered westward, with a fresh gale.

On the 15th of April we saw an egg-bird and a gannet, and as these are birds that never go far from the land, we continued to sound all night, but had no ground with 130 fathom. At noon, on the 16th, a small land-bird perched upon the rigging, but we had no ground with 120 fathom. At eight we wore, and stood to the southward till twelve at night, and then wore and stood to the N.W. till four in the morning, when we again stood to the southward, having a fresh gale, with squalls and dark weather till nine, when the weather became clear, and there being little wind, we had an opportunity to take several observations of the sun and moon. We had now a hard gale from the southward, and a great sea from the same quarter, which obliged us to run under our fore-sail and mizen all night, during which we sounded every two hours, but had no ground with 120 fathom.

In the morning of the 18th, we saw two Port Egmont hens, and a pintado bird, which are certain signs of approaching land, and, indeed, by our reckoning, we could not be far from it, for our longitude was now one degree to the westward of the east side of Van Dieman's Land, according to the longitude laid down by Tasman, whom we could not suppose to have erred much in so short a run as from this land to New Zealand; and by our latitude, we could not be above fifty or fifty-five leagues from the place whence he took his departure. At six we saw land extending from N.E. to W. at the distance of five or six leagues, having eighty fathom water, with a fine sandy bottom.

We continued standing westward till eight, when we made all the sail we could, and bore away along the shore N.E. for the easternmost land in sight. The southernmost point in view I gave the name of Point Hicks, because Mr. Hicks, the first lieutenant, was the first who discovered it.

We continued to sail along the shore to the northward, with a southerly wind, and saw smoke in several places near the beach. About two leagues to the northward of Cape George, the shore seemed to form a bay, which promised shelter from the north-east winds; but as the wind was with us, it was not in my power to look into it without beating up, which would have cost me more time than I was willing to spare. The north point of this bay, on account of its figure, I named Long Nose; and about eight leagues north of it there lies a point, which, from the colour of the land about it, I called Red Point. To the north-west of Red Point, and a little way inland, stands a round hill, the top of which looks like the crown of a hat. We continued at the distance of between two and four miles from the shore, when we saw several of the natives walking briskly along, four of whom carried a small canoe upon their shoulders. We flattered ourselves that they were going to put her into the water and come off to the ship, but finding ourselves disappointed, I determined to pull for that part of the shore where they appeared, near which four small canoes were lying at the water's edge. The Indians sat down upon the rocks, and seemed to wait for our landing; but to our great regret, when we came within about a quarter of a mile, they ran away into the woods. We determined, however, to go on shore, and procure an interview: but in this we were again disappointed, for we found so great a surf beating upon every part of the beach, that, after many a wishful look, we were obliged to return to the ship with our curiosity rather excited than satisfied. At daybreak we discovered a bay, which seemed to be well sheltered from all winds, and into which, therefore, I determined to go with the ship. On directing our glasses to the shore we discovered ten people, who, upon our nearer approach, left their fire, and retired to a little eminence, whence they could conveniently observe our motions. As the pinnace proceeded along the shore to sound, most of the people took the same route, and kept abreast of her at a distance. When she came back, the master told us, that in a cove a little within the harbour, some of them had come down to the beach, and invited him to land by many signs and words, of which he knew not the meaning; but that all of them were armed with long pikes, and a wooden weapon shaped somewhat like a scymitar. The Indians who had not followed the boat, seeing the ship approach, used many threatening gestures and brandished their weapons; particularly two who made a very singular appearance, for their faces seemed to have been dusted with a white powder, and their bodies painted with broad streaks of the same colour, which passing obliquely over their breasts and backs, looked not unlike the cross-belts worn by our soldiers; the same kind of streaks were also drawn round their legs and thighs, like broad garters. Each of these men held in his hand the weapon that had been described to us as like a scymitar,* which appeared to be about two feet and a half long; and they seemed to talk to each other with great earnestness.

The place where the ship had anchored was abreast of a small village, consisting of about six or eight houses; and while we were preparing to hoist out the boat, we saw an old woman, followed by three children, come out of the wood; she was loaded with fire-wood, and each of the children had also its little burden. When she came to the houses, three more children, younger than the others, came out to meet her; she often looked at the ship, but expressed neither fear nor surprise. In a short time she kindled a fire, and the four canoes came in from fishing. The men landed, and having hauled up their boats, began to dress their dinner, to all appearance, wholly unconcerned about us, though we were within half a mile of them. We thought it remarkable that all of the people we had yet seen, not one had the least appearance of clothing.

COURAGE OF THE NATIVES.

After dinner the boats were manned, and we set out from the ship, having Tupia of our party. We intended to land where we saw the people, and began to hope that as they had so little regard to the ship's coming into the bay, they would as little regard our coming on shore. In this, however, we were disappointed; for as soon as we approached the rocks, two of the men came down upon them to dispute our landing, and the rest ran away. Each of the two champions was armed with a lance about ten feet long, and a short stick, which he seemed to handle as if it was a machine to assist him in managing or

* The *boomerang*.

throwing the lance. They called to us in a very loud tone, and in a harsh dissonant language, of which neither we nor Tupia understood a single word: they brandished their weapons, and seemed resolved to defend their coast to the uttermost, though they were but two, and we were forty. I could not but admire their courage, and being very unwilling that hostilities should commence with such inequality of force between us, I ordered the boat to lie upon her oars: we then parleyed by signs for about a quarter of an hour, and to bespeak their good-will, I threw them nails, beads, and other trifles, which they took up, and seemed to be well pleased with. I then made signs that I wanted water, and, by all the means that I could devise, endeavoured to convince them that we would do them no harm. They now waved to us, and I was willing to interpret it as an invitation; but upon our putting the boat in, they came again to oppose us. One appeared to be a youth about nineteen or twenty, and the other a man of middle age; as I had now no other resource, I fired a musket between them.

Upon the report, the youngest dropped a bundle of lances upon the rock, but recollecting himself in an instant, he snatched them up again with great haste. A stone was then thrown at us, upon which I ordered a musket to be fired with small-shot, which struck the eldest upon the legs, and he immediately ran to one of the houses, which was distant about a hundred yards. I now hoped that our contest was over, and we immediately landed; but we had scarcely left the boat when he returned, and we then perceived that he had left the rock only to fetch a shield or target for his defence. As soon as he came up, he threw a lance at us, and his comrade another; they fell where we stood thickest, but happily hurt nobody. A third musket with small-shot was then fired at them, upon which one of them threw another lance, and both immediately ran away; if we had pursued, we might probably have taken one of them; but Mr. Banks suggesting that the lances might be poisoned, I thought it not prudent to venture into the woods. We repaired immediately to the huts, in one of which we found the children, who had hidden themselves behind a shield and some bark; we peeped at them, but left them in their retreat, without their knowing that they had been discovered, and we threw into the house, when we went away, some beads, ribbons, pieces of cloth, and other presents, which we hoped would procure us the goodwill of the inhabitants when they should return; but the lances which we found lying about, we took away with us, to the number of about fifty: they were from six to fifteen feet long, and all of them had four prongs in the manner of a fish-gig, each of which was pointed with fish-bone, and very sharp; we observed that they were smeared with a viscous substance of a green colour, which favoured the opinion of their being poisoned, though we afterwards discovered that it was a mistake; they appeared, by the sea-weed that we found sticking to them, to have been used in striking fish.

While Mr. Banks was gathering plants near the watering-place, I went with Solander and Monkhouse to the head of the bay, that I might examine that part of the country, and make farther attempts to form some negociation with the natives. In our way we met with eleven or twelve small canoes, with each a man in it, probably the same that were afterwards abreast of the shore, who all made into shoal water upon our approach. We met other Indians on shore the first time we landed, who instantly took to their canoes and paddled away. We went up the country to some distance, and found the face of it nearly the same with that which has been described already, but the soil was much richer; for, instead of sand, I found a deep black mould, which I thought very fit for the production of grain of any kind. In the woods we found a tree which bore fruit that in colour and shape resembled a cherry: the juice had an agreeable tartness, though but little flavour. We found also interspersed some of the finest meadows in the world: some places, however, were rocky, but these were comparatively few; the stone is sandy, and might be used with advantage for building.

The great quantity of plants which Mr. Banks and Dr. Solander collected in this place, induced me to give it the name of

BOTANY BAY.*

All the inhabitants that we saw were stark naked: they did not appear to be numerous, nor to live in societies, but, like other animals, were scattered about along the coast, and in the woods. Of their manner of life, however, we could know but little, as we were never able to form the least connection with them. After the first contest at our landing, they would never come near enough to parley; nor did they touch a single article of all that we had left at their huts, and the places they frequented, on purpose for them to take away.

During my stay in this harbour I caused the English colours to be displayed on shore every day, and the ship's name and the date of the year to be inscribed upon one of the trees near the watering-place.

At daybreak, on Sunday the 6th of May, 1770, we set sail from Botany Bay, and steered along the shore N.N.E., until we

---

* For many years a penal settlement for our convicts, but no longer so.

came abreast of a bay or harbour, in which there appeared to be good anchorage, and which I called Port Jackson
(Now the town of Sydney).

The wind continuing northerly till the morning of the 10th, we continued to stand in and off the shore, with very little change of situation in other respects; but a gale then springing up at S.W., we made the best of our way along the shore to the northward.

At latitude 30° 43′ S., and longitude 206° 45′ W., we were between three and four leagues from the shore, the northernmost part of which bore from us N. 13 W., and a point, or headland, on which we saw fires that produced a great quantity of smoke, bore W., distant four leagues. To this point I gave the name of Smoky Cape.*

We advanced to the northward by Point Look-out, Moreton's Bay, Double Island Point, Indian Head, Sandy Cape, Hervey's Bay (so named in honour of Captain Hervey), Bustard Bay, Cape Capricorn, Cape Manifold, Keppel Bay, Cape Townshend, Thirsty Sound (because it afforded us no fresh water), Cape Palmerston, Cape Conway, Repulse Bay, Whitsunday's Passage, Cape Gloucester, Cape Grafton, and Trinity Bay (discovered on Trinity Sunday).

Hitherto we had safely navigated this dangerous coast, where the sea in all parts conceals shoals that suddenly project from the shore, and rocks that rise abruptly like a pyramid from the bottom, for an extent of two-and-twenty degrees of latitude, more than one thousand three hundred miles; and therefore none of the names which distinguish the several parts of the country that we saw are memorials of distress; but here we became acquainted

* The present Port Macquarrie.

with misfortune, and we therefore called the point which we had just seen farthest to the northward

CAPE TRIBULATION.

It was my design here to stretch off all night, as well to avoid the danger we saw ahead as to see whether any islands lay in the offing, especially as we were now near the latitude assigned to the islands which were discovered by Quiros, and which some geographers, for what reason I know not, have thought fit to join to this land. We had the advantage of a fine breeze and a clear moonlight night, and in standing off from six till near nine o'clock, we deepened our water from fourteen to twenty-one fathom ; but while we were at supper, it suddenly shoaled, and we fell into twelve, ten, and eight fathom, within the space of a few minutes. I immediately ordered everybody to their station, and all was ready to put about and come to an anchor, but meeting at the next cast of the lead with deep water again, we concluded that we had gone over the tail of the shoals which we had seen at sunset, and that all danger was past. Before ten we had twenty and one-and-twenty fathom, and this depth continuing, the gentlemen left the deck in great tranquillity, and went to bed ; but a few minutes before eleven, the water shallowed at once from twenty to seventeen fathom, and before the lead could be cast again, the ship struck, and remained immovable, except by the heaving of the surge that beat her against the crags of the rock upon which she lay.

PRECARIOUS POSITION OF THE SHIP.

In a few moments everybody was upon the deck, with countenances which sufficiently expressed the horrors of our situation.

We had stood off the shore three hours and a half, with a pleasant breeze, and therefore knew that we could not be very near it, and we had too much reason to conclude that we were upon a rock of coral, which is more fatal than any other, because the points of it are sharp, and every part of the surface so rough, as to grind away whatever is rubbed against it, even with the gentlest motion. In this situation all the sails were immediately taken in, and the boats hoisted out to examine the depth of water round the ship: we soon discovered that our fears had not aggravated our misfortune, and that the vessel had been lifted over a ledge of the rock, and lay in a hollow within it: in some places there was from three to four fathom, and in others not so many feet. The ship lay with her head to the N.E.; and at the distance of about thirty yards on the starboard side, the water deepened to eight, ten, and twelve fathom. As soon as the long-boat was out, we struck our yards and top-masts, and carried out the stream anchor on the starboard bow, got the coasting-anchor and cable into the boat, and were going to carry it out the same way; but upon sounding a second time round the ship, the water was found to be deepest astern: the anchor, therefore, was carried out from the starboard quarter instead of the starboard bow—that is, from the stern instead of the head—and having taken ground, our utmost force was applied to the capstan, hoping that if the anchor did not come home, the ship would be got off; but, to our great misfortune and disappointment, we could not move her. During all this time she continued to beat with great violence against the rock, so that it was with the utmost difficulty that we kept upon our legs; and to complete the scene of distress, we saw by the light of the moon the sheathing-boards from the bottom of the vessel floating away all round her, and at last her false keel, so that every moment was making way for the sea to rush in which was to swallow us up. We had now no chance but to lighten her, and we had lost the opportunity of doing that to the greatest advantage, for unhappily we went on shore just at high water, and by this time it had considerably fallen, so that after she should be lightened so as to draw as much less water as the water had sunk, we should be but in the same situation as at first; and the only alleviation of this circumstance was, that as the tide ebbed the ship settled to the rocks, and was not beaten against them with so much violence. We had indeed some hope from the next tide, but it was doubtful whether she would hold together so long, especially as the rock kept grating her bottom under the starboard bow with such force as to be heard in the fore store-room. This, however, was no time to indulge conjecture, nor was any effort remitted in despair of success: that no time might be lost, the water was immediately started in the hold, and pumped up; six of our guns, being all we had upon the deck, our iron and stone ballast, casks, hoop-staves, oil-jars, decayed stores, and many other things that lay in the way of heavier materials, were thrown overboard with the utmost expedition, every one exerting himself with an alacrity almost approaching to cheerfulness, without the least repining or discontent; yet the men were so far impressed with a sense of their situation, that not an oath was heard among them, the habit of profaneness, however strong, being instantly subdued by the dread of incurring guilt when death seemed to be so near.

While we were thus employed day broke upon us, and we saw the land at about eight leagues distance, without any island in the intermediate space, upon which, if the ship should have gone to pieces, we might have been set ashore by the boats, and from which they might have taken us by different turns to the main; the wind, however, gradually died away, and early in the forenoon it was a dead calm; if it had blown hard the ship must inevitably have been destroyed. At eleven in the forenoon we expected high water, and anchors were got out, and everything made ready for another effort to heave her off if she should float, but to our inexpressible surprise and concern, she did not float by a foot and a half, though we had lightened her near fifty ton; so much did the day-tide fall short of that in the night. We now proceeded to lighten her still more, and threw overboard everything that it was possible for us to spare; hitherto she had not admitted much water, but as the tide fell, it rushed in so fast, that two pumps, incessantly worked, could scarcely keep her free. At two o'clock she lay heeling two or three streaks to starboard, and the pinnace, which lay under her bows, touched the ground; we had now no hope but from the tide at midnight, and to prepare for it we carried out our two bower-anchors, one on the starboard quarter, and the other right astern, got the blocks and tackle which were to give us a purchase upon the cables in order, and brought the falls, or ends of them, in abaft, straining them tight, that the next effort might operate upon the ship, and by shortening the length of the cable between that and the anchors, draw her off the ledge upon which she rested, towards the deep water. About five o'clock in the afternoon, we observed the tide begin to rise, but we observed at the same time that the leak increased to a most alarming degree, so that two more pumps were manned, but unhappily only one of them would work. Three of the pumps, however, were kept going, and at nine o'clock the ship righted; but the leak had gained upon us so considerably, that it was imagined she must go to the bottom as soon as she ceased to be supported by the rock.

HORRORS OF SHIPWRECK.

This was a dreadful circumstance, so that we anticipated the floating of the ship not as an earnest of deliverance, but as an event that would probably precipitate our destruction. We well knew that our boats were not capable of carrying us all on shore, and that when the dreadful crisis should arrive, as all command and subordination would be at an end, a contest for preference would probably ensue, that would increase even the horrors of shipwreck, and terminate in the destruction of us all by the hands of each other; yet we knew that if any should be left on board to perish in the waves, they would probably suffer less upon the whole than those who should get on shore, without any lasting or effectual defence against the natives, in a country where even nets and fire-arms would scarcely furnish them with food; and where, if they should find the means of subsistence, they must be condemned to languish out the remainder of life in a desolate wilderness, without the possession, or even hope, of any domestic comfort, and cut off from all commerce with mankind, except the naked savages who prowled the desert, and who perhaps were some of the most rude and uncivilized upon the earth.

To those only who have waited in a state of such suspense, death has approached in all his terrors; and as the dreadful moment that was to determine our fate came on, every one saw his own sensations pictured in the countenances of his companions; however, the capstan and windlass were manned with as many hands as could be spared from the pumps, and the ship floating about twenty minutes after ten o'clock, the effort was made, and she was heaved into deep water. It was some comfort to find that she did not now admit more water than she had done upon the rock; and though, by the gaining of the leak upon the pumps, there was no less than three feet nine inches water in the hold, yet the men did not relinquish their labour, and we held the water as it were at bay; but having now endured excessive fatigue of body and agitation of mind for more than four-and-twenty hours, and having but little hope of succeeding at last, they began to flag; none of them could work at the pump for more than five or six minutes together, and then, being totally exhausted, they threw themselves down upon the deck, though a stream of water was running over it from the pumps, between three and four inches deep; when those who succeeded them had worked their spell, and were exhausted in their turn, they threw themselves down in the same manner, and the others started up again and renewed their labour; thus relieving each other till an accident was very near putting an end to their efforts at once. The planking which lines the inside of the ship's bottom is called the ceiling, and between this and the outside planking there is a space of about eighteen inches; the man who till this time had attended the well to take the depth of water, had taken it only to the ceiling, and gave the measure accordingly; but he being now relieved, the person who came in his stead reckoned the depth to the outside planking, by which it appeared in a few minutes to have gained upon the pumps eighteen inches, the difference between the planking without and within. Upon this, even the bravest was upon the point of giving up his labour with his hope, and in a few minutes everything would have been involved in all the confusion of despair. But this accident, however dreadful in its first consequences, was eventually the cause of our preservation; the mistake was soon detected, and the sudden joy which every man felt upon finding his situation better than his fears had suggested, operated like a charm, and seemed to possess him with a strong belief that scarcely any real danger remained.

New confidence and new hope, however founded, inspired new vigour; and though our state was the same as when the men first began to slacken in their labour through weariness and despondency, they now renewed their efforts with such alacrity and spirit, that before eight o'clock in the morning the leak was so far from having gained upon the pumps, that the pumps had gained considerably upon the leak. Everybody now talked of getting the ship into some harbour as a thing not to be doubted, and as hands could be spared from the pumps, they were employed in getting up the anchors; the stream-anchor and best bower we had taken on board; but it was found impossible to save the little bower, and therefore it was cut away at a whole cable; we lost also the cable of the stream-anchor among the rocks; but in our situation these were trifles which scarcely attracted our notice. Our next business was to get up the fore-topmast and foreyard, and warp the ship to the south-east, and at eleven, having now a breeze from the sea, we once more got under sail and stood for the land.

INGENIOUS MANNER OF STOPPING A LEAK.

It was, however, impossible long to continue the labour by which the pumps had been made to gain upon the leak; and as the exact situation of it could not be discovered, we had no hope of stopping it within. In this situation Monkhouse, one of my midshipmen, came to me, and proposed an expedient that he had once seen used on board a merchant-ship, which sprung a leak that admitted above four feet of water an hour, and which, by this expedient, was brought safely from Virginia to London; the master having such confidence in it, that he took her out of harbour, knowing her condition, and did not think it worth while to wait till the leak could be otherwise stopped. To this man, therefore, the care of the expedient, which is called fothering the ship, was immediately committed, four or five of the people being appointed to assist him, and he performed it in this manner: he took a lower studdingsail, and having mixed together a large quantity of oakum and wool, chopped pretty small, he stitched it down in handfuls upon the sail, as lightly as possible, and over this he spread the dung of our sheep and other filth; but horse-dung, if we had had it, would have been better. When the sail was thus prepared, it was hauled under the ship's bottom by ropes, which kept it extended, and when it came under the leak, the suction which carried in the water, carried in with it the oakum and wool from the surface of the sail, which in other parts the water was not sufficiently agitated to wash off. By the success of this expedient our leak was so far reduced, that instead of gaining upon three pumps, it was easily kept under with one. This was a new source of confidence and comfort; the people could scarcely have expressed more joy if they had been already in port; and their views were so far from being limited to running the ship ashore in some harbour, either of an island or the main, and building a vessel out of her materials to carry us to the East Indies, which had so lately been the utmost object of our hope, that nothing was now thought of but ranging along the shore in search of a convenient place to repair the damage she had sustained, and then prosecuting the voyage upon the same plan as if nothing had happened. In the meantime, we got up the main-top-mast and main-yard, and kept edging in for the land, when we came to an anchor in seventeen fathom water, at a distance of seven leagues from the shore, and one from the ledge of rocks upon which we had struck.

The pinnace was sent out with one of the mates, who reported on his return that about two leagues to leeward he had discovered just such a harbour as we wanted, in which there was a sufficient rise of water, and every other convenience that could be desired, either for laying the ship ashore, or heaving her down.

In consequence of this information I weighed at six o'clock in the morning, and having sent two boats ahead to lie upon the shoals that we saw in our way, we ran down to the place; but notwithstanding our precaution we were once in three fathom water. It was happy for us that a place of refuge was at hand; for we soon found that the ship would not work, having twice missed stays: our situation, however, though it might have been much worse, was not without danger; we were entangled among shoals, and I had great reason to fear being driven to leeward before the boats could place themselves so as to prescribe our course. I therefore anchored in four fathom about a mile from the shore, and then made the signal for the boats to come on board. When this was done I went myself and buoyed the channel, which I found very narrow; the harbour also I found smaller than I expected, but most excellently adapted to our purpose; and it is remarkable that in the whole course of our voyage we had seen no place which, in our present circumstances, could have afforded us the same relief. For our farther security we got down the topgallant yards, unbent the mainsail and some of the small sails; got down the fore-topgallant-mast, and the jib-boom and spritsail, with a view to lighten the ship forwards as much as possible, in order to come at her leak, which we supposed to be somewhere in that part; for in all the joy of our unexpected deliverance we had not forgot that at this time there was

Nothing but a lock of wool between us and destruction.

The scurvy now began to make its appearance among us with many formidable symptoms. Our poor Indian, Tupia, who had some time before complained that his gums were sore and swelled, and who had taken plentifully of our lemon juice by the surgeon's directions, had now livid spots upon his legs, and other indubitable testimonies that the disease had made a rapid progress, notwithstanding all our remedies, among which the bark had been liberally administered. Mr. Green, our astronomer, was also declining; and these, among other circumstances, embittered the delay which prevented our going ashore.

In the morning of the 17th, though the wind was still fresh, we ventured to weigh, and push in for the harbour; but in doing this we twice ran the ship aground: the first time she went off without any trouble, but the second time she stuck fast. We now got down the fore-yard, fore-top-masts, and booms, and taking them overboard made a raft of them alongside of the ship. The tide was happily rising, and about one o'clock in the afternoon she floated. We soon warped her into the harbour, and having moored her alongside of a steep beach to the south, we got the anchors, cables, and all the hawsers on shore before night.

A stage was then made from the ship to the shore which was so bold that she floated at twenty feet distance: two tents were also set up, one for the sick and the other for stores and provisions, which were landed in the course of the day. We also landed all the empty water-casks, and part of the stores. As soon as the tent for the sick was got ready for their reception, they were sent ashore to the number of eight or nine, and the boat was despatched to haul the seine, in hopes of procuring some fish for their refreshment; but she returned without success. In the mean time I climbed one of the highest hills among those that overlooked the harbour, which afforded by no means a comfortable prospect: the low land near the river is wholly overrun with mangroves, among which the salt-water flows every tide; and the high land appeared to be everywhere stony and barren. Mr. Banks had also taken a walk up the country, and met with the frames of several old Indian houses, and places where they had dressed shell-fish; but they seemed not to have been frequented for some months. Tupia, who had employed himself in angling, and lived entirely upon what he caught, recovered in a surprising degree; but Mr. Green still continued to be extremely ill.

The next morning I got the four remaining guns out of the hold, and mounted them upon the quarter-deck; I also got a spare anchor and anchor-stock ashore, and the remaining part of the stores and ballast that were in the hold; set up the smith's forge, and employed the armourer and his mate to make nails and other necessaries for the repair of the ship. In the afternoon, all the officers' stores and the ground tier of water were got out; so that nothing remained in the fore and main hold but the coals and a small quantity of stone ballast.

On the 20th we landed the powder, and got out the stone ballast and wood, which brought the ship's draught of water to eight feet ten inches forward, and thirteen feet abaft; and this, I thought, with the difference that would be made by trimming the coals aft, would be sufficient; for I found that the water rose and fell perpendicularly eight feet at the spring tides: but as soon as the coals were trimmed from over the leak, we could hear the water rush in a little abaft the foremast, about three feet from the keel : this determined me to clear the hold entirely, which I accomplished the next day.

CURIOUS DISCOVERY ABOUT THE LEAK.

At two o'clock in the morning of the 22d the tide left her, and gave us an opportunity to examine the leak, which we found to be at her floor heads, a little before the starboard forechains. In this place the rocks had made their way through four planks, and even into the timbers; three more planks were much damaged, and the appearance of these breaches was very extraordinary : there was not a splinter to be seen, but all was as smooth as if the whole had been cut away by an instrument : the timbers in this place were happily very close, and if they had not, it would have been absolutely impossible to have saved the ship. But after all her preservation depended upon a circumstance still more remarkable: one of the holes, which was big enough to have sunk us if we had had eight pumps instead of four, and been able to keep them incessantly going, was in great measure plugged up by a fragment of the rock, which, after having made the wound, was left sticking in it; so that the water, which at first had gained upon our pumps, was what came in at the interstices between the stone and the edges of the hole that received it. We found also several pieces of the fothering, which had made their way between the timbers, and in a great measure stopped those parts of the leak which the stone had left open. Upon further examination we found that, besides the leak, considerable damage had been done to the bottom.

This day almost everybody had seen the animal which a pigeon shooting-party had brought an account of the day before; and one of the seamen who had been rambling in the woods told us at his return that he verily believed

He had seen the devil:

we naturally inquired in what form he had appeared, and his answer was, "He was as large as a one-gallon keg, and very like it; he had horns and wings, yet he crept so slowly through the grass that if I had not been *afeard* I might have touched him." This formidable apparition we afterwards discovered to be a bat; and the bats here must be acknowledged to have a frightful appearance, for they are nearly black, and full as large as a partridge; they have indeed no horns, but the fancy of a man who thought he saw the devil might easily supply that defect.

Early in the morning of July 2d, I sent the master in the pinnace out of the harbour, to sound about the shoals in the offing, and look for channel to the northward, but our utmost efforts were still ineffectual.

He returned the next day at noon, and reported that he had found a passage out to sea between the shoals, which he described as consisting of coral rocks, many of which were dry at low water, and upon one of which he had been ashore. He found there some cockles of so enormous a size, that one of them was more than two men could eat, and a great variety of other shell-fish, of which he brought us a plentiful supply: in the evening he had also landed in a bay about three leagues to the northward of our station, where he disturbed some of the natives who were at supper: they all fled with the greatest precipitation at his approach, leaving some fresh sea eggs, and a fire ready kindled behind them, but there was neither house nor hovel near the place.

SHOOTING EXCURSION.

The next morning, Mr. Banks, with Lieutenant Gore, and three men, set out in a small boat up the river, with a view to spend two or three days in an excursion, to examine the country, and kill some of the animals which had been so often seen at a distance.

Having proceeded about three leagues among swamps and mangroves, they went up into the country, which they found to differ but little from what they had seen before: they pursued their course, therefore, up the river, which at length was contracted into a narrow channel, and was bounded, not by swamps and mangroves, but by steep banks, covered with trees of a most beautiful verdure, among which was the mohoe, or the bark-tree of the West Indies. The land within was in general low, and had a thick covering of long grass: the soil seemed to be such as promised great fertility, to any who should plant and improve it. At night they took up their lodging close to the banks of the river, and made a fire, but the mosquitoes swarmed about them in such numbers that their quarters were almost untenable: they followed them into the smoke, and almost into the fire, which, hot as the climate was, they could better endure

K

than the stings of these insects, which were an intolerable torment. The fire, the flies, and the want of a better bed than the ground, rendered the night extremely uncomfortable, so that they passed it, not in sleep, but in restless wishes for the return of day.

With the first dawn they set out in search of game, and in a walk of many miles they saw four animals of the same kind, two of which Mr. Banks's greyhound fairly chased, but they threw him out at a great distance, by leaping over the long thick grass, which prevented his running. This animal (the kangaroo) was observed, not to run upon four legs, but to bound or hop forward upon two, like the *Jerboa*, or *Mus Jaculus*. As evening approached, it became low water, and the river was then so shallow that they were obliged to get out of the boat and drag her along, till they could find a place in which they might, with some hope of rest, pass the night. Such a place at length offered; and, while they were getting the things out of the boat, they observed a smoke at the distance of about a furlong; as they did not doubt but that some of the natives, with whom they had so long and earnestly desired to become personally acquainted, were about the fire, three of the party went immediately towards it, hoping that so small a number would not put them to flight: when they came up to the place, however, they found it deserted, and therefore they conjectured, that before they had discovered the Indians, the Indians had discovered them. They found the fire still burning in the hollow of an old tree that had become touchwood, and several branches of trees newly broken down, with which children appeared to have been playing: they observed also many footsteps upon the sand, below high-water mark, which were certain indications that the

Indians had been recently upon the spot. Several houses were found at a little distance, and some ovens dug in the ground, in the same manner as those of Otaheite, in which victuals appeared to have been dressed since the morning; and scattered about them lay some shells of a kind of clam, and some fragments of roots, the refuse of the meal. After regretting their disappointment, they repaired to their quarters, which was a broad sandbank, under the shelter of a bush. Their beds were plantain leaves, which they spread upon the sand, and which were as soft as a mattress; their cloaks served them for bed-clothes, and some bunches of grass for pillows: with these accommodations they hoped to pass a better night than the last, especially as, to their great comfort, not a mosquito was to be seen.

THE FORCE OF HABIT.

Here they lay down, and, such is the force of habit, they resigned themselves to sleep, without once reflecting upon the probability and danger of being found by the Indians in that situation. If this appears strange, let us for a moment reflect, that every danger, and every calamity, after a time, becomes familiar, and loses its effect upon the mind. If it were possible that a man should first be made acquainted with his mortality, or even with the inevitable debility and infirmities of old age, when his understanding had arrived at its full strength, and life was endeared by the enjoyments of youth, and vigour, and health, with what an agony of terror and distress would the intelligence be received! yet, being gradually acquainted with these mournful truths, by insensible degrees, we scarce know when, they lose all their force, and we think no more of the approach of old age and death, than these wanderers of an unknown desert did of a less obvious and certain evil—the approach of the native savages, at a time when they must have fallen an easy prey to their malice or their fears. And it is remarkable, that the greater part of those who have been condemned to suffer a violent death, have slept the night immediately preceding their execution, though there is perhaps no instance of a person accused of a capital crime having slept the first night of his confinement. Thus is the evil of life in some degree a remedy for itself, and though every man at twenty deprecates fourscore, almost every man is as tenacious of life at fourscore as at twenty; and if he does not suffer under any painful disorder, loses as little of the comforts that remain by reflecting that he is upon the brink of the grave, where the earth already crumbles under his feet, as he did of the pleasures of his better days, when his dissolution, though certain, was supposed to be at a distance.

The party having slept, without once awaking, till the morning, examined the river, and finding the tide favoured their return, and the country promised nothing worthy of a farther search, they re-embarked in their boat, and made the best of their way to the ship.

Soon after the arrival of this party, the master also returned, having been seven leagues out to sea; and he was now of opinion that there was no getting out where before he thought there had been a passage. His expedition, however, was by no means without its advantage; for having been a second time upon the rock where he had seen the large cockles, he met with a great number of turtle, three of which he caught, that together weighed seven hundred and ninety-one pounds, though he had no better instrument than a boat-hook.

THE NATIVES AT LAST PROPITIATED.

Soon after four of the natives appeared upon the sandy point, on the north side of the river, having with them a small wooden canoe, with out-riggers: they seemed for some time to be busily employed in striking fish: some of our people were for going over to them in a boat; but this I would by no means permit, repeated experience having convinced me that it was more likely to prevent than to procure an interview. I was determined to try what could be done by a contrary method, and accordingly let them alone, without appearing to take the least notice of them: this succeeded so well, that at length two of them came in the canoe within a musket-shot of the ship, and there talked a great deal in a very loud tone: we understood nothing that they said, and therefore could answer their harangue only by shouting, and making all the signs of invitation and kindness that we could devise. During this conference they came insensibly nearer and nearer, holding up their lances, not in a threatening manner, but as if to intimate that if we offered them any injury, they had weapons to revenge it. When they were almost alongside of us, we threw them some cloth, nails, beads, paper, and other trifles, which they received without the least appearance of satisfaction: at last one of the people happened to throw them a small fish; at this they expressed the greatest joy imaginable, and intimating by signs that they would fetch their companions, immediately paddled away towards the shore. In the mean time, some of our people, and among them Tupia, landed on the opposite side of the river: the canoe, with all the four Indians, very soon returned to the ship, and came quite alongside, without expressing any fear or distrust. We distributed some more presents among them, and soon after they left us, and landed on the same side of the river where our people had gone ashore: every man carried in his hand two lances, and a stick, which is used in throwing them, and advanced to the place where Tupia and the rest of our people were sitting. Tupia soon prevailed upon them to lay down their arms, and come forward without them: he then made signs that they should sit down by him, with which they complied, and seemed to be under no apprehension or constraint: several more of us then going ashore, they expressed some jealousy lest we should get between them and their arms; we took care, however, to show them that we had no such intention, and, having joined them, we made them some more presents, as a farther testimony of our goodwill, and our desire to obtain theirs. We continued together, with the utmost cordiality, till dinner-time, and then giving them to understand that we were going to eat, we invited them by signs to go with us: this, however, they declined, and as soon as we left them, they went away in their canoe. One of these men was somewhat above the middle age, the other three were young; they were in general of the common stature, but their limbs were remarkably small; their skin was of the colour of wood-soot, or what would be called a dark chocolate colour; their hair was black, but not woolly; it was short-cropped, in some lank, and in others curled. Dampier says that the people whom he saw on the western coast of this country wanted two of their fore teeth, but these had no such defect: some part of their bodies had been painted red, and the upper lip and breast of one of them was painted with streaks of white, which he called *Carbanda;* their features were far from disagreeable, their eyes were lively, and their teeth even and white;

their voices were soft and tunable, and they repeated many words after us with great facility.

The next morning we had another visit from four of the natives; three of them had been with us before, but the fourth was a stranger, whose name, as we learned from his companions who introduced him was Yaparico. This gentleman was distinguished by an ornament of a very striking appearance: it was the bone of a bird, nearly as thick as a man's finger, and five or six inches long, which he had thrust into a hole made in the gristle that divides the nostrils; of this we had seen one instance, and only one, in New Zealand; but, upon examination, we found that among all these people this part of the nose was perforated, to receive an ornament of the same kind: they had also holes in their ears, though nothing was then hanging to them, and had bracelets upon the upper part of their arms, made of platted hair, so that, like the inhabitants of Terra del Fuego, they seem to be fond of ornament, though they are absolutely without apparel; and one of them, to whom I had given part of an old shirt, instead of throwing it over any part of his body, tied it as a fillet round his head. They brought with them a fish, which they gave us, as we supposed, in return for the fish that we had given them the day before. They seemed to be much pleased, and in no haste to leave us; but seeing some of our gentlemen examine their canoe with great curiosity and attention, they were alarmed, and jumping immediately into it, paddled away without speaking a word.

We observed that all of them were remarkably clean-limbed, and exceedingly active and nimble. One had a necklace of shells, very prettily made, and a bracelet upon his arm, formed of several strings, so as to resemble what in England is called gymp: others had a piece of bark tied over the forehead, and were disfigured by the bone in the nose. We thought their language more harsh than that of the islanders in the South Sea, and they were continually repeating the word *chercau*, which we imagined to be a term expressing admiration, by the manner in which it was uttered: they also cried out, when they saw anything new, *cher, tut, tut, tut, tut!* which probably had a similar signification.

THE KANGAROO.

Mr. Gore, who went out this day with his gun, had the good fortune to kill one of the animals which had been so much the subject of our speculation, the *Kangaroo*. In form, it is most like the Jerboa, which it also resembles in its motion, as has been observed already; but it greatly differs in size, the Jerboa not being larger than a common rat, and this animal, when full grown, being as big as a sheep: this was a young one, much under its full growth, weighing only thirty-eight pounds. The head, neck, and shoulders are very small in proportion to the other parts of the body; the tail is nearly as long as the body, thick near the rump, and tapering towards the end: the fore-legs of this individual were only eight inches long, and the hind-legs two-and-twenty: its progress is by successive leaps or hops, of a great length, in an erect posture; the fore-legs are kept bent close to the breast, and seemed to be of use only for digging: the skin is covered with a short fur, of a dark mouse or gray colour, excepting the head and ears, which bear a slight resemblance to those of a hare.

TURTLE.

The next day our kangaroo was dressed for dinner, and proved most excellent meat; we might now indeed be said to fare sumptuously every day; for we had turtle in great plenty, and we all agreed that they were much better than any we had tasted in England, which we imputed to their being eaten fresh from the sea, before their natural fat had been wasted, or their juices changed by a diet and situation so different from what the sea affords them, as garbage and a tub. Most of those that we caught here were of the kind called green turtle, and weighed from two to three hundredweight, and when these were killed, they were always found to be full of turtle grass, which our naturalists took to be a kind of *conferva*: two of them were logger-heads, the flesh of which was much less delicious, and in their stomachs nothing was to be found but shells.

AFFRAY WITH THE NATIVES.

On the 19th, in the morning, we were visited by ten of the natives, and, like all the rest of the people we had seen in this country, they were stark naked. Our guests brought with them a greater number of lances than they had ever done before, and having laid them up in a tree, they set a man and a boy to watch them: the rest then came on board, and we soon perceived that they had determined to get one of our turtle, which was probably as great a dainty to them as to us. They first asked us by signs to give them one; and being refused, they expressed, both by looks and gestures, great disappointment and anger. At this time we happened to have no victuals dressed, but I offered one of them some biscuit, which he snatched and threw overboard with great disdain. One of them renewed his request to Mr. Banks, and upon a refusal stamped with his foot, and pushed him from him in a transport of resentment and indignation. Having applied by turns to almost every person who appeared to have any command in the ship, without success, they suddenly seized two of the turtles and dragged them towards the side of the ship where their canoe lay: our people soon forced them out of their hands, and replaced them with the rest. They would not however relinquish their enterprize, but made several other attempts of the same kind, in all which being equally disappointed, they suddenly leaped into their canoe in a rage, and began to paddle towards the shore. At the same time, I went into the boat with Mr. Banks and five or six of the ship's crew, and we got ashore before them, where many more of our people were already engaged in various employments.

As soon as they landed, they seized their arms, and before we were aware of their design, they snatched a brand from under a pitch-kettle which was boiling, and making a circuit to the windward of the few things we had on shore, they set fire to the grass in their way, with surprising quickness and dexterity: the grass, which was five or six feet high, and as dry as stubble, burnt with amazing fury; and the fire made a rapid progress towards a tent of Mr. Banks's, which had been set up for Tupia when he was sick, taking in its course a sow and pigs, one of which it scorched to death. Mr. Banks leaped into a boat, and fetched some people from on board, just time enough to save his tent, by hauling it down upon the beach; but the smith's forge, at least such part of it as would burn, was consumed. While this was doing, the Indians went to a place at some distance, where several of our people were washing, and where our nets, among which was the seine and a great quantity of linen, were laid out to dry; here they again set fire to the grass, entirely disregarding both threats and entreaties. We were therefore obliged to discharge a musket, loaded with small shot, at one of them, which drew blood at the distance of about forty yards, and thus putting them to flight, we extinguished the fire at this place before it had made much progress; but where the grass had been first kindled, it spread into the woods to a great distance. As the Indians were still in sight, I fired a musket, charged with ball, abreast of them among the mangroves, to convince them that they were not yet out of our reach: upon hearing the ball they quickened their pace, and we soon lost sight of them. We thought they would now give us no more trouble; but soon after we heard their voices in the woods, and perceived that they came nearer and nearer. I set out, therefore, with Mr. Banks, and three or four more to meet them. When our parties came in sight of each other, they halted, except one old man, who came forward to meet us: at length he stopped, and having uttered some words, which we were very sorry we could not understand, he went back to his companions, and the whole body slowly retreated. We found means, however, to seize some of their darts, and continued to follow them about a mile: we then sat down upon some rocks, from which we could observe their motions, and they also sat down at about a hundred yards' distance. After a short time, the old man again advanced towards us, carrying in his hand a lance without a point; he stopped several times, at different distances, and spoke; we answered by beckoning, and making such signs of amity as we could devise; upon which the messenger of peace, as we supposed him to be, turned and spoke aloud to his companions, who then set up their lances against a tree, and advanced towards us in a friendly manner: when they came up, we returned the darts or lances that we had taken from them, and we perceived with great satisfaction that this rendered the reconciliation complete. We found in this party four persons whom we had never seen before, who as usual were introduced to us by name; but the man who had been wounded in the attempt to burn our nets and linen was not among them; we knew, however, that he could not be dangerously hurt, by the distance at which the shot reached him. We made all of them presents of such trinkets as we had about us, and they walked back with us towards the ship. As we went along, they told us, by signs, that they would not set fire to the grass any more; and we distributed among them some musket-balls, and endeavoured to make them understand their use and effect. When they came abreast of the ship, they sat down, but could not be prevailed upon to come on board; we therefore left them, and in about two hours they went away, soon after which we perceived the woods on fire at about two miles' distance. If this accident had happened a very little while sooner, the consequence might have been dreadful; for our powder had been aboard but a few days, and the store-tent, with many valuable things which it contained, had not been removed many hours. We had no idea of the fury with which grass would burn in this hot climate, nor consequently of the difficulty of extinguishing it; but we determined that if it should ever again be necessary for us to pitch our tents in such a situation, our first measure should be to clear the ground round us.

DEPARTURE FROM THE COAST OF NEW SOUTH WALES.

Having got everything on board the ship, new berthed her, and let her swing with the tide; at night the master returned with the discouraging account that there was no passage for the ship to the northward.

The next morning, at low water, I went and sounded and buoyed the bar, the ship being now ready for sea.

At six o'clock in the morning of Friday, 3d August, we made a second unsuccessful attempt to warp the ship out of the harbour; but at five o'clock in the morning of the 4th, our efforts had a better effect, and about seven we got once more under sail, with a light air from the land, which soon died away, and was followed by the sea-breezes from S.E. by S., with which we stood off to sea, having the pinnace ahead, which was ordered to keep sounding continually. To the harbour which we had now left, I gave the name of

ENDEAVOUR RIVER.

ENTANGLED AMONG THE SHOALS.

In the afternoon of the 4th, we had a gentle breeze at S.E., and clear weather; but as I did not intend to sail till the morning, I sent all the boats to the reef to get what turtle and shell-fish they could. At low-water I went up to the mast-head, and took a view of the shoals, which made a very threatening appearance: I could see several at a remote distance, and part of many of them was above water.

In the morning of the 6th we had a strong gale, so that we

were obliged to veer away more cable, and strike our top-gallant yards. At low water, myself, with several of the officers, kept a look out at the mast-head, to see if any passage could be discovered between the shoals, but nothing was in view except breakers, and out to sea beyond the reach of our sight. Convinced that there was no passage but through the labyrinth formed by these shoals, I was altogether at a loss which way to steer, when the weather should permit us to get under sail. It was the master's opinion, that we should beat back the way we came, but this would have been an endless labour, as the wind blew strongly from that quarter, almost without intermission; on the other hand, if no passage could be found to the northward, we should be compelled to take that measure at last. These anxious deliberations engaged us till eleven o'clock at night, when the ship drove, and obliged us to veer away to a cable and one-third, which brought her up; but in the morning, the gale increasing, she drove again, and we therefore let go the the small bower, and veered away to a whole cable upon it, and two cables on the other anchors, yet she still drove, though not so fast; we then got down top-gallant masts, and struck the yards and top-masts close down, and at last had the satisfaction to find that she rode. As the gale continued, with little remission, we rode till seven o'clock in the morning of the 10th, when, it being more moderate, we weighed, and stood in for the land, having at length determined to seek a passage along the shore to the northward, still keeping the small boat sounding ahead. At noon we were got between the headland and three islands: from the headland we were distant two leagues, and from the islands four. We now thought we saw a clear opening before us, and hoped that we were once more out of danger; in this hope, however, we soon found ourselves disappointed, and for that reason I called the headland

CAPE FLATTERY.

As soon as I got down from the mast-head, the master and some others went up, who all insisted that the land ahead was not islands, as I thought, but the main, and to make their report still more alarming, they said that they saw breakers all round us. In this dilemma we hauled upon a wind in for the land, and made the signal for the boat that was sounding ahead to come on board, but as she was far to leeward, we were obliged to edge away to take her up, and soon after we came to an anchor, under a point of the main, which I called Point Look-out, in somewhat less than five fathom, and at about the distance of a mile from the shore. I went ashore upon the point. Upon this point, which was high and narrow, and consisted of the finest white sand we had ever seen, we discovered the footsteps of people, and we saw also smoke and fire at a distance up the country.

In the evening I returned to the ship, and resolved the next morning to visit one of the high islands in the offing, from the top of which, as they lay five leagues out to sea, I hoped to discover more distinctly the situation of the shoals, and the channel between them.

In the morning, therefore, of the 11th I set out in the pinnace, accompanied by Mr. Banks (whose fortitude and curiosity made him a party in every expedition), for the northernmost and largest of these islands. On reaching it, we immediately ascended the highest hill, with a mixture of hope and fear, proportioned to the importance of our business, and the uncertainty of the event.

When I looked round, I discovered a reef of rocks lying between two and three leagues without the islands, and extending in a line farther than I could see, upon which the sea broke in a dreadful surf; this, however, made me think that there were no shoals beyond them, and I conceived hopes of getting without these, as I perceived several breaks or openings in the reef, and deep water between that and the islands. I continued upon this hill till sunset, but the weather was so hazy during the whole time, that I came down much disappointed. After reflecting upon what I had seen, and comparing the intelligence I had gained with what I expected, I determined to stay upon the island all night, hoping that the morning might be clearer, and afford me a more distinct and comprehensive view. We therefore took up our lodging under the shelter of a bush which grew upon the beach, and at three in the morning, having sent the pinnace with one of the mates whom I had brought out with me to sound between the island and the reefs, and examine what appeared to be a channel through them, I climbed the hill a second time, but to my great disappointment found the weather much more hazy than it had been the day before. About noon the pinnace returned, having been as far as the reef, and found between fifteen and twenty-eight fathom of water; but it blew so hard that the mate did not dare to venture into one of the channels, which he said appeared to him to be very narrow: this, however, did not discourage me, for I judged from his description of the place he had been at, that he had seen it to disadvantage. While I was busy in my survey, Mr. Banks was attentive to his favourite pursuit, and picked up several plants which he had not before seen; and as we saw no animals upon this place but lizards, I called it Lizard Island.

Returning to the ship, we landed in our way upon a low sandy island with trees upon it, upon which we saw an incredible number of sea-fowl: we found also the nest of an eagle, with young ones, which we killed; and the nest of some other bird, we knew not what, of a most enormous size: it was built with sticks upon the ground, and was no less than six-and-twenty feet in circumference, and two feet eight inches high. We found that this, as well as the other island, had been visited by the Indians, probably to eat turtle, many of which we saw upon the island, and a great number of their shells, piled one upon another in different places. To this spot we gave the name of EAGLE ISLAND.

After considering what I hàd seen myself, and the report of the master, who had been down to the low islands, I was of opinion that the passage to leeward would be dangerous, and that, by keeping in with the main, we should run the risk of being locked in by the great reef, and at last be compelled to return back in search of another passage, by which, or any other accident that should cause the same delay, we should infallibly lose our passage to the East Indies, and endanger the ruin of the voyage, as we had now but little more than three months' provisions on board at short allowance. Having stated this opinion, and the facts and appearances upon which it was founded, to the officers, it was unanimously agreed, that the best thing we could do would be to quit the coast altogether, till we could approach it with less danger.

In the morning, therefore, at break of day, we got under sail, and stood out for the north-west end of Lizard Island, leaving Eagle Island to windward, and some other islands and shoals to the leeward, and having the pinnace ahead to ascertain the depth of water in every part of our course. As soon as we had got without the breakers, we had no ground with one hundred and fifty fathom, and found a large sea rolling in from the S.E., a certain sign that neither land nor shoals were near us in that direction.

HOPES AND FEARS.

Our change of situation was now visible in every countenance, for it was most sensibly felt in every breast: we had been little less than three months entangled among shoals and rocks, that every moment threatened us with destruction; frequently passing our nights at anchor within hearing of the surge that broke over them; sometimes driving towards them even while our anchors were out, and knowing that if by any accident, to which an almost continual tempest exposed us, they should not hold, we must in a few minutes inevitably perish. But now, after having sailed no less than three hundred and sixty leagues, without once having a man out of the chains heaving the lead, even for a minute, which perhaps never happened to any other vessel, we found ourselves in an open sea, with deep water; and enjoyed a flow of spirits, which was equally owing to our late dangers and our present security: yet the very waves, which by their swell convinced us that we had no rocks or shoals to fear, convinced us also that we could not safely put the same confidence in our vessel as before she had struck; for the blows she received from them so widened her leaks, that she admitted no less than nine inches water an hour, which, considering the state of our pumps, and the navigation that was still before us, would have been a subject of more serious consideration to people whose danger had not so lately been so much more imminent.

When we had stood about two miles it fell calm; we had

sounded several times during the night, but had no bottom with one hundred and forty fathom, neither had we any ground now with the same length of line; yet, about four in the morning, we plainly heard the roaring of the surf, and at break of day saw it foaming to a vast height, at not more than a mile's distance. Our distress now returned upon us with double force; the waves, which rolled in upon the reef, carried us towards it very fast; we could reach no ground with an anchor, and had not a breath of wind for the sail. In this dreadful situation, no resource was left us but the boats; and to aggravate our misfortune, the pinnace was under repair: the long-boat and yawl, however, were put into the water, and sent ahead to tow, which, by the help of our sweeps abaft, got the ship's head round to the northward; which, if it could not prevent our destruction, might at least delay it. But it was six o'clock before this was effected, and we were not then a hundred yards from the rock upon which the same billow which washed the side of the ship, broke to a tremendous height the very next time it rose; so that

> Between us and destruction there was only a dreary valley,
> no wider than the base of one wave;

And even now the sea under us was unfathomable, at least no bottom was to be found with a hundred and twenty fathom. During this scene of distress the carpenter had found means to patch up the pinnace; so that she was hoisted out, and sent ahead, in aid of the other boats, to tow; but all our efforts would have been ineffectual, if, just at this crisis of our fate, a light air of wind had not sprung up—so light, that at any other time we should not have observed it, but which was enough to turn the scale in our favour, and, in conjunction with the assistance which was afforded us by the boats, to give the ship a perceptible motion obliquely from the reef.

Our hopes now revived; but in less than ten minutes it was again a dead calm, and the ship was again driven towards the breakers, which were not now two hundred yards distant. The same light breeze, however, returned before we had lost all the ground it had enabled us to gain, and lasted about ten minutes more. During this time we discovered a small opening in the reef, at about the distance of a quarter of a mile: I immediately sent one of the mates to examine it, who reported that its breadth was not more than the length of the ship, but that within it there was smooth water: this discovery seemed to render our escape possible, and that was all, by pushing the ship through the opening, which was immediately attempted. It was uncertain, indeed, whether we could reach it; but if we should succeed thus far, we made no doubt of being able to get through: in this, however, we were disappointed, for having reached it by the joint assistance of our boats and the breeze, we found that in the meantime it had become high water, and to our great surprise we met the tide of ebb rushing out of it like a mill-stream. We gained, however, some advantage, though in a manner directly contrary to our expectations; we found it impossible to go through the opening, but the stream that prevented us, carried us out about a quarter of a mile; it was too narrow for us to keep in it longer; yet this tide of ebb so much assisted the boats, that by noon we had got an offing of near two miles. We had, however, reason to despair of deliverance, even if the breeze, which had now died away, should revive, for we were still embayed in the reef; and the tide of ebb being spent, the tide of flood, notwithstanding our utmost efforts, again drove the ship into the bight. About this time, however, we saw another opening, near a mile to the westward, which I immediately sent Hicks, first lieutenant, in a small boat to examine: in the meantime we struggled hard with the flood, sometimes gaining a little, and sometimes losing; but every man still did his duty, with as much calmness and regularity as if no danger had been near. About two o'clock Hicks returned, with an account that the opening was narrow and dangerous, but that it might be passed: the possibility of passing it was sufficient encouragement to make the attempt, for all danger was less imminent than that of our present situation. A light breeze now sprung up, with which, by the help of our boats, and the very tide of flood that, without an opening, would have been our destruction, we entered it, and were hurried through with amazing rapidity, by a torrent that kept us from driving against either side of the channel, which was not more than a quarter of a mile in breadth. While we were shooting this gulf, our soundings were from thirty to seven fathom, very irregular, and the ground at bottom very foul.* As soon as we had got within the reef, we anchored in nineteen fathom, over a bottom of coral and shells.

Danger in Navigating Unknown Seas.

And now, such is the vicissitude of life, we thought ourselves happy in having regained a situation which, but two days before, it was the utmost object of our hope to quit. Rocks and shoals are always dangerous to the mariner, even where their situation has been ascertained; they are more dangerous in seas which

---

* "In this truly terrible situation not one man ceased to do his utmost, and that with as much calmness as if no danger had been near."—*Extract, Captain Cook's Journal—Records, Admiralty, Whitehall*, p. 289.

have never before been navigated, and in this part of the globe they are more dangerous than in any other; for here they are reefs of coral rock, rising like a wall almost perpendicularly out of the unfathomable deep, always overflowed at high water, and at low water dry in many places; and here the enormous waves of the vast Southern Ocean meeting with so abrupt a resistance, break, with inconceivable violence, in a surf which no rocks or storms in the northern hemisphere can produce. The danger of navigating unknown parts of this ocean was now greatly increased by our having a crazy ship, and being short of provisions and every other necessary; yet the distinction of a first discoverer made us cheerfully encounter every danger, and submit to every inconvenience: and we chose rather to incur the censure of imprudence and temerity, which the idle and voluptuous so liberally bestow upon unsuccessful fortitude and perseverance, than leave a country which we had discovered unexplored, and give colour to a charge of timidity and irresolution.

Having now congratulated ourselves upon getting within the reef, notwithstanding we had so lately congratulated ourselves upon getting without it, I resolved to keep the main land on board in my future route to the northward, whatever the consequence might be; for if we had now gone without the reef again, it might have carried us so far from the coast as to prevent my being able to determine, whether this country did, or did not join to New Guinea; a question which I was determined to resolve from my first coming within sight of land.

The next morning we again got under sail, and stood away to the N.W., having two boats ahead to direct us; our soundings were very irregular, varying five or six fathom every cast, between ten and twenty-seven.

Passing through numerous channels, we at length anchored in a passage among a group of islands, on one of which we resolved to go ashore. We immediately climbed the highest hill, which was not more than three times as high as the mast-head, and the most barren of any we had seen. From this hill, no land could be seen between the S.W. and W.S.W., so that I had no doubt of finding a channel through. The land to the north-west of it consisted of a great number of islands of various extent, and different heights, ranged one behind another, as far to the northward and westward as I could see, which could not be less than thirteen leagues.

Taking Possession of New South Wales.

As I was now about to quit the eastern coast of New Holland, which I had coasted from latitude 38 to this place, and which I am confident no European had ever seen before, I once more hoisted English colours, and though I had already taken possession of several particular parts, I now took possession of the whole eastern coast, from latitude 38° to this place, latitude $10\frac{1}{2}°$ S., in right of his Majesty King George III., by the name of NEW SOUTH WALES, with all the bays, harbours, rivers, and islands situated upon it: we then fired three volleys of small arms, which were answered by the same number from the ship. Having performed this ceremony upon the island, we called it POSSESSION ISLAND.

Description of N. S. Wales.

New Holland, or, as I have now called the eastern coast, New South Wales, is of a larger extent than any other country in the known world that does not bear the name of a continent; the length of coast along which we sailed, reduced to a straight line, is no less than twenty-seven degrees of latitude, amounting to near 2000 miles, so that its square surface must be much more than equal to all Europe. To the southward of 33 or 34, the land in general is low and level; farther northward it is hilly, but in no part can be called mountainous; and the hills and mountains, taken together, make but a small part of the surface, in comparison with the valleys and plains. It is, upon the whole, rather barren than fertile: yet the rising ground is chequered by woods and lawns, and the plains and valleys are in many places covered with herbage: the soil, however, is frequently sandy, and many of the lawns, or savannahs, are rocky and barren, especially to the northward, where, in the best spots, vegetation was less vigorous than in the southern part of the country; the trees were not so tall, nor was the herbage so rich. The grass in general is high, but thin, and the trees, where they are largest, are seldom less than fifty feet asunder; nor is the country inland, as far as we could examine it, better clothed than the sea-coast. The banks of the bays are covered with mangroves, to the distance of a mile within the beach, under which the soil is a rank mud, that is always overflowed by a spring-tide; farther in the country we sometimes met with a bog, upon which the grass was very thick and luxuriant, and sometimes with a valley, that was clothed with underwood: the soil in some parts seemed to be capable of improvement, but the far greater part is such as can admit of no cultivation. The coast, at least that part of it which lies to the northward of 25° S., abounds with fine bays and harbours, where vessels may lie in perfect security from all winds.

If we may judge by the appearance of the country while we

were there, which was in the very height of the dry season, it is well watered: we found innumerable small brooks and springs, but no great rivers; these brooks, however, probably become large in the rainy season. Thirsty Sound was the only place where fresh water was not to be procured for the ship, and even there one or two small pools were found in the woods, though the face of the country was everywhere intersected by salt creeks and mangrove land.

Of trees, there is no great variety. Of those that could be called timber, there are but two sorts: the largest is the gum-tree, which grows all over the country, and has been mentioned already: it has narrow leaves, not much unlike a willow; and the gum, or rather resin, which it yields, is of a deep red, and resembles the *sanguis draconis;* possibly it may be the same, for this substance is known to be the produce of more than one plant. It is mentioned by Dampier, and is perhaps the same that Tasman found upon Diemen's Land, where he says he saw "gum of the trees, and gum lac of the ground." The other timber tree is that which grows somewhat like our pines. The wood of both these trees, as I have before remarked, is extremely hard and heavy. Besides these, there are trees covered with a soft bark that is easily peeled off, and is the same that in the East Indies is used for calking of ships.

We found here the palm of three different sorts. The first, which grows in great plenty to the southward, has leaves that are platted like a fan: the cabbage of these is small, but exquisitely sweet; and the nuts, which it bears in great abundance, are very good food for hogs. The second sort bore a much greater resemblance to the true cabbage-tree of the West Indies; its leaves were large and pinnated, like those of the cocoa-nut; and these also produced a cabbage, which, though not so sweet as the other, was much larger. The third sort, which, like the second, was found only in the northern parts, was seldom more than ten feet high, with small pinnated leaves, resembling those of some kind of fern: it bore no cabbage, but a plentiful crop of nuts, about the size of a large chesnut, but rounder.

There are plants in great variety to enrich the collection of a botanist, but very few of them are of the esculent kind. A small plant, with long, narrow, grassy leaves, resembling that kind of bulrush which in England is called the Cat's-tail, yields a resin of a bright yellow colour, exactly resembling gamboge, except that it does not stain; it has a sweet smell, but its properties we had no opportunity to discover, any more than those of many others with which the natives appear to be acquainted, as they have distinguished them by names.

THE AUSTRALIAN ANT.

Among other reptiles, here are serpents. The principal insects are the mosquito and the ant. Of the ant there are several sorts; some are as green as a leaf, and live upon trees, where they build their nests of various sizes, between that of a man's head and his fist. These nests are of a very curious structure: they are formed by bending down several of the leaves, each of which is as broad as a man's hand, and gluing the points of them together, so as to form a purse; the viscus used for this purpose is an animal juice, which nature has enabled them to elaborate. Their method of first bending down the leaves, we had not an opportunity to observe; but we saw thousands uniting all their strength to hold them in this position, while other busy multitudes were employed within, in applying the gluten that was to prevent their returning back. To satisfy ourselves that the leaves were bent and held down by the efforts of these diminutive artificers, we disturbed them in their work, and as soon as they were driven from their station, the leaves on which they were employed sprung up with a force much greater than we could have thought them able to conquer by any combination of their strength. But, though we gratified our curiosity at their expense, the injury did not go unrevenged; for thousands immediately threw themselves upon us, and gave us intolerable pain with their stings, especially those who took possession of our necks and our hair, from whence they were not easily driven: the sting was scarcely less painful than that of a bee; but, except it was repeated, the pain did not last more than a minute.

Another sort are quite black, and their operations and manner of life are not less extraordinary. Their habitations are the inside of the branches of a tree, which they contrive to excavate by working out the pith almost to the extremity of the slenderest twig; the tree at the same time flourishing, as if it had no such inmate. When we first found the tree we gathered some of the branches, and were scarcely less astonished than we should have been to find that we had profaned a consecrated grove, where every tree, upon being wounded, gave signs of life; for we were instantly covered with legions of these animals, swarming from every broken bough, and inflicting their stings with incessant violence.

A third kind we found nested in the root of a plant, which grows on the bark of trees in the manner of mistletoe, and which they had perforated for that use.

We found a fourth kind, which are perfectly harmless, and almost exactly resemble the white ants of the East Indies; the architecture of these is still more curious than that of the others.

They have houses of two sorts; one is suspended on the branches of trees, and the other erected upon the ground: those upon the trees are about three or four times as big as a man's head, and are built of a brittle substance, which seems to consist of small parts of vegetables kneaded together with a glutinous matter, which their bodies probably supply: upon breaking this crust, innumerable cells, swarming with inhabitants, appear in a great variety of winding directions, all communicating with each other, and with several apertures that lead to other nests upon the same tree; they have also one large avenue, or covered way, leading to the ground, and carried on under it to the other nest or house that is constructed there. This house is generally at the root of a tree, but not of that upon which their other dwellings are constructed: it is formed like an irregularly-sided cone, and sometimes is more than six feet high, and nearly as much in diameter. Some are smaller; and these are generally flat-sided, and very much resemble in figure the stones which are seen in many parts of England, and supposed to be the remains of druidical antiquity. The outside of these is of well-tempered clay, about two inches thick; and within are the cells, which have no opening outwards, but communicate only with the subterranean way to the houses on the tree, and to the tree near which they are constructed, where they ascend up the root, and so up the trunk and branches, under covered ways of the same kind as those by which they descended from their other dwellings. To these structures on the ground they probably retire in the winter, or rainy seasons, as they are proof against any wet that can fall; which those in the tree, though generally constructed under some overhanging branch, from the nature and thinness of their crust or wall, cannot be.

The sea is much more liberal of food to the inhabitants than the land; and though fish is not quite so plenty here as they generally are in higher latitudes, yet we seldom hauled the seine without taking from fifty to two hundred weight. They are of various sorts; but except the mullet, and some of the shellfish, none of them are known in Europe: most of them are palatable, and some are very delicious. Upon the shoals and reef there are incredible numbers of the finest green turtle in the world, and oysters of various kinds, particularly the rock oyster and the pearl-oyster. The gigantic cockles have been already mentioned.

THE NATIVES.

The only tribe with which we had any intercourse we found where the ship was careened: it consisted of one-and-twenty persons—twelve men, seven women, one boy, and one girl: the women we never saw but at a distance; for when the men came over the river they were always left behind. The men, here and in other places, were of a middle size, and in general well made, clean-limbed, and remarkably vigorous, active, and nimble; their countenances were not altogether without expression, and their voices were remarkably soft and effeminate.

Their skins were so uniformly covered with dirt, that it was very difficult to ascertain their true colour: we made several attempts, by wetting our fingers and rubbing it, to remove the incrustations, but with very little effect. With the dirt, they appear nearly as black as a negro, and according to our best discoveries, the skin itself is of the colour of wood soot, or what is commonly called a chocolate colour. Their features are far from being disagreeable; their noses are not flat, nor are their lips thick; their teeth are white and even, and their hair naturally long and black, it is, however, universally cropped short; in general, it is straight, but sometimes it has a slight curl; we saw none that was not matted and filthy, though without oil or grease, and to our great astonishment free from lice. Their beards were of the same colour with their hair, and bushy and thick; they are not, however, suffered to grow long. A man, whom we had seen one day with his beard somewhat longer than his companions, we saw the next with it somewhat shorter, and upon examination found the ends of the hairs burnt; from this incident, and our having never seen any sharp instrument among them, we concluded that both the hair and the beard were kept short by singeing them.

Their principal ornament is the bone which they thrust through the cartilage that divides the nostrils from each other. What perversion of taste could make them think this a decoration, or what could prompt them, before they had worn it or seen it worn, to suffer the pain and inconvenience that must of necessity attend it, is perhaps beyond the power of human sagacity to determine. As this bone is as thick as a man's finger, and between five and six inches long, it reaches quite across the face, and so effectually stops up both the nostrils, that they are forced to keep their mouths wide open for breath, and snuffle so when they attempt to speak, that they are scarcely intelligible even to each other. Our seamen, with some humour, called it their spritsail-yard; and, indeed, it had so ludicrous an appearance, that till we were used to it, we found it difficult to refrain from laughter.

Though these people wear no clothes, their bodies have a covering besides the dirt, for they paint them both white and red: the red is commonly laid on in broad patches upon the shoulders and breast, and the white in stripes, some narrow, and some broad:

the narrow were drawn over the limbs, and the broad over the body, not without some degree of taste. The white was also laid on in small patches upon the face, and drawn in a circle round each eye. The red seemed to be ochre, but what the white was we could not discover: it was close-grained, saponaceous to the touch, and almost as heavy as white lead; possibly it might be a kind of *Steatites*, but to our great regret we could not procure a bit of it to examine. They have holes in their ears, but we never saw anything worn in them.

Upon their bodies we saw no marks of disease or sores, but large scars in irregular lines, which appeared to be the remains of wounds which they had inflicted upon themselves with some blunt instrument, and which we understood by signs to have been memorials of grief for the dead.

They appeared to have no fixed habitations, for we saw nothing like a town or village in the whole country. Their houses, if houses they may be called, seemed to be formed with less art and industry than any we had seen, except the wretched hovels at Terra del Fuego, and in some respects they are inferior even to them. At Botany Bay, where they were best, they were just high enough for a man to sit upright in, but not large enough for him to extend himself in his whole length in any direction: they are built with pliable rods about as thick as a man's finger, in the form of an oven, by sticking the two ends into the ground, and then covering them with palm-leaves and broad pieces of bark: the door is nothing but a large hole at one end, opposite to which the fire is made, as we perceived by the ashes. Under these houses or sheds, they sleep, coiled up with their heels to their head, and in this position one of them will hold three or four persons.

Manner of Producing Fire.

They produce fire with great facility, and spread it in a wonderful manner. To produce it they take two pieces of dry soft wood—one is a stick about eight or nine inches long, the other piece is flat: the stick they shape into an obtuse point at one end, and pressing it upon the other, turning it nimbly by holding it between both their hands as we do a chocolate mill, often shifting their hands up, and then moving them down upon it, to increase the pressure as much as possible.* By this method they get fire in less than two minutes, and from the smallest spark, they increase it with great speed and dexterity. We have often seen one of them run along the shore to all appearance with nothing in his hand, who stooping down for a moment, at the distance of every fifty or hundred yards, left fire behind him, as we could see first by the smoke, and then by the flame among the drift wood, and other litter which was scattered along the place. We had the curiosity to examine one of these planters of fire, when he set off, and we saw him wrap up a small spark in dry grass, which, when he had run a little way, having been fanned by the air that his motion produced, began to blaze; he then laid it down in a place convenient for his purpose, inclosing a spark of it in another quantity of grass, and so continued his course.

There are perhaps few things in the history of mankind more extraordinary than the discovery and application of fire: it will scarcely be disputed that the manner of producing it, whether

---

* Similar implements (obtained from the Esquimaux in Pond's Bay, by Sir Edward Belcher, C.B.) may be seen in the "Arctic Collection" presented by Mr Barrow to the British Museum, and deposited in the Ethnographical Room.

by collision or attrition, was discovered by chance: but its first effects would naturally strike those to whom it was a new object with consternation and terror: it would appear to be an enemy to life and nature, and to torment and destroy whatever was capable of being destroyed or tormented; and therefore it seems not easy to conceive what should incline those who first saw it receive a transient existence from chance, to reproduce it by design.

Their weapons are spears or lances, of different kinds: some that we saw upon the southern part of the coast had four prongs, pointed with bone, and barbed; the points were also smeared with a hard resin, which gave them a polish, and made them enter deeper into what they struck. These are thrown with great force and dexterity: if intended to wound at a short distance, between ten and twenty yards, simply with the hand; but if at the distance of forty or fifty, with an instrument which we called a throwing stick. They have shields made of the bark of a tree: one of these was fetched out of a hut by one of the men that opposed our landing, who, when he ran away, left it behind him, and upon taking it up, we found that it had been pierced through with a single-pointed lance near the centre.

RETURN TO ENGLAND BY NEW GUINEA AND CAPE OF GOOD HOPE.

At this time we made sail and stood to the north, in order to make the land of New Guinea, and it is sufficient to say, that we continued our course to the northward with very shallow water, upon a bank of mud, at such a distance from the shore as that it could scarcely be seen from the ship, till the 3d of September. During this time we made many attempts to get near enough to go on shore, but without success; and having now lost six days of fair wind, at a time when we knew the south-east monsoon to be nearly at an end, we began to be impatient of farther delay, and determined to run the ship in as near to the shore as possible, and then land with the pinnace, while she kept plying off and on, to examine the produce of the country, and the disposition of the inhabitants. For the last two days we had early in the morning a light breeze from the shore, which was strongly impregnated with the fragrance of the trees, shrubs, and herbage that covered it, the smell being something like that of Gum Benjamin. On the 3d of September, at daybreak, we saw the land at about four leagues' distance, and we then kept standing in for it with a fresh gale till nine o'clock, when being within about three or four miles of it, and in three fathom water, we brought to. The pinnace being hoisted out, I set off from the ship with the boat's crew, accompanied by Mr. Banks, who also took his servants, and Dr. Solander, being in all twelve persons well armed; we rowed directly towards the shore, but the water was so shallow that we could not reach it by about two hundred yards: we waded, however, the rest of the way, having left two of the seamen to take care of the boat.

ALARMING ATTACK BY SAVAGES.

Hitherto we had seen no signs of inhabitants at this place; but as soon as we got ashore we discovered the prints of human feet, which could not long have been impressed upon the sand, as they were below high-water mark: we therefore concluded that the people were at no great distance, and, as a thick wood came down within a hundred yards of the water, we thought it necessary to proceed with caution, lest we should fall into an ambuscade, and our retreat to the boat be cut off. We walked along the skirts of the wood, and at the distance of about two hundred yards from the place where we landed, we came to a grove of cocoa-nut trees, which stood upon the banks of a little brook of brackish water. The trees were of a small growth, but well hung with fruit; and near them was a shed or hut, which had been covered with their leaves, though most of them were now fallen off: about the hut lay a great number of the shells of the fruit, some of which appeared to be just fresh from the tree. We looked at the fruit very wishfully, but not thinking it safe to climb, we were obliged to leave it without tasting a single nut. At a little distance from this place we found plantains, and a bread-fruit tree, but it had nothing upon it; and having now advanced about a quarter of a mile from the boat, three Indians rushed out of the wood with a hideous shout, at about the distance of a hundred yards; and as they ran towards us, the foremost threw something out of his hand, which flew on one side of him, and burnt exactly like gunpowder, but made no report: the other two instantly threw their lances at us; and, as no time was now to be lost, we discharged our pieces, which were loaded with small shot. It is probable that they did not feel the shot, for though they halted a moment, they did not retreat; and a third dart was thrown at us. As we thought their farther approach might be prevented with less risk of life, than it would cost to defend ourselves against their attack if they should come nearer, we loaded our pieces with ball, and fired a second time: by this discharge it is probable that some of them were wounded; yet we had the satisfaction to see that they all ran away with great agility. As I was not disposed forcibly to invade this country, either to gratify our appetites or our curiosity, and perceived that nothing was to be done upon friendly terms, we improved this interval, in which the destruction of the natives was no longer necessary to our own defence, and with all expedition returned towards our boat. We there took a view of them at our leisure; they made much the some appearance as the New Hollanders, being nearly of the same stature, and having their hair short-cropped: like them also they were all stark naked, but we thought the colour of their skin was not quite so dark; this, however, might perhaps be merely the effect of their not being quite so dirty. All this while they were shouting defiance, and letting off their fires by four or five at a time. What these fires were, or for what purpose intended, we could not imagine: those who discharged them had in their hands a short piece of stick, possibly a hollow cane, which they swung sideways from them, and we immediately saw fire and smoke, exactly resembling those of a musket, and of no longer duration. This wonderful phenomenon was observed from the ship, and the deception was so great, that the people on board thought they had fire-arms; and in the boat, if we had not been so near as that we must have heard the report, we should have thought they had been firing volleys. After we had looked at them attentively some time, without taking any notice of their flashing and vociferation, we fired some muskets over their heads: upon hearing the balls rattle among the trees, they walked leisurely away.

The place where this occurred lies about sixty-five leagues to the N.E. of Port St. Augustine, or Walche Caep, and is near what is called in the charts C. de la Colta de St. Bonaventura. The land, like that in every other part of the coast, is very low, but covered with a luxuriance of wood and herbage that can scarcely be conceived. We saw the cocoa-nut, the bread-fruit, and the plantain-tree, all flourishing in a state of the highest perfection, though the cocoa-nuts were green, and the bread-fruit not in season: besides, most of the trees, shrubs, and plants that are common to the South Sea Islands, New Zealand, and New Holland.

REGARD FOR THE RIGHTS OF PROPERTY.

Soon after our return to the ship we made sail to the westward, being resolved to spend no more time upon this coast, to the great satisfaction of a very considerable majority of the ship's company. But I am sorry to say that I was strongly urged by some of the officers to send a party of men ashore, and cut down the cocoa-nut trees for the sake of the fruit. This I peremptorily refused, as equally unjust and cruel. The natives had attacked us merely for landing upon their coast, when we attempted to take nothing away; and it was therefore morally certain that they would have made a vigorous effort to defend their property, if it had been invaded, in which case many of them must have fallen a sacrifice to our attempt, and perhaps also some of our own people. I should have regretted the necessity of such a measure, if I had been in want of the necessaries of life; and certainly it would have been highly criminal, when nothing was to be obtained but two or three hundred of green cocoa-nuts, which would at most have procured us a mere transient gratification. I might indeed have proceeded farther along the coast to the northward and westward, in search of a place where the ship might have lain so near the shore as to cover the people with her guns when they landed; but this would have obviated only part of the mischief, and though it might have secured us, would probably in the very act have been fatal to the natives.

ESTABLISHMENT OF FACT THAT NEW HOLLAND AND NEW GUINEA WERE TWO DISTINCT COUNTRIES.

Besides, we had reason to think that before such a place would have been found, we should have been carried so far to the westward as to have been obliged to go to Batavia, by the north side of Java; which I did not think so safe a passage as to the south of Java, through the Straits of Sunda: the ship also was so leaky that I doubted whether it would not be necessary to heave her down at Batavia, which was another reason for making the best of our way to that place; especially as no discovery could be expected in seas which had already been navigated, and where every coast had been laid down by the Dutch geographers. The Spaniards indeed, as well as the Dutch, seem to have circumnavigated all the islands in New Guinea, as almost every place that is distinguished in the chart has a name in both languages. The charts with which I compared such part of the coast as I visited, are bound up with a French work, entitled "Histoire des Navigations aux Terres Australes," which was published in 1756, and I found them tolerably exact; yet I know not by whom, nor when they were taken: and though New Holland and New Guinea are in them represented as two distinct countries, the very History in which they are bound up leaves it in doubt. I pretend, however, to no more merit in this part of the voyage, than to have established the fact beyond all controversy.

ISLAND OF SAVU—TEMPTATION OF FRESH MUTTON.

Being clear of all the islands which are laid down in the maps we had on board, between Timor and Java, we steered a west course till six o'clock the next morning, when we unexpectedly saw an island bearing W.S.W., and at first I thought we had made a new discovery. We steered directly for it, and by ten o'clock were close in with the north side of it, where we saw houses, cocoa-nut trees, and to our very agreeable surprise, numerous flocks of sheep. This was a temptation not to be resisted by people in our situation, especially as many of us were in a bad state of health, and many still repining at my not having touched at Timor : it was therefore soon determined to attempt a commerce with people who appeared to be so well able to supply our many necessities, and remove at once the sickness and discontent that had got footing among us.

ARRIVAL AT SAVU.

Just as we got round the north point, and entered the bay, we discovered a large Indian town or village, upon which we stood on, hoisting a jack on the fore top-mast head : soon after, to our great surprise, Dutch colours were hoisted in the town, and three guns fired ; we stood on, however, till we had soundings, and then anchored.

As soon as it was light in the morning, we saw the same colours hoisted upon the beach, abreast of the ship ; supposing therefore that the Dutch had a settlement here, I sent Lieutenant Gore ashore, to wait upon the governor, or the chief person residing upon the spot, and acquaint him who we were, and for what purpose we had touched upon the coast. As soon as he came ashore, he was received by a guard of between twenty and thirty Indians, armed with muskets, who conducted him to the town, where the colours had been hoisted the night before, carrying with them those that had been hoisted upon the beach, and marching without any military regularity. As soon as he arrived, he was introduced to the raja, or king of the island; and by a Portuguese interpreter told him that the ship was a man-of-war belonging to the king of Great Britain, and that she had many sick on board, for whom we wanted to purchase such refreshments as the island afforded. His Majesty replied, that he was willing to supply us with whatever we wanted, but that, being in alliance with the Dutch East India Company, he was not at liberty to trade with any other people, without having first procured their consent, for which, however, he said, he would immediately apply to a Dutchman who belonged to the company, and who was the only white man upon the island. To this man, who resided at some distance, a letter was immediately despatched, acquainting him with our arrival and request. In about three hours, the Dutch resident answered the letter that had been sent him, in person: he proved to be a native of Saxony, and his name is Johan Christopher Lange. He behaved with great civility to Mr. Gore, assuring him, that we were at liberty to purchase of the natives whatever we pleased. After a short time, he expressed a desire of coming on board, so did the king also, and several of his attendants: Mr. Gore intimated that he was ready to attend them, but they desired that two of our people might be left ashore as hostages: and in this also they were indulged.

ROYAL SCRUPLES.

About two o'clock, they all came aboard the ship, and our dinner being ready, they accepted our invitation to partake of it: I expected them immediately to sit down, but the king seemed to hesitate, and at last, with some confusion, said, he did not imagine that we, who were white men, would suffer him, who

First Voyage. 169

was of a different colour, to sit down in our company; a compliment soon removed his scruples, and we all sat down together with great cheerfulness and cordiality: happily we were at no loss for interpreters, both Dr. Solander and Mr. Sporing understanding Dutch enough to keep up a conversation with Mr. Lange, and several of the seamen were able to converse with such of the natives as spoke Portuguese. Our dinner happened to be mutton, and the king expressed a desire of having an English sheep: we had but one left, however, that was presented to him: the facility with which this was procured encouraged him to ask for an English dog, and Mr. Banks politely gave up his greyhound: Mr. Lange then intimated that a spying-glass would be acceptable, and one was immediately put into his hand. Our guests then told us, that the island abounded with buffaloes, sheep, hogs, and fowls, plenty of which should be driven down to the beach the next day, that we might purchase as many of them as we should think fit. This put us all into high spirits, and the liquor circulated rather faster than either the Indians or the Saxon could bear. They intimated their desire to go away, before they were quite drunk, and were received upon deck, as they had been when they came aboard, by the marines under arms. The king expressed a curiosity to see them exercise, in which he was gratified, and they fired three rounds: he looked at them with great attention, and was much surprised at their regularity and expedition, especially in cocking their pieces; the first time they did it, he struck the side of the ship with a stick that he had in his hand, and cried out with great vehemence, that all the locks made but one clink. They were dismissed with many presents, and when they went away saluted with nine guns: Mr. Banks and Dr.

Solander went ashore with them; and as soon as they put off they gave us three cheers.

In the morning of the 19th, I went ashore with Mr. Banks, and several of the officers and gentlemen, to return the king's visit; but my chief business was to procure some of the buffaloes, sheep, and fowls, which we had been told should be driven down to the beach. We were, however, greatly mortified to find that no steps had been taken to fulfil this promise.

LUXURY OF DINNER ON SHORE AFTER A LONG VOYAGE.

As the morning was now far advanced, and we were very unwilling to return on board and eat salt provisions, when so many delicacies surrounded us ashore, we petitioned his majesty for liberty to purchase a small hog and some rice, and to employ his subjects to dress them for us. He answered very graciously, that if we could eat victuals dressed by his subjects, which he could scarcely suppose, he would do himself the honour of entertaining us. We expressed our gratitude, and immediately sent on board for liquors. About five o'clock, dinner was ready; it was served in six-and-thirty dishes, or rather baskets, containing alternately rice and pork; and three bowls of earthenware, filled with the liquor in which the pork had been boiled; these were ranged upon the floor, and mats laid round them for us to sit upon. We were then conducted by turns to a hole in the floor, near which stood a man with water in a vessel, made of the leaves of the fan-palm, who assisted us in washing our hands. When this was done, we placed ourselves round the victuals, and waited for the king. As he did not come, we inquired for him, and were told that the custom of the country did not permit the person who gave the entertainment to sit down with his guests; but that, if we suspected the victuals to be poisoned, he would come and taste them. We immediately declared that we had no such suspicion, and desired that none of the rituals of hospitality might be violated on our account. The prime minister and Mr. Lange were of our party, and

> We made a most luxurious meal.

We thought the pork and rice excellent, and the broth not to be despised; but the spoons, which were made of leaves, were so small, that few of us had patience to use them. After dinner, our wine passed briskly about, and we again inquired for our royal host, thinking that though the custom of his country would not allow him to eat with us, he might at least share in the jollity of our bottle; but he again excused himself, saying, that the master of a feast should never be drunk, which there was no certain way to avoid but by not tasting the liquor.

As wine generally warms and opens the heart, we took an opportunity, when we thought its influence began to be felt, to revive the subject of the buffaloes and sheep, of which we had not in all this time heard a syllable, though they were to have been brought down early in the morning. But our Saxon Dutchman, with great phlegm, began to communicate to us the contents of a letter which he pretended to have received from the governor of Concordia, which letter, it was the general opinion, was a fiction; that the prohibitory orders were feigned with a view to get money from us for breaking them; and that, by precluding our liberality to the natives, this man hoped more easily to turn it into another channel.

STRATAGEM TO SECURE PROVISIONS—EFFECT OF AN OLD BROADSWORD.

The next morning we went ashore again; Dr. Solander went up to the town to speak to Lange, and I remained upon the beach, to see what could be done in the purchase of provisions. I found here an old Indian, who, as he appeared to have some authority, we had among ourselves called the prime minister; to engage this man in our interest, I presented him with a spying-glass, but I saw nothing at market except one small buffalo. I inquired the price of it, and was told five guineas: this was twice as much as it was worth; however, I offered three, which I could perceive the man who treated with me thought a good price; but he said he must acquaint the king with what I had offered before he could take it. A messenger was immediately despatched to his majesty, who soon returned, and said, that the buffalo would not be sold for anything less than five guineas. This price I absolutely refused to give; and another messenger was sent away with an account of my refusal: this messenger was longer absent than the other, and while I was waiting for his return, I saw, to my great astonishment, Dr. Solander coming from the town, followed by above a hundred men, some armed with muskets, and some with lances. When I inquired the meaning of this hostile appearance, the Doctor told me, that Mr. Lange had interpreted to him a message from the king, purporting that the people would not trade with us, because we had refused to give them more than half the value of what they had to sell; and that we should not be permitted to trade upon any terms longer than this day. Besides the officers who commanded the party, there came a man who was born at Timor, of Portuguese parents, and who, as we afterwards discovered, was a kind of colleague to the Dutch factor; by this man, the pretended king's order was delivered to me, of the same purport with that which Dr. Solander had received from Lange. We were all clearly of opinion that this was a mere artifice of the factors to extort money from us, for which we had been prepared by the account of a letter from Concordia; and while we were hesitating what step to take, the Portuguese, that he might the sooner accomplish his purpose, began to drive away the people who had brought down poultry and syrup, and others that were now coming in with buffaloes and sheep.

At this time, I glanced my eye upon the old man whom I had complimented in the morning with the spying-glass, and I thought, by his looks, that he did not heartily approve of what was doing; I therefore took him by the hand, and presented him with an old broadsword. This instantly turned the scale in our favour; he received the sword with a transport of joy, and flourishing it over the busy Portuguese, who crouched like a fox to a lion, he made him, and the officer who commanded the party, sit down upon the ground behind him, and the people, eager to supply us with whatever we wanted, and seemingly more desirous of goods than money, instantly improved the advantage that had been procured them, and the market was stocked almost in an instant. To establish a trade for buffaloes, however, which I most wanted, I found it necessary to give ten guineas for two, one of which weighed no more than a hundred and sixty pounds; but I bought seven more much cheaper, and might afterwards have purchased as many as I pleased almost upon my own terms, for they were now driven down to the water side in herds.

The houses of Savu are all built upon posts, or piles, about four feet high, one end of which is driven into the ground, and upon the other end is laid a substantial floor of wood, so that there is a vacant space of four feet between the floor of the house and the ground.

PALM-TREE TODDY.

The fan-palm tree furnishes the inhabitants with a kind of wine, called toddy, which is obtained by cutting the buds which are to produce flowers, and tying under them small baskets, made of the leaves, which are so close as to hold liquids without leaking. The juice which trickles into these vessels is collected by persons who climb the trees for that purpose, morning and evening, and is the common drink of every individual upon the island; yet a much greater quantity is drawn off than is consumed in this use, and of the surplus they make both a syrup and coarse sugar. The liquor is called *dua*, or *duac*, and both the syrup and sugar, *gula*. The syrup is prepared by boiling the liquor down in pots of earthen-ware, till it is sufficiently inspissated; it is not unlike treacle in appearance, but is somewhat thicker, and has a much more agreeable taste: the sugar is of a reddish brown, perhaps the same with the Jugata sugar upon the continent of India, and it was more agreeable to our palates than any cane sugar, unrefined, that we had ever tasted. We were at first afraid that the syrup, of which some of our people ate very great quantities, would have brought on fluxes, but its aperient quality was so very slight, that what effect it produced was rather salutary than hurtful.

EFFECT OF SUGAR ON THE TEETH.

Both sexes are enslaved by the hateful and pernicious habit

First Voyage. 175

of chewing betel and areca, which they contract even while they are children, and practise incessantly from morning till night. With these they always mix a kind of white lime, made of coral stone and shells, and frequently a small quantity of tobacco, so that their mouths are disgustful in the highest degree both to the smell and the sight; the tobacco taints their breath, and the betel and lime make the teeth not only as black as charcoal, but as rotten too. I have seen men between twenty and thirty, whose fore-teeth have been consumed almost down to the gums, though no two of them were exactly of the same length or thickness, but irregularly corroded like iron by rust. This loss of teeth is, I think, by all who have written upon the subject, imputed to the tough and stringy coat of the areca-nut; but I impute it wholly to the lime: they are not loosened, or broken, or forced out, as might be expected, if they were injured by the continual chewing of hard and rough substances, but they are gradually wasted like metals that are exposed to the action of powerful acids; the stumps always adhering firmly to the socket in the jaw, when there is no part of the tooth above the gums: and possibly those who suppose that sugar has a bad effect upon the teeth of Europeans, may not be mistaken, for it is well known that refined loaf sugar contains a considerable quantity of lime; and he that doubts whether lime will destroy bone of any kind, may easily ascertain the fact by experiment. If the people here are at any time without this odious mouthful, they are smoking.

PRIDE OF PEDIGREE—MONUMENTAL STONES.

The chief object of pride among these people, like that of a Welshman, is a long pedigree of respectable ancestors, and, indeed, a veneration for antiquity seems to be carried farther here than in any other country: even a house that has been well inhabited for many generations, becomes almost sacred, and few articles either of use or luxury bear so high a price as stones, which having been long sat upon, are become even and smooth: those who can purchase such stones, or are possessed of them by inheritance, place them round their houses, where they serve as seats for their dependants.

Every raja sets up in the principal town of his province, or nigree, a large stone, which serves as a memorial of his reign. In the principal town of Seba, where we lay, there are thirteen such stones, besides many fragments of others, which had been set up in earlier times, and are now mouldering away: these monuments seem to prove that some kind of civil establishment here is of considerable antiquity. The last thirteen reigns in England make something more than 276 years. Many of these stones are so large, that it is difficult to conceive by what means they were brought to their present station, especially as it is the summit of a hill; but the world is full of memorials of human strength, in which the mechanical powers that have been since added by mathematical science seem to be surpassed; and of such monuments there are not a few among the remains of barbarous antiquity in our own country, besides those upon Salisbury Plain. These stones not only record the reigns of successive princes, but serve for a purpose much more extraordinary, and probably altogether peculiar to this country. When a raja dies, a general feast is proclaimed throughout his dominions, and all his subjects assemble round these stones; almost every living creature that can be caught is then killed, and the feast lasts for a less or greater number of weeks or months, as the kingdom happens to be more or less furnished with live stock at the time;

the stones serve for tables. When this madness is over, a fast must necessarily ensue, and the whole kingdom is obliged to subsist upon syrup and water, if it happens in the dry season, when no vegetables can be procured, till a new stock of animals can be raised from the few that have escaped by chance, or been preserved by policy from the general massacre, or can be procured from the neighbouring kingdoms. Such, however, is the account that we received from Mr. Lange.

The religion of these people, according to the same gentleman's information, is an absurd kind of paganism, every man choosing his own god, and determining for himself how he should be worshipped; so that there are almost as many gods and modes of worship as people. In their morals, however, they are said to be irreproachable, even upon the principles of Christianity.

This island was settled by the Portuguese almost as soon as they first found their way into this part of the ocean; but they were in a short time supplanted by the Dutch, who placed three persons upon the island; Mr. Lange, his colleague, a native of Timor, and one Frederick Craig, the son of an Indian woman by a Dutchman.

Dutch Christianity.

The office of Mr. Frederick Craig is to instruct the youth of the country in reading and writing, and the principles of the Christian religion; the Dutch having printed versions of the New Testament, a catechism, and several other tracts, in the language of this and the neighbouring islands. Dr. Solander, who was at his house, saw the books, and the copy-books also, of his scholars, many of whom wrote a very fair hand. He boasted that there were no less than six hundred Christians in the township of Seba; but what the Dutch Christianity of these Indians may be, it is not perhaps very easy to guess, for there was not a church, nor even a priest, in the whole island.

ISLAND OF JAVA AND BATAVIA.

In the morning of Friday, the 21st of September 1770, we got under sail, and stood away to the westward, along the north side of the island of Savu, and of the smaller that lies to the westward of it; and at four o'clock in the morning of the 2d October, we fetched close in with the coast of Java, in fifteen fathom; we then stood along the coast, and early in the forenoon I sent the boat ashore to try if she could procure some fruit for Tupia, who was very ill, and some grass for the buffaloes that were still alive. In an hour or two she returned with four cocoa-nuts, and a small bunch of plantains, which had been purchased for a shilling, and some herbage for the cattle, which the Indians not only gave us, but assisted our people to cut. The country looked like one continued wood, and had a very pleasant appearance.

Having again weighed, we stood to the N.E. between Thwart-the-way-Island and the Cap, sounding from eighteen to twenty-eight fathom: we had but little wind all night, and having a strong current against us, we got no further by eight in the morning than Bantam Point. At this time the wind came to the N.E., and obliged us to anchor in two-and-twenty fathom, at about the distance of two miles from the shore; with a strong current setting to the N.W.

DUTCH QUESTIONS.

Having made several attempts to sail with a wind that

would not stem the current, and as often come to an anchor, a proa* came alongside of us in the morning of the 5th, in which was a Dutch officer, who sent me down a printed paper in English, duplicates of which he had in other languages, particularly in French and Dutch, all regularly signed, in the name of the Governor and Council of the Indies, by their secretary: it contained nine questions, very ill expressed in the following terms:—

" 1. To what nation the ship belongs, and its name?

" 2. If it comes from Europe, or any other place?

" 3. From what place it lastly departed from?

" 4. Whereunto designed to go?

" 5. What and how many ships of the Dutch Company by departure from the last shore there layed, and their names?

" 6. If one or more of these ships in company with this, is departed for this or any other place?

" 7. If during the voyage any particularities is happened or seen?

" 8. If not any ships in sea, or the Straits of Sunda, have seen or hailed in, and which?

" 9. If any other news worth of attention, at the place from whence the ship lastly departed, or during the voyage, is happened?

"BATAVIA, in the Castle.
"By order of the Governor-General
"and the Counsellors of India,
"J. BRANDER BUNGL, Sec."

Of these questions I answered only the first and the fourth;

* A long narrow sail canoe used in the south seas.

which when the officer saw, he said answers to the rest were of no consequence: yet he immediately added, that he must send that very paper away to Batavia, and that it would be there the next day at noon.

Having alternately weighed and anchored several times, we at length stood in for Batavia road, where we arrived at four o'clock on the 9th October.

ARRIVAL AT BATAVIA AND PRESAGE OF SUFFERINGS.

We found here the Harcourt Indiaman from England, two English private traders of that country, thirteen sail of large Dutch ships, and a considerable number of small vessels. A boat came immediately on board from a ship which had a broad pendant flying, and the officer who commanded, having inquired who we were, and whence we came, immediately returned with such answers as we thought fit to give him: both he and his people were as pale as spectres, a sad presage of our sufferings in so unhealthy a country.

As it was the universal opinion that the ship could not safely proceed to Europe without an examination of her bottom, I determined to apply for leave to heave her down at this place. With this view we repaired immediately to the house of Mr. Leith, the only Englishman of any credit who is resident at this place, who received us with great politeness, and engaged us to dinner. At five o'clock in the afternoon I was introduced to the governor-general, who received me very courteously; he told me that I should have everything I wanted, and that in the morning my request to repair the ship should be laid before the council, which I was desired to attend.

BENEFIT OF A LIGHTNING-CONDUCTOR.

About nine o'clock, we had a dreadful storm of thunder, lightning, and rain, during which the mainmast of one of the Dutch East Indiamen was split, and carried away by the deck; the main-top-mast and top-gallant mast were shivered all to pieces; she had an iron spindle at the main-top-gallant masthead, which probably directed the stroke. This ship lay not more than the distance of two cables' length from ours, and in all probability we should have shared the same fate, but for the electrical chain which we had but just got up, and which conducted the lightning over the side of the ship; but though we escaped the lightning, the explosion shook us like an earthquake, the chain at the same time appearing like a line of fire. A sentinel was in the action of charging his piece, and the shock forced the musket out of his hand, and broke the rammer rod. Upon this occasion, I cannot but earnestly recommend chains of the same kind to every ship, whatever be her destination, and I hope that the fate of the Dutchman will be a warning to all who shall read this narrative, against having an iron spindle at the masthead.*

In the meantime, I procured an order to the superintendent of the island of Onrust, where it was arranged the ship was to be repaired, to receive her there; and sent, by one of the ships that sailed for Holland, an account of our arrival here, to Mr. Stephens,

* N. B.—This recommendation was not attended to for more than half a century. All ships of the Royal Navy are, however, now fitted with Sir Wm. Snow Harris' conductors, and no accident has ever occurred, so far as the editor is aware, with any so fitted, though many ships have been struck. Vessels not so fitted had previously suffered great damage, and many gallant lives were lost.—ED.

the secretary to the admiralty.* The expenses that would be incurred by repairing and refitting the ship rendered it necessary for me to take up money in this place, which I imagined might

* This interesting letter from Captain Cook, dated October 23d 1770, detailing his successful voyage, and that he "had not lost a man by sickness," is sadly corroborative of the ill effects of the climate of Batavia, aided possibly by the excesses of the men, on the arrival of the ship at that place :—

Endeavour Bark, near Batavia,
23d October 1770.

Sir,—Please to acquaint my Lords Commissioners of the Admiralty that I left Rio de Janeiro the 28th of December 1768, and on the 16th of January following arrived in Success Bay, in Straits La Maire, where we recruited our wood and water, and on the 21st of the same month, we quitted Straits La Maire, and arrived at George's on the 13th of April. In our passage to this island I made a far more westerly track than any ship had ever done before, yet it was attended with no discovery until we arrived within the tropick, where we discovered several islands. We met with as friendly a reception by the natives of George's Island as I could wish, and I took care to secure ourselves in such a manner as to put it out of the power of the whole island to drive us off. Some days preceding the June 3d, I sent Lieut. Hicks to the eastern part of this island, and Lieut. Gore to York island, with others of the officers (Mr. Green having furnished them with instruments), to observe the transit of Venus, that we may have the better chance of succeeding should the day prove unfavourable, but in this we were so fortunate that the observations was everywhere attended with every favourable circumstance. It was the 13th of July before I was ready to quit this island, after which I spent near a month exploring some other islands which lay to the westward before we steered to the southward. On the 14th of August we discovered a small island laying in the latitude of 22° 27′ south, longitude 150° 47 west. After quitting this island I steered to the south, inclining a little to the east, until we arrived in the latitude of 40° 12′ south, without seeing the least signs of land. After this I steered to the westward, between the latitude of 30° and 40°, until the 6th of October, on which day we discovered the east coast of New Zealand, which I found to consist of two large islands extending from 34° to 48° of south latitude, both of which I circumnavigated. On the 1st of April 1770, I quitted New Zealand and steered to the westward until I fell in with the east coast of New

First Voyage.

be done without difficulty : but I found myself mistaken ; for, after the most diligent inquiry, I could not find any private person that had ability and inclination to advance the sum that I

Holland, in the latitude of 38° south. I coasted the shore of this country to the north, putting in at such places as I saw convenient, until we arrived in the latitude of 15° 45' south, where on the night of the 10th of June we struck upon a reef of rocks, where we lay twenty-three hours and received some very considerable damage, this proved a fatal stroke to the remainder of the voyage, as we were obliged to take shelter in the first port we met with, where we were detained repairing the damage we had sustained, until the 4th of August, and after all put to sea with a leaky ship, and afterwards coasted the shore to the northward through the most dangerous navigation that ever perhaps ship was in, until the 22d of same month, when being in the latitude of 10° 30' south, we found a passage into the Indian Sea, between the northern extremity of New Holland and New Guinea. After getting through this passage I stood over for the coast of New Guinea, which we made on the 29th ; but as we found it absolutely necessary to heave the ship down to stop her leak before we proceeded home, I made no stay here, but quitted this coast on the 3d of September, and made the best of my way to Batavia, where we arrived on the 10th instant, and soon after obtained leave of the governor and council to be hove down at Onrust, where we have but just got alongside of the wharf in order to take out our stores, etc.

I send herewith a copy of my journal containing the proceedings of the whole voyage, together with such charts as I have had time to copy, which I judge will be sufficient for the present to illustrate said journal. I have with undisguised truth and without gloss inserted the whole transactions of the voyage, and made such remarks and have given such description of things as I thought was necessary, in the best manner I was capable of. Although the discoveries made in this voyage are not great, I flatter myself they are such as may merit the attention of their Lordships. Although I have failed in discovering the so much talked of southern continent, which perhaps do not exist, and which I myself have much at heart, yet I am confident that no part of the failure of such discovery can be laid to my charge ; had we been so fortunate not to have run ashore, much more would have been done in the latter part of the voyage than what was ; but as it is, I presume this voyage will be found as complete as any before made to the South Seas on the same account. The plans I have drawn of the places where I

wanted. In this difficulty I applied to the governor himself, by a written request; in consequence of which, the Shebander had orders to supply me with what money I should require out of the Company's treasury.

FATAL EFFECT OF THE CLIMATE.

On the 18th, as soon as it was light, having by several accidents and mistakes suffered a delay of many days, I took up the anchor, and ran down to Onrust: a few days afterwards we went alongside of the wharf, on Cooper's Island, which lies close to Onrust, in order to take out our stores. By this time, having been here only nine days, we began to feel the fatal effects of the climate and situation. Tupia, after the flow of spirits which the

have been at were made with all the care and accuracy that time and circumstances would admit of thus; for I am certain that the latitude and longitude of few parts of the world are better settled than these. In this I was very much assisted by Mr. Green, who let slip no opportunity for making observations for settling the longitude during the whole course of the voyage, and the many valuable discoveries made by Mr. Banks and Dr. Solander in natural history, and other things useful to the learned world, cannot fail of contributing very much to the success of the voyage.

In justice to the officers and the whole crew, I must say they have gone through the fatigues and dangers of the whole voyage with that cheerfulness and alertness that will always do honour to British seamen, and I have the satisfaction to say that I have not lost one man by sickness during the whole voyage.

I hope the repairs wanted to the ship will not be so great as to detain us any length of time. You may be assured that I shall make no unnecessary delay, either here or any other place, but shall make the best of my way home.

I have the honour to be, with the greatest respect, Sir, your most obedient humble servant, (Signed) JAMES COOK.

(*From the original letter of Captain Cook. Records of the Admiralty, Whitehall. Captain's letters, C. vol. 22.*)

novelties of the place produced upon his first landing, sunk on a sudden, and grew every day worse and worse. Tayeto was seized with an inflammation upon his lungs, Mr. Banks's two servants became very ill, and himself and Dr. Solander were attacked by fevers: in a few days almost every person both on board and ashore was sick; affected, no doubt, by the low, swampy situation of the place, and the numberless dirty canals which intersect the town in all directions. On the 26th, I set up the tent for the reception of the ship's company, of whom there was but a small number able to do duty. Poor Tupia, of whose life we now began to despair, and who till this time had continued ashore with Mr. Banks, desired to be removed to the ship, where, he said, he should breathe a freer air than among the numerous houses which obstructed it ashore: on board the ship, however, he could not go, for she was unrigged, and preparing to be laid down at the careening place: but on the 28th, Mr. Banks went with him to Cooper's Island, or, as it is called here, Kuypor, where she lay; and as he seemed pleased with the spot, a tent was there pitched for him: at this place both the sea-breeze and the land-breeze blew directly over him, and he expressed great satisfaction in his situation. Mr. Banks, whose humanity kept him two days with this poor Indian, returned to the town on the 30th, and the fits of his intermittent, which was now become a regular tertian, were so violent as to deprive him of his senses while they lasted, and leave him so weak that he was scarcely able to crawl down stairs: at this time Dr. Solander's disorder also increased, and Mr. Monkhouse the surgeon was confined to his bed.

On the 5th of November, after many delays, in consequence of the Dutch ships coming alongside the wharfs to load pepper, the ship was laid down, and the same day Mr. Monkhouse, our surgeon, a sensible, skilful man, fell the first sacrifice to this fatal country, a loss which was greatly aggravated by our situation. Dr. Solander was just able to attend his funeral, but Mr. Banks was confined to his bed. Our distress was now very great, and the prospect before us discouraging in the highest degree: our danger was not such as we could surmount by any efforts of our own; courage, skill, and diligence, were all equally ineffectual, and death was every day making advances upon us, where we could neither resist nor fly. Malay servants were hired to attend the sick, but they had so little sense either of duty or humanity, that they could not be kept within call, and the patient was frequently obliged to get out of bed to seek them. On the 9th we lost our poor Indian boy Tayeto, and Tupia was so much affected, that it was doubted whether he would survive till the next day.

MELANCHOLY REFLECTION.

In the meantime, the bottom of the ship being examined, was found to be in a worse condition than we apprehended: the false keel was all gone to within twenty feet of the stern-post; the main keel was considerably injured in many places; and a great quantity of the sheathing was torn off, and several planks were much damaged; two of them, and the half of a third, under the main channel near the keel, were for the length of six feet so worn, that they were not above an eighth part of an inch thick, and here the worms had made their way quite into the timbers; yet in this condition she had sailed many hundred leagues, where navigation is as dangerous as in any part of the world: how much misery did we escape, by being ignorant that so considerable a part of the bottom of the vessel was thinner than the sole of a shoe, and that every life on board depended upon

So slight and fragile a barrier between us and the unfathomable ocean!

It seemed, however, that we had been preserved only to perish here: Mr. Banks and Dr. Solander were so bad, that the physician declared they had no chance for recovery but by removing into the country; a house was therefore hired for them at the distance of about two miles from the town, which belonged to the master of the hotel, who engaged to furnish them with provisions, and the use of slaves. As they had already experienced their want of influence over slaves that had other masters, and the unfeeling inattention of these fellows to the sick, they bought each of them a Malay woman, which removed both the causes of their being so ill served; the women were their own property, and the tenderness of the sex, even here, made them good nurses. While these preparations were making, they received an account of the death of Tupia, who sunk at once after the loss of the boy, whom he loved with the tenderness of a parent.

By the 14th, the bottom of the ship was thoroughly repaired, and very much to my satisfaction; it would, indeed, be injustice to the officers and workmen of this yard, not to declare that, in my opinion, there is not a marine yard in the world where a ship can be laid down with more convenience, safety, and despatch, nor repaired with more diligence and skill.

Mr. Banks and Dr. Solander recovered slowly at the country-house: but I was now taken ill myself; Mr. Sporing and a seaman who had attended Mr. Banks were also seized with intermittents; and, indeed, there were not more than ten of the whole ship's company that were able to do duty.*

On the 8th of December, the ship being perfectly refitted, and having taken in most of her water and stores, and received the sick on board, we ran up to Batavia Road, and anchored in four fathom and a half of water. From this time to the 24th, we were employed in getting on board the remainder of our water and provisions, with some new pumps, and in several other operations that were necessary to fit the ship for the sea—all which would have been effected much sooner, if sickness and death had not disabled or carried off a great number of our men.

While we lay here, the "Earl of Elgin," Captain Cook, a ship belonging to the English East India Company, came to an anchor in the road. She was bound from Madras to China, but having lost her passage, put in here to wait for the next season. The "Phœnix," Captain Black, an English country ship, from Bencoolen also came to an anchor at this place.

BATAVIA, the capital of the Dutch dominions in India, and generally supposed to have no equal among all the possessions of the Europeans in Asia, is situated on the north side of the island of Java, in a low fenny plain, where several small rivers, which take their rise in the mountains called Blaeuwen Berg,

* "The mortality of Europeans in Batavia is far beyond what is known in any other settlement, exceeding those in the most fatal of the West India Islands. We had indeed, in our own instance, a fatal proof of the malignancy of the climate notwithstanding every precaution that was taken for preserving the health of the crew. A dysentery, accompanied with typhus fever, was here brought on board, which continued with more or less severity during the remaining part of the voyage. We had not lost a man on our arrival at this place, but from hence to the end of the voyage there died not fewer than fifty men."—*Barrow's Voyage to Cochin-china, in H.M.S. Lion,* P. 179.

about forty miles up the country, empty themselves into the sea, and where the coast forms a large bay, called the Bay of Batavia, at the distance of about eight leagues from the Strait of Sunda.

The Dutch seem to have pitched upon this spot for the convenience of water-carriage; and in that it is, indeed, a second Holland, and superior to every other place in the world. There are very few streets that have not a canal of considerable breadth running through them, or rather stagnating in them, and continued for several miles in almost every direction beyond the town, which is also intersected by five or six rivers, some of which are navigable thirty or forty miles up the country. As the houses are large, and the streets wide, it takes up a much greater extent, in proportion to the number of houses it contains, than any city in Europe.

In the afternoon of Christmas Eve, the 24th, I took leave of the governor, and several of the principal gentlemen of the place, with whom I had formed connections, and from whom I received every possible civility and assistance.

At six in the morning of the 26th, we weighed and set sail; the number of sick on board amounting to forty, and the rest of the ship's company in a very feeble condition. Every individual had been sick except the sail-maker, an old man between seventy and eighty years of age; and it is very remarkable that this old man, during our stay at this place, was constantly drunk every day: we had buried seven—the surgeon, three seaman, Mr Green's servant, Tupia, and Tayeto his boy. All but Tupia fell a sacrifice to the unwholesome, stagnant, putrid air of the country; and he who, from his birth, had been used to subsist chiefly upon vegetable food, particularly ripe fruit, soon contracted all the disorders that are incident to a sea life, and would probably have sunk under them before we could have completed our voyage, if we had not been obliged to go to Batavia to refit.

We now made the best of our way for the Cape of Good Hope, but the seeds of disease which we had received at Batavia began to appear with the most threatening symptoms in dysenteries and slow fevers.* Lest the water which we had taken in at Prince's Island should have had any share in our sickness, we purified it with lime, and we washed all parts of the ship between decks with vinegar, as a remedy against infection. Mr. Banks was among the sick, and for some time there was no hope of his

---

* " 30th January 1771. In the course of this twenty-four hours, we have had four men died of the flux, a melancholy proof of the calamitous situation we are at present in, having hardly well men enough to tend the sails and look after the sick, many of whom are so ill that we have not the least hopes of their recovery."— *Extract Captain Cook's Journal.—Records, Admiralty, Whitehall.*

" 12th February 1771.—Died of the flux, after a long and painful illness, Mr. John Satterly, a man much esteemed by me and every gentleman on board."— *Ibid.*

" 27th February. Died of the flux, H. Jeffs, E. Parrey, and P. Morgan, seamen. The death of these three men in one day did not in the least alarm us. On the contrary, we are in hopes that they will be the last that will fall a sacrifice to this fatal disorder, for such as are now ill of it are in a fair way of recovery."— *Ibid.*

N.B.—These were happily the last deaths recorded.

In a letter in the Records of the Admiralty, dated Endeavour Bark, 9th May 1771, Captain Cook makes mention of the deplorable sickness on board in the following terms :—" That uninterrupted state of health we had all along enjoyed was soon after our arrival at Batavia succeeded by a general sickness, which delayed us there so much, that it was the 26th of December before we were able to leave this place. We were fortunate enough to lose but few men at Batavia, but in our passage from thence to the Cape of Good Hope we had twenty-four men died —all, or most of them, of the bloody flux. The fatal disorder reigned in the ship with such obstinacy that medicine, however skilfully administered, had not the least effect."

life. We were very soon in a most deplorable situation; the ship was nothing better than an hospital, in which those that were able to go about were too few to attend the sick, who were confined to their hammocks; and we had almost every night a dead body to commit to the sea. In the course of about six weeks, we buried Sporing, a gentleman who was in Mr. Banks' retinue; Parkinson, his natural history painter; Green, the astronomer; the boatswain; the carpenter and his mate; Monkhouse, the midshipman, who had fothered the ship after she had been stranded on the coast of New Holland; our old jolly sailmaker and his assistant, the ship's cook, the corporal of the marines, two of the carpenter's crew, a midshipman, and nine seamen; in all three-and-twenty persons, besides the seven that we buried at Batavia.

THE CAPE OF GOOD HOPE.

Our run from Java Head to this place afforded very few subjects of remark that can be of use to future navigators.

On Friday, the 15th of March, about ten o'clock in the morning, we anchored off the Cape of Good Hope. My first care was to provide a proper place ashore for the sick, which were not a few; and a house was soon found, where it was agreed they should be lodged and boarded at the rate of two shillings a-head per day.

Having lain here to recover the sick, procure stores, and perform several necessary operations upon the ship and rigging, till the 13th of April, I then got all the sick on board, several of whom were still in a dangerous state, and having taken leave of the governor, I unmoored the next morning, and got ready to sail.

On the morning of the 14th, we weighed and stood out of the bay; and at five in the evening anchored under Penquin, or Robin Island; we lay here all night, and as I could not sail in the morning for want of wind, I sent a boat to the island for a few trifling articles which we had forgot to take in at the Cape.

On the 25th, at three o'clock in the afternoon, we weighed, with a light breeze at S.E., and put to sea. About an hour afterwards, we lost our master, Mr. Robert Mollineux, a young man of good parts, but unhappily given up to intemperance, which brought on disorders that put an end to his life.

We proceeded in our voyage homeward without any remarkable incident; and in the morning of the 29th we crossed our first meridian, having circumnavigated the globe in the direction from east to west, and consequently lost a day, for which we made an allowance at Batavia.

At daybreak, on the 1st of May, we saw the island of St. Helena; and at noon, we anchored in the road before James's Fort.

We staid here till the 4th, to refresh, and Mr. Banks improved the time in making the complete circuit of the island, and visiting the most remarkable places upon it.

At one o'clock in the afternoon of the 4th of May, we weighed and stood out of the road, in company with the "Portland" man-of-war, and twelve sail of Indiamen.

We continued to sail in company with the fleet, till the 10th in the morning, when, perceiving that we sailed much heavier than any other ship, and thinking it for that reason probable that the "Portland" would get home before us, I made the signal to speak with her, upon which Captain Elliot himself came on board, and I delivered to him a letter to the Admiralty, with a box, containing the common log-books of the ship, and the journals of some of the officers. We continued in company, however, till the 23d in the morning, and then there was not one of the ships in sight. About one o'clock in the afternoon we lost our first lieutenant Mr. Hicks, and in the evening we committed his body to the sea, with the usual ceremonies. The disease of which he died was a consumption, and as he was not free from it when he sailed from England, it may truly be said that he was dying during the whole voyage, though his decline was very gradual till we came to Batavia: the next day I gave Mr. Charles Clerke an order to act as lieutenant in his room, a young man who was extremely well qualified for that station.

Our rigging and sails were now become so bad, that something was giving way every day. We continued our course, however, in safety till the 10th of June, when land, which proved to be the Lizard, was discovered by Nicholas Young, the same boy that first saw new Zealand: on the 11th, we ran up the channel; at six in the morning of the 12th we passed Beachy Head; at noon we were abreast of Dover, and about three came to an anchor in the Downs, and went ashore at Deal.*

* Whoever has carefully read, and duly considered, the wonderful protection of this ship, in cases of danger the most imminent and astonishing, particularly when encircled in the wide ocean with rocks of coral, her sheathing beaten off, her false keel floating by her side, and a hole in her bottom, will naturally turn his thoughts with adoration to that Divine Being, whose mercies are over all his works.

The grand object of Captain Cook's expedition will be found detailed in the sixty-first volume of the Philosophical Transactions. But independent of this, no navigator, since the time of Columbus, had made more important original discoveries. Exclusive of several islands, never visited before, he ascertained New Zealand to be composed of two islands, by sailing between them; and he explored an immense tract of the coast of New Holland, till then little known by Europeans.

These are the appropriate merits of Captain Cook's first and glorious voyage; and though the sequel will shew that he improved on himself, he still remains unrivalled for what he had already accomplished.

The curiosities alluded to in the following letter from Captain Cook, will be found in the Ethnographical Collection in the British Museum :—

Mile End, 13*th August* 1771.

SIR,—Herewith you will receive the bulk of the curiosities I have collected in the course of the voyage, as undermentioned, which you will please to dispose of as you think proper.

I am, Sir, your most humble servant,   JAMES COOK.

One chest of So. Sea Islands cloth, breast-plates, and New Zeland clothing, etc.
One long-box or So. Sea Island chest, sundry small articles.
One cask, a small carved box from New Zeland, full of several small articles from the same place, 1 drum, 1 wooden tray, 5 pillows, 2 scoops, 2 stone and 2 wooden axes, 2 cloth beaters, 1 fish hook, 3 carved images and 8 paste beaters, all from the So. Sea Islands; 5 wooden, 3 bone, and 4 stone patta pattows, and 5 buga bugaes from New Zeland.
One bundle of New Zeland weapons.
One do   of South Sea Islands.
One do   of New Holland fish gigs.
One do   of a head ornament worn at the Heivas at Ulietea.

N.B.—There are many of the articles (engraved in the quarto edition of Cook's Voyages) in the national collection at the British Museum, and shewn in the cases, which can readily be identified. The original drawings from which the plates in Cook's Voyages were engraved, are now in the Banksean collection, and many drawings of articles which have not yet been copied; this is more particularly the case with the animals, plants, etc.

In the secretary's house at the Admiralty at Whitehall, as also in the building, there are several of the original portraits of native chiefs and others, taken by the artist who accompanied the Endeavour, all of which ought to be removed to the British Museum, as the only proper place for them, and where they may be seen, not only by the public, but by all foreigners visiting that noble institution.

The following is Captain Cook's letter reporting his arrival :—

Endeavour Bark, Downs, 12*th July* 1771.

SIR,—It is with pleasure I have to request that you will be pleased to acquaint my Lords Commissioners of the Admiralty with the arrival of H. M. bark under my command at this place, where I shall leave her to wait until further orders, and in obedience to their Lordships' orders immediately, and with this letter, repair to their office in order to lay before them a full account of the proceedings of the whole voyage.

I make no doubt but that you have received my letters and journal forwarded from Batavia in Dutch ships in October last, and likewise my letter of the 10th of May, together with some of the officers' journals, which I put on board his majesty's ship Portland, since which time nothing material hath happened, excepting the death of Lieut. Hicks. The vacancy made on this occasion I filled up by appointing Mr. Charles Clerke, a young man well worthy of it, and as such, must beg leave to recommend him to their Lordships. This, as well as all other appointments made in the bark vacant by the death of former officers, agreeable to the inclosed list, will I hope meet their Lordships' approbation.

You will herewith receive my journals containing an account of the proceedings of the whole voyage, together with all the charts, plans, and drawings I have made of the respective places we touched at, which you will be pleased to lay before their Lordships. I flatter myself that the latter will be found sufficient to convey a tolerable knowledge of the places they are intended to illustrate, and that the discoveries we have made, though not great, will apologize for the length of the voyage.

I have the honour to be, Sir, your most obedient humble servant,

Philip Stephens, Esq.   ·   JAMES COOK.

(*Captain's letters, C. vol. 22. Records of the Admiralty, Whitehall.*)

LIST of OFFICERS appointed to His Majesty's bark, the "Endeavour," by Lieutenant James Cook, commander, in the room of others, deceased.

1770, Nov. 6, William Perry, surgeon, in the room of Wm. B. Munkhouse, dd. 5th Nov. 1770, at Batavia.

1771, Feb. 5, Samuel Evans, boatswain, in the room of John Gathrey, dd. 4th Feb. 1771.

,, ,, 13, George Nowell, carpenter, in the room of John Satterley, dd. 12th Feb.

,, April 16, Richard Pickersgill, master, in the room of Robt. Molineux, dd. 15th April.

,, May 26th, John Gore, 2d lieut., in the room of Zachariah Hicks, dd. 25th May.

,, ,, 26th, Charles Clerke, 3d lieut., in the room of John Gore, appointed 2d lieut.

} At Sea

                                            JAMES COOK.

Second Voyage

TOWARDS THE SOUTH POLE, AND ROUND THE WORLD,

IN 1772, 1773, 1774, AND 1775.   THREE YEARS 18 DAYS.

WHETHER the unexplored part of the *Southern Hemisphere* were only an immense mass of water, or contained another continent, as speculative geography seemed to suggest, was a question which had long engaged the attention, not only of learned men, but of most of the maritime powers of Europe. To put an end to all diversity of opinion about a matter so curious and important was his Majesty's principal motive in directing this voyage to be undertaken.

The nature of this voyage required ships of a particular construction, and the "Endeavour" being gone to Falkland Isles, as a store-ship, the Navy-board was directed to purchase two such ships as were most suitable for this service.

Accordingly, two were purchased of Captain William Hammond of Hull. They were both built at Whitby, by the same person who built the "Endeavour," being about fourteen or sixteen months old at the time they were purchased, and were in my opinion as well adapted to the intended service as if they had been built for the purpose. The largest of the two was four hundred and sixty-two tons burthen. She was named "Resolution," and sent to Deptford to be equipped. The other was three hundred and thirty-six tons burthen. She was named "Adventure," and sent to be equipped at Woolwich.

It was first proposed to sheath them with copper; but, on considering that copper corrodes the iron-work, especially about the rudder, this intention was laid aside, and the old method of sheathing and fitting pursued, as being the most secure; for, although it is usual to make the rudder-bands of the same composition, it is not, however, so durable as iron, nor would it, I am well assured, last out such a voyage as the "Resolution" performed. Therefore, till a remedy is found to prevent the effect of copper upon the iron-work, it would not be advisable to use it on a voyage of this kind, as the principal fastenings of the ship being iron, they may be destroyed.

On the 28th of November 1771, I was appointed to the command of "the Resolution;" and Tobias Furneaux (who had been second lieutenant with Captain Wallis) was promoted, on this occasion, to the command of "the Adventure."

I had all the reason in the world to be perfectly satisfied with the choice of the officers. The second and third lieutenants, the lieutenant of marines, two of the warrant officers, and several of the petty officers, had been with me during the former voyage. The others were men of known abilities; and all of them, on every occasion, shewed their zeal for the service in which they were employed during the whole voyage.

"The Resolution" had 112 persons on board, officers included, and "the Adventure" 81. Mr. Forster and his son, both eminent naturalists, and Mr. Wales, afterwards mathematical master of Christ's Hospital, accompanied them. The following were the principal officers :—

"RESOLUTION."

R. P. Cooper, Charles Clerke, Richard Pickersgill, lieutenants.
Joseph Gilbert, master.
James Patten, surgeon.
John Edgecumbe, lieutenant, royal marines.

"ADVENTURE."

Joseph Shank, Arthur Kempe, lieutenants.
Peter Fannin, master.
Thomas Andrews, surgeon.
James Scott, lieutenant, royal marines.

And now it may be necessary to say, that, as I am on the point of sailing on a third expedition, I leave this account of my last voyage in the hands of some friends, who in my absence have kindly accepted the office of correcting the press for me; who are pleased to think, that what I have here to relate is better to be given in my own words, than in the words of another person, especially as it is a work designed for information and not merely for amusement; in which it is their opinion, that candour and fidelity will counterbalance the want of ornament.

I shall, therefore, conclude this introductory discourse with desiring the reader to excuse the inaccuracies of style, which doubtless he will frequently meet with in the following narrative; and that, when such occur, he will recollect that it is the production of a man who has not had the advantage of much school education, but who has been constantly at sea from his youth; and though, with the assistance of a few good friends, he has passed through all the stations belonging to a seaman, from an apprentice boy in the coal trade, to a post captain in the Royal Navy, he has had no opportunity of cultivating letters. After this account of myself, the public must not expect from me the elegance of a fine writer, or the plausibility of a professed book-maker; but will, I hope, consider me as a plain man, zealously exerting himself in the service of his country, and determined to give the best account he is able of his proceedings.

Plymouth Sound,
July 7, 1776.

CHAPTER IV.

(1772.)

ON the 22d of June the ship was completed for sea, when I sailed from Sheerness; and on the 3d of July, joined the "Adventure" in Plymouth Sound. The evening before, we met, off the Sound, Lord Sandwich, in the "Augusta" yacht (who was on his return from visiting the several dockyards), with the "Glory" frigate and "Hazard" sloop. We saluted his lordship with 17 guns; and soon after he and Sir Hugh Palliser gave us the last mark of the very great attention they had paid to this equipment, by coming on board, to satisfy themselves that everything was done to my wish, and that the ship was found to answer to my satisfaction.

On the 13th, at six o'clock in the morning, I sailed from Plymouth Sound, with the "Adventure" in company; and on the evening of the 29th, anchored in Funchal Road, in the island of Madeira. Having got on board a supply of water, wine, and other necessaries, we left Madeira on the 1st of August, and stood to the southward, with a fine gale. On the 4th we passed Palma, one of the Canary Isles.

On finding that our stock of water would not last us to the Cape of Good Hope, without putting the people to a scanty allowance, I resolved to stop at St. Jago for a supply. On the 9th we made the island of Bonavista; the next day passed the island of Mayo on our right; and the same evening anchored in Port Praya, in the island of St. Jago.

MAN OVERBOARD.

We had no sooner got clear of Port Praya, when we got a fresh gale which blew in squalls, attended with showers of rain. But the next day the wind and showers abated, and veered to the south. It was, however, variable and unsettled for several days, accompanied with dark gloomy weather, and showers of rain. On the 19th, in the afternoon, one of the carpenter's mates fell overboard and was drowned. He was over the side, fitting in one of the scuttles, from whence, it was supposed, he had fallen: for he was not seen till the very instant he sunk under the ship's stern, when our endeavours to save him were too late. This loss was sensibly felt during the voyage, as he was a sober man and a good workman. About noon the next day the rain poured down upon us, not in drops, but in streams. The wind, at the same time, was variable and squally, which obliged the people to attend the decks, so that few in the ships escaped a good soaking. We, however, benefited by it, as it gave us an opportunity of filling all our empty water-casks. At length, on the 8th of September, we crossed the line in the longitude of 8° west; after which the ceremony of ducking, etc., generally practised on this occasion, was not omitted.

On the 29th October we made the Cape of Good Hope, where, by the healthy condition of the crews of both ships, I thought to have made my stay very short. But, as the bread we wanted was unbaked, and the spirit, which I found scarce, to be collected from different parts out of the country, it was the 18th of November before we had got everything on board, and the 22d before we could put to sea. During this stay the crews of both ships were served every day with fresh beef or mutton, new baked bread, and as much greens as they could eat. The ships were caulked and painted; and, in every respect, put in as good a condition as when they left England.

Mr. Forster, whose whole time was taken up in the pursuit of natural history and botany, met with Mr. Sparrman, a Swedish gentleman, who had studied under Dr. Linnæus. Mr. Forster strongly importuned me to take him on board; thinking that he would be of great assistance to him in the course of the voyage. I at last consented, and he embarked with us accordingly, as an assistant to Mr. Forster, who bore his expenses.

I now directed my course for Cape Circumcision, and judging that we should soon come into cold weather, ordered slops to be served to such as were in want; and gave to each man the fearnought jacket and trousers allowed them by the Admiralty.*

A Storm.

The wind, which had for two days blown a moderate gale, increased on the 29th to a storm, which continued, with few intervals, till the 6th of December. This gale, which was attended with rain and hail, blew at times with such violence that we could carry no sails; we were driven far to the eastward of our intended course, and no hopes were left me of reaching Cape Circumcision. But the greatest misfortune was the loss of great part of our live stock, which we had brought from the Cape; and which consisted of sheep, hogs, and geese. Indeed this sudden transition from warm mild weather to extreme cold and wet, made every man in the ship feel its

* All ships recently employed in the Arctic Seas received a similar indulgence. Indeed, it is an invariable custom to issue warm clothing gratis on voyages of discovery.

effects. For by this time the mercury in the thermometer had fallen to 38; whereas at the Cape it was generally at 67 and upwards. I now made some addition to the people's allowance of spirit, by giving them a dram whenever I thought it necessary, and ordered Captain Furneaux to do the same.

First Contact with Islands of Ice.

On the morning of the 10th December we saw an island of ice to the westward of us, and made the signal for the "Adventure" to make sail and lead. I judged it to be about 50 feet high, and half a mile in circuit. It was flat at top, and its sides rose in a perpendicular direction, against which the sea broke exceedingly high. Captain Furneaux at first took this ice for land, and hauled off from it, until called back by signal.

On the 12th, we had still thick hazy weather, with sleet and snow; so that we were obliged to proceed with great caution on account of the ice islands; six of these we passed this day; some of them near two miles in circuit, and 60 feet high. And yet, such was the force and height of the waves, that the sea broke quite over them—a sight which was pleasing to the eye; but when we reflected on the danger, the mind was filled with horror; for, were a ship to get against the weather-side of one of these islands when the sea runs high, she would be dashed to pieces in a moment.* Upon our getting among the ice islands, the

* This would not be inevitably the case. When Sir James Ross's ships came into collision on the windward side of a chain of icebergs, in the South Atlantic, on the 13th of March 1842, in a heavy gale of wind, the lower yardarms scraped against the berg; but the "undertow," or reaction of the wave from the vertical side of the berg, saved the ships from being driven to atoms against it. The sternboard made by the Erebus on that occasion was one of the most difficult, dangerous, and daring efforts of navigation ever attempted and successfully accomplished. It is considered by all scamen as a masterpiece of intrepidity and skill.

arbatrosses left us; nor did our other companions, the pintadoes, sheerwaters, small grey birds, and fulmars, appear in such numbers; on the other hand, penguins began to make their appearance.

Having come to a resolution to run as far west as the meridian of Cape Circumcision, provided we met with no impediment, as the distance was not more than eighty leagues, the wind favourable, and the sea seemed to be pretty clear of ice, I sent on board for Captain Furneaux, to make him acquainted therewith; and after dinner he returned to his ship.

EXPEDITIOUS WAY OF WATERING.

By the 8th January 1773, ice islands were so familiar to us, that they were often passed unnoticed, but more generally unseen, on account of the thick weather. On coming to one which had a quantity of loose ice about it, we shortened sail, and stood off and on, with a view to take some on board. We brought to, hoisted out three boats, and, in about five or six hours, took up as much ice as yielded fifteen tons of good fresh water. The pieces we took up were hard and solid as a rock; some of them were so large that we were obliged to break them with pickaxes before they could be taken into the boats.

The salt water which adhered to the ice was so trifling as not to be tasted, and after it had lain on deck a short time entirely drained off; and the water which the ice yielded was perfectly sweet and well-tasted. Part of the ice we broke in pieces and put into casks, some we melted in the coppers, and filled up the casks with the water, and some we kept on deck for present use. The melting and stowing away the ice is a little tedious, and takes up some time, otherwise this is the most expeditious way of watering I ever met with.

AMONG THE ICEBERGS.

On the 23d February we were in the latitude 61° 52′ south, longitude 95° 2′ east. As it blew a fresh gale, we tacked, and spent the night, which was exceedingly stormy, thick, and hazy, with sleet and snow, in making short boards.

SURROUNDED ON EVERY SIDE WITH DANGER,

It was natural for us to wish for daylight; this, when it came, served only to increase our apprehensions, by exhibiting to our view those huge mountains of ice which, in the night, we had passed without seeing.

These unfavourable circumstances, together with dark nights, at this advanced season of the year, quite discouraged me from putting in execution a resolution I had taken of crossing the Antarctic circle once more. Accordingly, at four o'clock in the morning, we stood to the north, with a very hard gale at E.S.E, accompanied with snow and sleet, and a very high sea, from the same point, which made great destruction among the ice islands. This circumstance, far from being of any advantage to us, greatly increased the number of pieces we had to avoid. The large pieces which break from the ice islands are much more dangerous than the islands themselves; the latter are so high out of water, that we can generally see them, unless the weather be very thick and dark, before we are very near them; whereas the others cannot be seen in the night, till they are under the ship's bows. These dangers were, however, now become so familiar to us, that the apprehensions they caused were never of long duration, and were, in some measure, compensated, both by the seasonable supplies of fresh water these ice islands afforded us

"Surrounded on every side with danger," p. 206.

(without which we must have been greatly distressed), and also by their very romantic appearance, greatly heightened by the foaming and dashing of the waves into the curious holes and caverns which are formed in many of them; the whole exhibiting a view which at once filled the mind with admiration and horror, and can only be described by the hand of an able painter.

I now came to the resolution to quit the high southern latitudes, and to proceed to New Zealand, to look for the "Adventure," and to refresh my people.* I had also some thoughts, and even a desire, to visit the east coast of Van Diemen's Land, in order to satisfy myself if it joined the coast of New South Wales, but as the wind, continuing between the north and the west, would not permit of this, I shaped my course to New Zealand; and, being under no apprehensions of meeting with any danger, I was not backward in carrying sail, as well by night as day, having the advantage of a very strong gale, which was attended with hazy rainy weather, and a very large swell from the W. and W.S.W.

* He had penetrated further towards the South Pole than any previous navigator; but, in 1823, Weddell, just fifty years after, attained the latitude of 74° 15', being 214 geographical miles further south than Captain Cook; and, in 1841, Captain Sir James Clark Ross reached the highest latitude that in all probability will ever be attained in the Antarctic Ocean, viz., 78° 4', when he discovered the South Polar Barrier, extending 450 miles in length, with a perpendicular face of ice 180 feet above the sea level. This voyage of Sir James C. Ross (already alluded to) in her Majesty's ships Erebus and Terror (the same ships in which Franklin, Crozier, Fitzjames, and their gallant associates nobly perished in the service of their country), will ever stand as one of the most remarkable in the maritime annals of England; and it is much to be regretted that no medal has been hitherto awarded to the gallant seamen who perilled their lives in this voyage in the Antarctic Ocean.

ARRIVAL AT NEW ZEALAND.

At ten o'clock in the morning of the 25th, the land of New Zealand was seen from the mast-head; and, as I intended to put into Dusky Bay, or any other port I could find, on the southern part of TAVAI POENAMMOO, we steered in for the land, under all the sail we could carry, having the advantage of a fresh gale at west, and tolerably clear weather, and anchored in 50 fathoms water, so near the shore as to reach it with a hawser. This was on Friday the 26th of March 1773, at three in the afternoon, after having been 117 days at sea; in which time we had sailed 3660 leagues, without having once sight of land.

After such a long continuance at sea, in a high southern latitude, it is but reasonable to think that many of my people must be ill of the scurvy. The contrary, however, happened. Sweet-wort being given to such as were scorbutic, had so far the desired effect, that we had only one man on board that could be called very ill of this disease; occasioned, chiefly, by a bad habit of body, and a complication of other disorders. We did not attribute the general good state of health in the crew wholly to the sweet-wort, but to the frequent airing and sweetening the ship by fires, etc. We must also allow portable broth and sourkrout to have had some share in it. This last can never be enough recommended.

TALKATIVENESS OF WOMEN ALL OVER THE WORLD.

Early in the morning of the 6th April, a shooting party, made up of the officers, went to Goose Cove; and myself, accompanied by the two Forsters and Hodges, set out to continue the survey of the bay. My attention was directed to the north side where I discovered a fine capacious cove, in the bottom of which is a fresh-water river; on the west side several beautiful small cascades; and the shores are so steep that a ship might lie near enough to convey the water into her by a hose. In this cove we shot fourteen ducks, besides other birds, which occasioned my calling it Duck Cove.

As we returned in the evening, we had a short interview with three of the natives, one man and two women. They were the first that discovered themselves on the N.E. point of Indian Island, named so on this occasion. We should have passed without seeing them, had not the man hallooed to us. He stood with his club in his hand upon the point of a rock, and behind him, at the skirts of the wood, stood the two women, with each of them a spear. The man could not help discovering great signs of fear when we approached the rock with our boat. He, however, stood firm; nor did he move to take up some things we threw him ashore. At length I landed, went up, and embraced him; and presented him with such articles as I had about me, which at once dissipated his fears. Presently after, we were joined by the two women, the gentlemen who were with me, and some of the seamen. After this, we spent about half an hour in chit-chat, little understood on either side, in which the youngest of the two women bore by far the greatest share. This occasioned one of the seamen to say, that women did not want tongue in any part of the world. We presented them with fish and fowl which we had in our boat; but these they threw into the boat again, giving us to understand that such things they wanted not. Night approaching obliged us to take leave of them; when the youngest of the two women, whose volubility of tongue exceeded everything I ever met with, gave us a dance; but the man viewed us with great attention.

SEAL-HUNTING.

In the afternoon of the 21st April, I went with a party out to the isles on seal-hunting. The surf run so high that we could only land in one place, where we killed ten. These animals served us for three purposes: the skins we made use of for our rigging; the fat gave oil for our lamps; and the flesh we ate. Their harslets (liver) are equal to that of a hog, and the flesh of some of them eats little inferior to beef-steaks.

WATERSPOUTS.

After leaving Dusky Bay, I directed my course along shore for Queen Charlotte's Sound, where I expected to find the "Adventure," and met with nothing worthy of notice till the 17th May. Being then about three leagues to the westward of Cape Stephens, having a gentle gale and clear weather, the wind at once flattened to a calm, the sky became suddenly obscured by dark, dense clouds, and seemed to forebode much wind. This occasioned us to clew up all our sails, and presently after, six waterspouts were seen. Four rose and spent themselves between us and the land; that is, to the S.W. of us; the fifth was without us; the sixth first appeared in the S.W. at the distance of two or three miles at least from us. Its progressive motion was to the N.E., not in a straight, but in a crooked line, and passed within fifty yards of our stern, without our feeling any of its effects. The diameter of the base of this spout I judged to be about fifty or sixty feet; that is, the sea within this space was much agitated, and foamed up to a great height. From this a tube or round body was formed, by which the water or air, or both, was carried in a spiral stream up to the clouds. Some of

Waterspout.

our people said they saw a bird in the one near us; which was whirled round like the fly of a jack as it was carried upwards. During the time these spouts lasted, we had, now and then, light puffs of wind from all points of the compass; with some few slight showers of rain, which generally fell in large drops; and the weather continued thick and hazy for some hours after, with variable light breezes of wind. At length the wind fixed in its old point, and the sky resumed its former serenity. Some of these spouts appeared, at times, to be stationary; and, at other times, to have a quick, but very unequal, progressive motion, and always in a crooked line, sometimes one way, and sometimes another; so that, once or twice, we observed them to cross one another. From the ascending motion of the bird, and several other circumstances, it was very plain to us that these spouts were caused by whirlwinds, and that the water in them was violently hurried upwards, and did not descend from the clouds, as I have heard some assert. The first appearance of them is by the violent agitation and rising up of the water; and, presently after, you see a round column or tube forming from the clouds above, which apparently descends till it joins the agitated water below. I say apparently, because I believe it not to be so in reality, but that the tube is already formed from the agitated water below, and ascends, though at first it is either too small or too thin to be seen. When the tube is formed, or becomes visible, its apparent diameter increases, until it is pretty large; after that it decreases, and at last it breaks or becomes invisible towards the lower part. Soon after the sea below resumes its natural state, and the tube is drawn, by little and little, up to the clouds, where it is dissipated. The same tube would sometimes have a vertical, and sometimes a crooked or inclined direction. The most rational account I have read of waterspouts is in *Falconer's Marine Dictionary*, which is chiefly collected from the philosophical writings of the ingenious Dr. Franklin. I have been told that the firing of a gun will dissipate them, and I am very sorry I did not try the experiment, as we were near enough, and had a gun ready for the purpose; but, as soon as the danger was past, I thought no more about it, being too attentive in viewing these extraordinary meteors.

The wind having returned to the west, we resumed our course to the east; and at daylight of the 18th, we appeared off Queen Charlotte's Sound, where we discovered our consort the "Adventure," by the signals which she made to us; an event which, after a separation of fourteen weeks, every one felt with agreeable satisfaction.

A Man's Head.

Captain Furneaux in the account of his voyage, since parting with the "Resolution," mentioned that, in clearing a place on Motuara Island for erecting tents for the sick, he was visited by three canoes with about sixteen of the natives: and to induce them to bring fish and other provisions he gave them several things, with which they seemed highly pleased. One of the young officers, seeing something wrapped up in a better manner than common, had the curiosity to examine what it was; and, to his great surprise, found it to be the head of a man lately killed. They were very apprehensive of its being forced from them; and particularly the man who seemed most interested in it, whose very flesh crept on his bones, for fear of being punished, as I had expressed great abhorrence of this unnatural act. They used every method to conceal the head, by shifting it from one to another; and by signs endeavouring to convince us that there was no such thing amongst them, though we had seen it but a few minutes before.

I now gave Captain Furneaux an account in writing of the route I intended to take; which was to proceed to the east, between the latitudes of 41° and 46° south, until I arrived in the longitude of 140° or 135° west; then, provided no land was discovered, to proceed to Otaheite; from thence back to this place by the shortest route; and after taking in wood and water, to proceed to the south, and explore all the unknown parts of the sea between the meridian of New Zealand and Cape Horn; therefore, in case of separation before we reached Otaheite, I appointed that island for the place of rendezvous, where he was to wait till the twentieth of August: if not joined by me before that time, he was then to make the best of his way back to Queen Charlotte's Sound, where he was to wait until the 20th of November; after which (if not joined by me), he was to put to sea, and carry into execution their Lordships' instructions.

Some may think it an extraordinary step in me to proceed on discoveries as far south as 46 degrees of latitude, in the very depth of winter. But though it must be owned that winter is by no means favourable for discoveries, it nevertheless appeared to me necessary that something should be done in it, in order to lessen the work I was upon, lest I should not be able to finish the discovery of the southern part of the South Pacific Ocean the ensuing summer. Besides, if I should discover any land in my route to the east, I should be ready to begin, with the summer, to explore it. Setting aside all these considerations, I had little to fear; having two good ships well provided, and healthy crews. Where then could I spend my time better? If I did nothing more, I was at least in hopes of being able to point out to posterity that these seas may be navigated, and that it is practicable to go on discoveries, even in the very depth of winter.

On the 7th of June 1773, at four in the morning, the wind being favourable, we unmoored, and at seven weighed and put to sea, with the "Adventure" in company.

Getting clear of the Straits, I directed my course S.E. by E. ; and on the 11th August, at daybreak, land was seen to the south. This, upon a nearer approach, we found to be one of those isles discovered by M. Bougainville, latitude of 17° 24', longitude 141° 39' west; and I called it, after the name of the ship, Resolution Island. The sickly state of the "Adventure's" crew made it necessary for me to make the best of my way to Otaheite, where I was sure of finding refreshments. Consequently, I did not wait to examine this island, which appeared too small to supply our wants, but continued my course to the west.

On the 15th August, I brought to and waited for the "Adventure" to come up with us, to acquaint Captain Furneaux that it was my intention to put into Oaiti-piha Bay, near the S.E. end of Otaheite, in order to get what refreshments we could from that part of the island, before we went down to Matavai. This done, we made sail, and at six in the evening saw the island bearing west.

Horrors of Shipwreck renewed.

At daybreak we found ourselves not more than half a league from the reef, in a calm. This made it necessary to hoist out our boats to tow the ships off; but all their efforts were not sufficient to keep them from being carried near the reef. We had been in hopes of getting round the western point of the reef and into the bay, through an opening or break in the reef. But on examining it, I found there was not a sufficient depth of water ; though it caused such an indraught of the tide of flood through it, as was very near proving fatal to the "Resolution ;" for as soon as the ships got into this stream, they were carried with great impetuosity towards the reef. The moment I perceived this, I ordered one of the warping machines, which we had in readiness, to be carried out with about four hundred fathoms of rope; but it had not the least effect. The horrors of shipwreck now stared us in the face. We were not more than two cables' length from the breakers; and yet we could find no bottom to anchor, the only probable means we had left to save the ships. We, however, dropped an anchor; but, before it took hold, and brought us up, the ship was in less than three fathoms water, and struck at every fall of the sea, which broke close under our stern in a dreadful surf, and threatened us every moment with shipwreck. The "Adventure," very luckily, brought up close upon our bow without striking.

We presently carried out two kedge anchors, with hawsers to each. These found ground a little without the bower, but in what depth we never knew. By heaving upon them, and cutting away the bower anchor, we got the ship afloat, where we lay some time in the greatest anxiety, expecting every minute that either the kedges would come home, or the hawsers be cut in two by the rocks. At length the tide ceased to act in the same direction. I ordered all the boats to try to tow off the "Resolution;" and when I saw this was practicable, we hove up the two kedges. At that moment, a light air came off from the land, which so much assisted the boats, that we soon got clear of all danger. Then I ordered all the boats to assist the "Adventure;" but before they reached her, she was under sail with the land-breeze, and soon after joined us, leaving behind her three anchors, her coasting cable, and two hawsers, which were never recovered. Thus we were once more safe at sea, after narrowly escaping being wrecked on the very island we, but a few days before, so ardently wished to be at. The calm, after bringing us into this dangerous situation, very fortunately continued; for, had the sea-breeze, as

Second Voyage.

is usual, set in, the "Resolution" must inevitably have been lost, and probably the "Adventure" too.

During the time we were in this critical situation, a number of the natives were on board and about the ships; they seemed to be insensible of our danger, showing not the least surprise, joy, or fear, when we were striking, and left us little before sunset, quite unconcerned.

It was not till the evening of the 25th that we arrived in Matavai Bay.

OTAHEITE AGAIN.

Before we got to an anchor, our decks were crowded with the natives; many of whom I knew, and almost all of them knew me. A great crowd were got together upon the shore; amongst whom was Otoo their king. I was just going to pay him a visit, when I was told he was *mataow'd* and gone to Oparree. I could not conceive the reason of his going off in a fright, as every one seemed pleased to see me. A chief whose name was Maritata was at this time on board, and advised me to put off my visit till the next morning, when he would accompany me; which I accordingly did.

Otoo, King of Otaheite.

After having given directions to pitch tents for the reception of the sick, coopers, sail-makers, and the guard, I set out on the 26th for Oparree; accompanied by Captain Furneaux, Forster, and others, Maritata and his wife. As soon as we landed, we were conducted to Otoo, whom we found seated on the ground under the shade of a tree, with an immense crowd round him. After the first compliments were over, I presented him with such articles as I guessed were most valuable in his eyes; well knowing that it was my interest to gain the friendship of this man. I also made presents to several of his attendants; and, in return, they offered me cloth, which I refused to accept; telling them that what I had given was for *tiyo* (friendship). The king inquired for Tupia, and all the gentlemen that were with me on my former voyage, by name; although I do not remember that he was personally acquainted with any of us. He promised that I should have some hogs the next day; but I had much ado to obtain a promise from him to visit on board. He said he was *mataou no to poupoue*, that is, afraid of the guns. Indeed, all his actions showed him to be a timorous prince. He was about thirty years of age, six feet high, and a fine, personable, well-made man as one can see. All his subjects appeared uncovered before him, his father not excepted. What is meant by uncovering, is the making bare the head and shoulders, or wearing no sort of clothing above the breast.

When I returned from Oparree, I found the tents, and the astronomer's observatories, set up on the same spot where we observed the transit of Venus in 1769. In the afternoon I had the sick landed; twenty from the "Adventure" all ill of the scurvy; and one from the "Resolution." I also landed some marines for a guard, and left the command to Lieutenant Edgcumbe of the marines.

On the 27th, early in the morning, Otoo, attended by a numerous train, paid me a visit. He first sent into the ship a large quantity of cloth, fruits, a hog, and two large fish; and, after some persuasion, came aboard himself, with his sister, a younger

brother, and several more of his attendants. To all of them I
made presents; and, after breakfast, took the king, his sister,
and as many more as I had room for, into my boat, and carried
them home to Oparree. I had no sooner landed than I was met
by a venerable old lady, the mother of the late Toutaha. She
seized me by both hands, and burst into a flood of tears, saying,
Toutaha Tiyo no Toutee matty Toutaha—(Toutaha, your friend,
or the friend of Cook, is dead). I was so much affected with her
behaviour, that it would have been impossible for me to have
refrained mingling my tears with hers, had not Otoo come and
taken me from her. I, with some difficulty, prevailed on him
to let me see her again, when I gave her an axe and some other
things. Captain Furneaux, who was with me, presented the king
with two fine goats, male and female, which, if taken care of, or
rather if no care at all is taken of them, will no doubt multiply.

DANCING AND COMEDY.

On another occasion, I entertained him and his people with
the bagpipes (of which music they are very fond), and dancing
by the seamen. He, in return, ordered some of his people to
dance also, which consisted chiefly of contortions. There were,
however, some who could imitate the seamen tolerably well, both
in country dances and hornpipes.

In their theatre we were entertained with a dramatic *heava*,
or *play*, in which were both dancing and comedy. The per-
formers were five men, and one woman, who was no less a
person than the king's sister. The music consisted of three
drums only; it lasted about an hour and a half, or two hours;
and, upon the whole, was well conducted. It was not possible
for us to find out the meaning of the play. Some part seemed

adapted to the present time, as my name was frequently mentioned. Other parts were certainly wholly unconnected with us. The dancing-dress of the lady was more elegant than any I saw there, by being decorated with long tassels, made of feathers, hanging from the waist downward.

Mr. Pickersgill, on a visit to Attahourou, to which place I had sent him, had seen old Oberea. She seemed much altered for the worse, poor, and of little consequence. The first words she said were *Earee mataou ina boa*—Earee is frightened; you can have no hogs. By this it appeared that she had little or no property, and was herself subject to the Earee; which I believe was not the case when I was here before.

HUMAN SACRIFICES.

As I had some reason to believe that amongst their religious customs human sacrifices were sometimes considered as necessary, I went one day to a *Marai* in Matavai, in company with Captain Furneaux; having with us, as I had upon all other occasions, one of my men who spoke their language tolerably well, and several of the natives, one of whom appeared to be an intelligent, sensible man. In the *Marai* was a *Tupapow*, on which lay a corpse and some viands; so that everything promised success to my inquiries. I began with asking questions relating to the several objects before me—If the plantains, etc., were for the *Eatua?* If they sacrificed to the *Eatua*, hogs, dogs, fowls, etc.? to all of which he answered in the affirmative. I then asked, If they sacrificed men to the *Eatua?* he answered, *Taata eno;* that is, Bad men they did, first *Tiparrahy*, or beating them till they were dead. I then asked him, If good men were put to death in this manner? his answer was, No, only *Taata eno*. I asked him,

If any *Earees* were? he said, they had hogs to give to the *Eatua;* and again repeated *Taata eno.* I next asked him, If *Towtows,* that is, servants or slaves, who had no hogs, dogs, or fowls, but yet were good men, if they were sacrificed to the *Eatua?* His answer was, No, only bad men. I asked him several more questions, and all his answers seemed to tend to this one point, that men for certain crimes were condemned to be sacrificed to the gods, provided they had not wherewithal to redeem themselves. This, I think, implies that, on some occasions, human sacrifices are considered as necessary; particularly when they take such men as have, by the laws of the country, forfeited their lives, and have nothing to redeem them; and such will generally be found among the lower class of people.

The man of whom I made these inquiries, as well as some others, took some pains to explain the whole of this custom to us; but we were not masters enough of their language to understand them. I have since learnt from Omai, that they offer human sacrifices to the Supreme Being. According to his account, what men shall be so sacrificed depends on the caprice of the high-priest, who, when they are assembled on any solemn occasion, retires alone into the house of god, and stays there some time. When he comes out he informs them, that he has seen and conversed with their great god (the high-priest alone having that privilege), and that he has asked for a human sacrifice, and tells them that he has desired such a person, naming a man present, whom most probably the priest has an antipathy against. He is immediately killed, and so falls a victim to the priest's resentment; who, no doubt (if necessary), has address enough to persuade the people that he was a bad man.

On the 1st September we put to sea, and left Otaheite.

Some hours before we got under sail, a young man, whose name was Poreo, came and desired I would take him with me. I consented, thinking he might be of service to us on some occasion. Many more offered themselves, but I refused to take them. This youth asked me for an axe and a spike-nail for his father, who was then on board. He had them accordingly, and they parted just as we were getting under sail, more like two strangers than father and son. This raised a doubt in me whether it was so; which was farther confirmed by a canoe, conducted by two men, coming alongside, as we were standing out of the bay, and demanding the young man in the name of Otoo. I now saw that the whole was a trick to get something from me; well knowing that Otoo was not in the neighbourhood, and could know nothing of the matter. Poreo seemed, however, at first undetermined whether he should go or stay; but he soon inclined to the former. I told them to return me the axe and nails, and then he should go (and so he really should), but they said they were ashore, and so departed. Though the youth seemed pretty well satisfied, he could not refrain from weeping, when he viewed the land astern.

HUAHEINE.

As soon as we were clear of the bay, and our boats in, I directed my course for the island of Huaheine, where I intended to touch. We made it the next day, and spent the night making short boards under the north end of the island. At daylight in the morning of the 3d September, we made sail for the harbour of Owharre; in which the "Resolution" anchored. As the wind blew out of the harbour, I chose to turn in by the southern channel, it being the widest. The "Resolution" turned in very well, but the "Adventure," missing stays, got ashore on the north side of the channel. I had the "Resolution's" launch in the water ready in case of an accident of this kind, and sent her immediately to the "Adventure." By this timely assistance, she was got off again, without receiving any damage. Several of the natives, by this time, had come off to us, bringing with them some of the productions of the island; and, as soon as the ships were both in safety, I landed with Captain Furneaux, and was received by the natives with the utmost cordiality. I learnt that my old friend Oree, chief of the isle, was still living, and that he was hastening to this part to see me.

INTERESTING PRESENTATION CEREMONY ON MY FIRST VISIT TO OREE.

We were conducted to the place by one of the natives, but not permitted to go out of our boat, till we had gone through some part of the following ceremony, usually performed at this isle, on such like occasions. The boat being landed before the chief's house, which stood close to the shore, five young plantain trees, which are their emblems of peace, were brought on board separately, and with some ceremony. Three young pigs, with their ears ornamented with cocoa-nut fibres, accompanied the first three; and a dog the fourth. Each had its particular name and purpose, rather too mysterious for us to understand. Lastly, the chief sent to me the inscription engraved on a small piece of pewter, which I left with him in July 1769. It was in the same bag I had made for it, together with a piece of counterfeit English coin, and a few beads, put in at the same time; which shows how well he had taken care of the whole. When they had made an end of putting into the boat the things just mentioned, our guide, who still remained with us, desired us to decorate three young plantain trees with looking-glasses, nails, medals, beads, etc. etc. This being accordingly done, we landed with these in our hands, and were conducted towards the chief, through the multitude; they making a lane, as it were, for us to pass through. We were made to sit down a few paces short of the chief, and our plantains were then taken from us, and one by one laid before him, as the others had been laid before us. One was for *Eatua* (or god), the second for the *Earee* (or king), and the third for *Tiyo* (or friendship.) This being done, I wanted to go to the king, but was told that he would come to me, which he accordingly did, fell upon my neck and embraced me. This was by no means ceremonious; the tears, which trickled plentifully down his venerable old cheeks, sufficiently bespoke the language of his heart. The whole ceremony being over, all his friends were introduced to us, to whom we made presents. Mine to the chief consisted of the most valuable articles I had; for I had regarded this man as a father. In return he gave me a hog and a quantity of cloth, promising that all our wants should be supplied; and it will soon appear how well he kept his word.

CONCERN OF THE NATIVES FOR THEIR KING.

One of the inhabitants, who had been very troublesome and insolent, was pointed out to me, completely equipped in the war habit with a club in each hand; and as he seemed bent on more mischief, I took these from him, broke them before his eyes, and, with some difficulty forced him to retire from the place. As they told me that he was a chief, I was the more suspicious of him, and sent for a guard, which till now I had thought unnecessary. About this time, Sparrman, having imprudently gone out alone, botanising, was set upon by two men, stripped of everything he had about him, except his trousers, struck several times with his own hanger, but happily without harm. They then made off; after which another of the natives brought a piece of cloth to cover him, and conducted him to the trading place, where there were a great number of the inhabitants. The very instant Sparrman appeared in the condition I have just mentioned, they fled to a man with the utmost precipitation. My first conjectures were, that they had stolen something; but we were soon undeceived, when we saw Sparrman, and the affair was related to us. As soon as I could recal a few of the natives, and had made them sensible that I should take no step to injure those who were innocent, I went to Oree to complain of this outrage, taking with us the man who came back with Sparrman, to confirm the complaint. As soon as the chief heard the whole affair related, he wept aloud, as did many others. After the first transports of his grief were over, he began to expostulate with his people, telling them (as far as we could understand) how well I had treated them, both in this and my former voyage, and how base it was in them to commit such actions. He then took a very minute account of the stolen articles, promised to do all in his power to recover them, and rising up, desired me to follow him to my boat. When the people saw this, being, as I supposed, apprehensive of his safety, they used every argument to dissuade him from what they, no doubt, thought a rash step. He hastened into the boat, notwithstanding all they could do or say. As soon as they saw their beloved chief wholly in my power, they set up a great outcry. The grief they showed was inexpressible; every face was bedewed with tears; they prayed, entreated—nay, attempted to pull him out of the boat. I even joined my entreaties to theirs, for I could not bear to see them in such distress.

All that could be said or done availed nothing; he insisted on my coming into the boat, which was no sooner done than he ordered it to be put off. His sister, with a spirit equal to that of her royal brother, was the only person who did not oppose his going. After some trouble, the stolen property was recovered.

On the 7th September, early in the morning, while the ships were unmooring, I went to pay my farewell visit to Oree, accompanied by Captain Furneaux and Mr. Forster. We took with us, for a present, such things as were not only valuable but useful. I also left with him the inscription-plate he had before in keeping, and another small copper-plate, on which were engraved these words, "Anchored here, his Britannic Majesty's ships 'Resolution' and 'Adventure,' September 1773," together with some medals, all put up in a bag; of which the chief promised to take care, and to produce to the first ship or ships that should arrive at the island.

During our short stay at this small but fertile isle, we procured to both ships not less than three hundred hogs, besides fowls and fruits; and, had we staid longer, might have got many more; for none of these articles of refreshment were seemingly diminished, but appeared everywhere in as great abundance as ever.

OMAI.

Before we quitted this island, Captain Furneaux agreed to receive on board his ship a young man named Omai, a native of Ulietea, where he had some property, of which he had been dispossessed by the people of Bolabola. I at first rather wondered that Captain Furneaux would encumber himself with this man, who, in my opinion, was not a proper sample of the inhabitants of these happy islands, not having any advantage of birth or acquired rank, nor being eminent in shape, figure, or complexion. For their people of the first rank are much fairer, and usually better behaved and more intelligent, than the middling class of people, among whom Omai is to be ranked. I have, however, since my arrival in England, been convinced of my error; for excepting his complexion (which is undoubtedly of a deeper hue than that of the *earees* or gentry, who, as in other countries, live a more luxurious life, and are less exposed to the heat of the sun), I much doubt whether any other of the natives would have given more general satisfaction by his behaviour among us.

Omai.

Soon after his arrival in London, the Earl of Sandwich, the First Lord of the Admiralty, introduced him to his Majesty at Kew, when he met with a most gracious reception. He embarked with me in the "Resolution," when she was fitted out for another voyage, loaded with presents from his several friends, and full of gratitude for the kind reception and treatment he had experienced among us.

PUBLIC DINNER AT ULIETEA—TWO WHOLE PIGS.

The chief was no sooner gone, than we made sail for Ulietea (where I intended to stop a few days).

Oreo the chief, and some of his friends, paid me a morning visit. I acquainted him that I would dine with him, and desired he would order two pigs to be dressed after their manner, which he accordingly did; and about one o'clock I and the officers of both ships went to partake of them. When we came to the chief's house, we found the cloth laid; that is, green leaves were strewed thick on the floor. Round them we seated ourselves:

presently one of the pigs came over my head souse upon the leaves, and immediately after the other; both so hot as hardly to be touched. The table was garnished round with hot bread-fruit and plantains, and a quantity of cocoa-nuts brought for drink. Each man being ready, with his knife in his hand, we turned to without ceremony; and it must be owned, in favour of their cookery, that victuals were never cleaner, nor better dressed. For though the pigs were served up whole, and the one weighed between fifty and sixty pounds, and the other about half as much, yet all the parts were equally well done, and ate much sweeter than if dressed in any of our methods. The chief and his son, and some other of his male friends, ate with us, and pieces were handed to others who sat behind: for we had a vast crowd about us; so that it might be truly said we dined in public. The chief never failed to drink his glass of Madeira whenever it came to his turn, not only now, but at all other times when he dined with us, without ever being once affected by it. As soon as we had dined, the boat's crew took the remainder; and by them, and those about them, the whole was consumed. When we rose up, many of the common people rushed in, to pick up the crumbs which had fallen, and for which they searched the leaves very narrowly. This leads me to believe that, though there is plenty of pork at these isles, but little falls to their share.

CHAPTER V.

FROM OUR DEPARTURE FROM THE SOCIETY ISLES, TO OUR RETURN TO AND LEAVING THEM THE SECOND TIME.

AFTER leaving Ulietea, I steered to the west, inclining to the south, to get clear of the tracks of former navigators, and to get into the latitude of the islands of Middleburg and Amsterdam; for I intended to run as far west as these islands, and to touch there if I found it convenient, before I hauled up for New Zealand. I generally lay to every night, lest we might pass any land in the dark.

On the 1st of October, we made the island of Middleburg, where I obtained the friendship of the chief, whose name was Tioony. On leaving this I sailed for Amsterdam.

These islands were first discovered by Captain Tasman, in January 1642-3; and were named by him.

CUSTOM OF MUTILATION.

We observed that the greater part of the people, both men and women, had lost one or both their little fingers. We endeavoured, but in vain, to find out the reason of this mutilation; for no one would take any pains to inform us. It was neither peculiar to rank, age, or sex; nor is it done at any certain age, as I saw those of all ages on whom the amputation had been just made; and, except some young children, we found few who had both hands perfect. As it was more common among the aged than the young, some of us were of opinion that it was occasioned by the death of their parents, or some other near relation. But Mr. Wales one day met with a man, whose hands were both perfect, of such an advanced age, that it was hardly possible his parents could be living. They also burn or make incisions in their cheeks, near the cheek-bone. The reason of this was equally unknown to us. In some, the wounds were quite fresh; in others, they could only be known by the scars, or colour of the skin. I saw neither sick nor lame amongst them: all appeared healthy, strong, and vigorous; a proof of the goodness of the climate in which they live.

WONDERFUL LUXURIOUSNESS OF NATURE.

Though benevolent nature has been very bountiful here, it cannot be said that the inhabitants are wholly exempt from the curse of our forefathers: part of their bread must be earned with the sweat of their brows. The high state of cultivation their lands are in must have cost them immense labour. This is now amply rewarded by the great produce, of which every one seems to partake. No one wants the common necessaries of life; joy and contentment are painted in every face. Indeed, it can hardly be otherwise: an easy freedom prevails among all ranks of people: they feel no wants which they do not enjoy the means of gratifying; and they live in a clime where the painful extremes of heat and cold are equally unknown. If nature has been wanting in anything, it is in the article of fresh water, which, as it is shut up in the bowels of the earth, they are obliged to dig for. A running stream was not seen, and but one well, at Amsterdam. At Middleburg, we saw no water but what the natives had in vessels; but as it was sweet and cool, I had no doubt of its being taken up upon the island, and probably not far from the spot where I saw it.

It being my intention to proceed directly to Queen Charlotte's Sound in New Zealand, there to take in wood and water, and then to go on further discoveries to the south and east, I sailed on the 8th; and on the morning of the 21st made the land of New Zealand. As soon as the "Adventure" was up with us, we made sail for Cape Kidnappers, which we passed, and continued our course alongshore.

It was evident the people here had not forgot the "Endeavour" being on their coast; for the first words they spoke to us were, *Mataou no te pow pow* (we are afraid of the guns). As they could be no strangers to the affair which happened off Cape Kidnapper in my former voyage, experience had taught them to have some regard to these instruments of death.

As soon as they were gone we stretched off to the southward, and the "Adventure," being a good way to leeward, we suppose did not observe the signal, but stood on, consequently was separated from us. I regretted her loss; for had she been with me, I should have given up all thoughts of going to Queen Charlotte's Sound to wood and water, and have sought for a place to get these articles farther south, as the wind was now favourable for ranging along the coast. But our separation made it necessary for me to repair to the Sound, that being the place of rendezvous.

NEW ZEALAND CANNIBALISM PUT TO THE TEST.

While lying here, in the month of November, some of the officers went on shore to amuse themselves among the natives, where they saw the head and bowels of a youth, who had lately been killed, lying on the beach, and the heart stuck on a forked stick which was fixed to the head of one of the largest canoes. One of the officers bought the head and brought it on board, where a piece of the flesh was broiled and eaten by one of the natives, before all the officers and most of the men. I was on shore at this time, but soon after returning on board, was informed of the above circumstances, and found the quarter-deck crowded with the natives, and the mangled head, or rather part of it (for the under jaw and lip were wanting), lying on the tafferel. The skull had been broken on the left side just above the temples, and the remains of the face had all the appearance of a youth under twenty.

The sight of the head, and the relation of the above circumstances, struck me with horror, and filled my mind with indignation against these cannibals. Curiosity, however, got the better of my indignation, especially when I considered that it would avail but little; and being desirous of becoming an eye-witness of a fact which many doubted, I ordered a piece of the flesh to be broiled and brought to the quarter-deck, where one of these cannibals ate it with surprising avidity. This had such an effect on some of our people as to make them sick. The account given of this in my former voyage, being partly founded on circumstances, was, as I afterwards understood, discredited by many persons. Few consider what a savage man is, in his natural state, and even after he is in some degree civilized. The New Zealanders are certainly in some state of civilization; their behaviour to us was manly and mild, showing on all occasions a readiness to oblige. They have some arts among them which they execute with great judgment and unwearied patience; they are far less addicted to thieving than the other islanders of the

South Sea; and I believe those in the same tribe, or such as are at peace one with another, are strictly honest among themselves. This custom of eating their enemies slain in battle (for I firmly believe they eat the flesh of no others) has, undoubtedly, been handed down to them from the earliest times; and we know it is not an easy matter to wean a nation from their ancient customs, let them be ever so inhuman and savage; especially if that nation has no manner of connection or commerce with strangers. For it is by this that the greatest part of the human race has been civilized; an advantage which the New Zealanders from their situation never had. An intercourse with foreigners would reform their manners, and polish their savage minds. Or, were they more united under a settled form of government, they would have fewer enemies; consequently, this custom would be less in use, and might in time be in a manner forgotten. At present, they have but little idea of treating others as themselves would *wish* to be treated, but treat them as they *expect* to be treated. If I remember right, one of the arguments they made use of to Tupia, who frequently expostulated with them against this custom, was, that there could be no harm in killing and eating the man who would do the same by them, if it was in his power. For, said they, " Can there be any harm in eating our enemies, whom we have killed in battle? Would not those very enemies have done the same to us?" I have often seen them listen to Tupia with great attention; but I never found his arguments have any weight with them, or that, with all his rhetoric, he could persuade any one of them that this custom was wrong; and when Oedidee and several of our people showed their abhorrence of it, they only laughed at them.

Among many reasons which I have heard assigned for the

prevalence of this horrid custom, the want of animal food has been one; but how far this is deducible either from facts or circumstances, I shall leave those to find out who advanced it. In every part of New Zealand where I have been, fish was in such plenty, that the natives generally caught as much as served both themselves and us. They have also plenty of dogs; nor is there any want of wild-fowl, which they know very well how to kill. So that neither this, nor the want of food of any kind, can in my opinion be the reason. But whatever it may be, I think it was but too evident that they have a great liking for this kind of food.

At daylight in the morning of the 26th November, we made sail round Cape Palliser, firing guns as usual as we ran along the shore. Every one was of opinion that the "Adventure" could neither be stranded on the coast, nor be in any of the harbours thereof. I therefore gave up looking for her, and all thoughts of seeing her any more during the voyage; as no rendezvous was absolutely fixed upon after leaving New Zealand. Nevertheless, this did not discourage me from fully exploring the southern parts of the Pacific Ocean, in the doing of which I intended to employ the whole of the ensuing season; and I had the satisfaction to find that not a man was dejected for the loss of our consort, or thought the dangers we had yet to go through were in the least increased by being alone; but as cheerfully proceeding to the south, or wherever I might think proper to lead them, as if the "Adventure," or even more ships, had been in our company.

We continued our course to the south until the 30th of January 1774, when we perceived the clouds over the horizon to the south to be of an unusual snow-white brightness, which we knew announced our approach to field-ice. Soon after, it was seen from the topmast head; and shortly we were close to its edge. It extended east and west, far beyond the reach of our sight. In the situation we were in, just the southern half of our horizon was illuminated by the rays of light reflected from the ice, to a considerable height. Ninety-seven ice-hills were distinctly seen within the field, besides those on the outside; many of them very large, and looking like a ridge of mountains, rising one above another till they were lost in the clouds. The outer or northern edge of this immense field was composed of loose or broken ice close packed together; so that it was not possible for anything to enter it. This was about a mile broad; within which was solid ice in one continued compact body. It was rather low and flat (except the hills), but seemed to increase in height, as you traced it to the south; in which direction it extended beyond our sight. Such mountains of ice as these were, I believe, never seen in the Greenland seas; at least, not that I ever heard or read of; so that we cannot draw a comparison between the ice here and there. It must be allowed that these prodigious ice mountains must add such additional weight to the ice-fields which inclose them, as cannot but make a great difference between the navigating this icy sea and that of Greenland.

Being at this time in the latitude of 71° 10′ S., longitude 106° 54′ W., I will not say it was impossible anywhere to get farther to the south; but the attempting it would have been a dangerous and rash enterprise, and what, I believe, no man in my situation would have thought of. It was, indeed, my opinion, as well as the opinion of most on board, that this ice extended quite to the pole, or perhaps joined to some land, to which it had been fixed from the earliest time; and that it is here—that is, to the south of this parallel—where all the ice we find scattered up and down to the north is first formed, and afterwards broken off by gales of wind, or other causes, and brought to the north by the currents, which we always found to set in that direction in the high latitudes. As we drew near this ice, some penguins were heard, but none seen; and but few other birds, or any other thing, that could induce us to think any land was near. And yet I think there must be some to the south behind this ice; but if there is, it can afford no better retreat for birds, or any other animals, than the ice itself, with which it must be wholly covered. I, who had ambition not only to go farther than any one had been before, but as far as it was possible for man to go, was not sorry at meeting with this interruption; as it, in some measure, relieved us; at least, shortened the dangers and hardships inseparable from the navigation of the southern polar regions. Since, therefore, we could not proceed one inch farther to the south, no other reason need be assigned for my tacking, and standing back to the north.*

I now came to a resolution to proceed to the north, and to spend the ensuing winter within the tropic, if I met with no employment before I came there.

My intention was first to go in search of the land, said to have been discovered by Juan Fernandez, above a century ago, in about the latitude of 38°; but as I failed in finding this, I went in search of Easter Island or Davis's Land, whose situation was known with so little certainty that the attempts lately made to find it had miscarried.

* Nothing could show a sounder judgment than this decision on the part of Captain Cook, who, having now penetrated to 71° 10' S., long. 106° 54' W., wisely left it to a future navigator to discover a continent in the Southern Atlantic Ocean, nearly a century afterwards—the present Admiral Sir James Clark Ross.

NECESSITY NO LAW.

At this time I was now taken ill of the bilious colic, which was so violent as to confine me to my bed; so that the management of the ship was left to Mr. Cooper, the first officer, who conducted her very much to my satisfaction. It was several days before the most dangerous symptoms of my disorder were removed; during which time Mr. Patten, the surgeon, was to me not only a skilful physician, but an affectionate nurse; and I should ill deserve the care he bestowed on me, if I did not make this public acknowledgment. When I began to recover, a favourite dog belonging to Mr. Forster fell a sacrifice to my tender stomach. We had no other fresh meat whatever on board; and I could eat of this flesh, as well as broth made of it, when I could taste nothing else. Thus I received nourishment and strength from food which would have made most people in Europe sick; so true it is, that necessity is governed by no law.

EASTER ISLAND.

On the morning of the 11th March 1774, land was seen from the mast-head, bearing west, which I made no doubt was Davis's Land, or Easter Island, as its appearance from this situation corresponded very well with Wafer's account.

Some of the officers at once made an excursion into the country to see what it produced, and returned again in the evening, with the loss only of a hat, which one of the natives snatched off the head of one of the party.

INCIDENTS OF AN EXCURSION.

On another occasion, they followed the direction of the coast to the north-east, and for about three miles found the country very barren, in some places stript even of the soil to the bare rock, which seemed to be a poor sort of iron ore. Beyond this they came to the most fertile part of the island they saw, it being interspersed with plantations of potatoes, sugar-canes, and plantain trees, and these not so much encumbered with stones as those which they had seen before; but they could find no water except what the natives twice or thrice brought them, which, though brackish and stinking, was rendered acceptable by the extremity of their thirst. They also passed some huts, the owners of which met them with roasted potatoes and sugar-canes, and placing themselves ahead of the foremost of the party (for they marched in a line in order to have the benefit of the path), gave one to each man as he passed by. They observed the same method in distributing the water which they brought; and were particularly careful that the foremost did not drink too much, lest none should be left for the hindmost. But at the very time these were relieving the thirsty and hungry, there were not wanting others who endeavoured to steal from them the very things which had been given them. At last, to prevent worse consequences, they

Monuments on Easter Island.

were obliged to fire a load of small shot at one who was so audacious as to snatch from one of the men the bag which contained everything they carried with them. The shot hit him on the back; on which he dropped the bag, ran a little way, and then fell; but he afterwards got up and walked; and what became of him they knew not, nor whether he was much wounded. As this affair occasioned some delay, and drew the natives together, they presently saw the man who had hitherto led the way, and one or two more, coming running towards them; but instead of stopping when they came up, they continued to run round them, repeating in a kind manner a few words, until our people set forwards again.

Towards the eastern end of the island, they met with a well whose water was perfectly fresh, being considerably above the level of the sea; but it was dirty, owing to the filthiness or cleanliness (call it which you will) of the natives, who never go to drink without washing themselves all over as soon as they have done; and if ever so many of them are together, the first leaps right into the middle of the hole, drinks, and washes himself without the least ceremony; after which another takes his place and does the same.

They observed that this side of the island was full of gigantic statues; some placed in groups on platforms of masonry; others single, fixed only in the earth, and that not deep; and these latter are in general much larger than the others. Having measured one which had fallen down, they found it very near twenty-seven feet long, and upwards of eight feet over the breast or shoulders; and yet this appeared considerably short of the size of one they saw standing; its shade, a little past two o'clock, being sufficient to shelter all the party, consisting of near thirty persons, from the rays of the sun. These statues are not, in my opinion, looked upon as idols by the present inhabitants, whatever they might have been in the days of the Dutch; at least, I saw nothing that could induce me to think so. On the contrary, I rather suppose that they are burying-places for certain tribes or families. Here they stopped to dine; after which they repaired to a hill, from whence they saw all the east and north shores of the isle, on which they could not see either bay or creek fit even for a boat to land in, nor the least signs of fresh water. What the natives brought them here was real salt water; but they observed that some of them drank pretty plentifully of it; so far will necessity and custom get the better of nature! On this account, they were obliged to return to the last-mentioned well; where, after having quenched their thirst, they directed their route across the island towards the ship.

In all this excursion, as well as the one made the preceding day, only two or three shrubs were seen. The leaf and seed of one (called by the natives *Torromedo*) were not much unlike those of the common vetch; but the pod was more like that of a tamarind in its size and shape. The seeds have a disagreeable bitter taste; and the natives, when they saw our people chew them, made signs to spit them out; from whence it was concluded that they think them poisonous.

Before I sailed from England, I was informed that a Spanish ship had visited this isle in 1769. Some signs of it were seen among the people now about us; one man had a pretty good broad-brimmed European hat on, another had a grego jacket, and another a red silk handkerchief. They also seemed to know the use of a musket, and to stand in much awe of it; but this they probably learnt from Roggewein, who, if we are to believe the authors of that voyage, left them sufficient tokens.

But no nation need contend for the honour of the discovery, as there can be few places which afford less convenience for shipping. There is no safe anchorage, no wood for fuel, nor any fresh water worth taking on board. As Nature has been exceedingly sparing of her favours, everything must be raised by dint of labour, and it cannot be supposed the inhabitants plant much more than is sufficient for themselves; and as they are but few in number, they cannot have much to spare to supply the wants of visitant strangers.

In general, the people are slender. I did not see a man that would measure six feet; so far are they from being giants, as one of the authors of Roggewein's voyage asserts. They are brisk and active, have good features, and not disagreeable countenances; are friendly and hospitable to strangers, but as much addicted to pilfering as any of their neighbours.

Their hair, in general, is black; the women wear it long, and sometimes tied up on the crown of the head; but the men wear it and their beards cropped short. Their head-dress is a round fillet adorned with feathers, and a straw bonnet something like a Scotch one; the former, I believe, being chiefly worn by the men, and the latter by the women. Both men and women have very large holes, or rather slits, in their ears, extended to near three inches in length. They sometimes turn this slit over the upper part, and then the ear looks as if the flap was cut off. The chief ear ornaments are the white down of feathers, and rings, which they wear in the inside of the hole, made of some elastic substance, rolled up like a watch-spring. I judged this was to keep the hole at its utmost extension.

R

After leaving Easter Island, I steered north-west by north, and north-north-west, with a fine easterly gale, for the Marquesas, discovered by Mendana in 1595. The first isle we reached was a new discovery, which I named Hood's Island, after the young gentleman who first saw it; the second was that of St. Pedro; the third, La Dominica; and the fourth, St. Christina. We ranged the south-east coast of La Dominica without seeing the least signs of anchorage, till we came to the channel that divides it from St. Christina, through which we passed, hauled over for the last-mentioned island, and ran along the coast to the south-west until we anchored in Mendana's Port.

This was no sooner done, than about thirty or forty of the natives came off to us in ten or twelve canoes; but it required some address to get them alongside. At last, a hatchet and some spike-nails induced the people in one canoe to come under the quarter-gallery; after which all the others put alongside, and having exchanged some bread-fruit and fish, for small nails, etc., retired ashore, the sun being already set. We observed a heap of stones in the bow of each canoe, and every man to have a sling tied round his hand.

Canoe of the Marquesas Islands.

The Marquesas were first discovered by Mendana, a Spaniard, and from him obtained the general name they now bear. They are five in number, viz., La Magdalena, St. Pedro, La Dominica, Santa Christina, and Hood's Island, which is the northernmost.

St. Christina stretches north and south, is nine miles long, and about seven leagues in circuit. A narrow ridge of hills of considerable height extends the whole length of the island. There are other ridges which, rising from the sea, and with an equal ascent, join the main ridge. These are disjoined by deep narrow valleys, which are fertile, adorned with fruit and other trees, and watered by fine streams of excellent water. La Magdalena we only saw at a distance. These isles occupy one degree in latitude,

Chief of the Island of St. Christina.

and near half a degree in longitude, viz., from 138° 47' to 139° 13' W., which is the longitude of the west end of La Dominica.

The port of Madre de Dios, which I named Resolution Bay, is situated near the middle of the west side of St. Christina, and under the highest land in the island.

The men are punctured, or curiously *tattooed*, from head to foot. But not the women and young children, who are therefore as fair as some Europeans. The men are in general tall; that is, about five feet ten inches or six feet; but I saw none that were fat and lusty like the *Earees* of Otaheite.

Their principal head-dress, and what appears to be their chief ornament, is a sort of broad fillet, curiously made of the fibres of the husk of cocoa-nuts. In the front is fixed a mother-of-pearl shell, wrought round to the size of a tea-saucer; before that, another, smaller, of very fine tortoise-shell, perforated into curious figures. Also before, and in the centre of that, is another round piece of mother-of-pearl, about the size of half-a-crown; and before this, another piece of perforated tortoise-shell, the size of a shilling. Besides this decoration in front, some have it also on each side, but in smaller pieces; and all have fixed to them the tail-feathers of cocks or tropic-birds, which, when the fillet is tied on, stand upright; so that the whole together makes a very sightly ornament. They wear round the neck a kind of ruff or necklace, call it which you please, made of light wood, the out and upper side covered with small red peas, which are fixed on with gum. They also wear small bunches of human hair, fastened to a string, and tied round the legs and arms.

When I found this island was not likely to supply us, on any conditions, with sufficient refreshments, such as we might expect to find at the Society Isles, nor very convenient for taking in wood and water, nor for giving the ship the necessary repairs she wanted, I resolved forthwith to leave it, and proceed to some other place where our wants might be effectually relieved. For, after having been nineteen weeks at sea, and living all the time upon salt diet, we could not but want some refreshments; although I must own, and that with pleasure, that on our arrival here, it could hardly be said we had one sick man, and but a few who had the least complaint. This was undoubtedly owing to the many antiscorbutic articles we had on board, and to the great attention of the surgeon, who was remarkably careful to apply them in time.

I therefore steered for Otaheite, falling in with some of those islands discovered by former navigators, especially the Dutch, whose situations are not well determined, and made the high land of Otaheite on the 21st April, anchoring in Matavai Bay as formerly. This was no sooner known to the natives than many of them made us a visit, and expressed not a little joy at seeing us again. As my chief reason for putting in at this place was to give Mr. Wales an opportunity to know the error of the watch by the known longitude, and to determine anew her rate of going, the first thing we did was to land his instruments, and to erect tents for the reception of a guard and such other people as it was necessary to have on shore. Sick we had none; the refreshments we got at the Marquesas had removed every complaint of that kind.

Our treatment at this isle was such as had induced one of our gunner's mates to form a plan to remain at it. He know he could not execute it with success while we lay in the bay, therefore took the opportunity, as soon as we were out, the boats in, and sails set, to slip overboard, being a good swimmer: but he was discovered before he got clear of the ship, and we presently hoisted a boat out and took him up. A canoe was observed, about half-way between us and the shore, seemingly coming after us; she was intended to take him up; but as soon as the people in her saw our boat they kept at a distance. This was a preconcerted plan between the man and them, which Otoo was acquainted with, and had encouraged. When I considered this man's situation in life, I did not think him so culpable, nor the resolution he had taken of staying here so extraordinary, as it may at first appear. He was an Irishman by birth, and had sailed in the Dutch service. I picked him up at Batavia on my return from my former voyage, and he had been with me ever since. I never learnt that he had either friends or connections to confine him to any particular part of the world : all nations were alike to him; where then could such a man be more happy than at one of these isles? where, in one of the finest climates in the world, he could enjoy not only the necessaries, but the luxuries of life, in ease and plenty. I know not, if he might not have obtained my consent, if he had applied for it in proper time. As soon as we had got him on board, and the boat in, I steered for Huaheine and Ulietea, in order to pay a visit to our friends there.

At one o'clock in the afternoon on the 15th we anchored in the north entrance of O'Wharre harbour, in the island of Huaheine; hoisted out the boats, warped into a proper berth, and moored with the bower and kedge anchor, not quite a cable's length from the shore. While this was doing, several of the natives made us a visit, amongst whom was old Oree, the chief, who brought a hog, and some other articles, which he presented to me, with the usual ceremony.

The people are, in general, more superstitious than at Otaheite. At the first visit I made the chief after our arrival, he desired I would not suffer any of my people to shoot herons and woodpeckers; birds as sacred with them as robin-redbreasts, swallows, etc., are with many old women in England. Tupia, who was a priest, and well acquainted with their religion, customs, traditions, etc., paid no regard to these birds.

When I first came here, I had some thought of visiting Tupia's famous Boḷabola. But as I had now got on board a plentiful supply of all manner of refreshments, and the route I had in view allowing me no time to spare, I laid this design aside, and directed my course to the west ; taking our final leave of these happy isles, on which benevolent nature has spread her luxuriant sweets with a lavish hand. The natives, copying the bounty of nature, are equally liberal; contributing plentifully and cheerfully to the wants of navigators. During the six weeks we remained at them, we had fresh pork, and all the fruits which were in season, in the utmost profusion ; besides fish at Otaheite, and fowls at the other isles. All these articles we got in exchange for axes, hatchets, nails, chisels, cloth, red feathers, beads, knives, scissars, looking-glasses, shirts, etc., articles which will ever be valuable here.

CHAPTER VI.

PASSAGE FROM ULIETEA TO THE FRIENDLY ISLES.

(1774.)

ON the 6th June, being the day after leaving Ulietea, we saw land bearing N.W., which, upon a nearer approach, we found to be a low reef island about four leagues in compass, and of a circular form. This is Howe Island, discovered by Captain Wallis, who, I think, sent his boat to examine it.

PALMERSTON ISLAND.

From this day we met with nothing remarkable, until the 16th, when, half an hour after sunrise, land was seen from the topmast head. We immediately altered the course, and steering for it, found it to be another reef island, composed of five or six woody islets, connected together by sand-banks and breakers, inclosing a lake, into which we could see no entrance. We ranged the West and N.W. coasts, from its southern to its northern extremity, which is about two leagues; and so near the shore, that at one time we could see the rocks under us; yet we found no anchorage, nor saw we any signs of inhabitants. There were plenty of various kinds of birds, and the coast seemed to abound with fish. The situation of this isle is not very distant from that assigned by Mr. Dalrymple for La Sagitaria, discovered by Quiros; but, by the description the discoverer has given of it, it cannot be the same. For this reason I looked upon it as a new discovery, and named it Palmerston Island, in honour of Lord Palmerston, one of the Lords of the Admiralty.

INCIDENT AT SAVAGE ISLAND, JUNE 1774.

As we drew near the shore, some of the inhabitants, who were on the rocks, retired to the woods, to meet us, as we supposed; and we afterwards found our conjectures right. We landed with ease in a small creek, took post on a high rock to prevent a surprise, displayed our colours, and Mr. Forster and his party began to collect plants. The coast was so overrun with woods, bushes, plants, stones, etc., that we could not see forty yards round us. I took two men, and with them entered a kind of chasm, which opened a way into the woods. We had not gone far before we heard the natives approaching; upon which I called to Mr. Forster to retire to the party, as I did likewise. We had no sooner joined, than the islanders appeared at the entrance of a chasm not a stone's throw from us. We began to speak, and make all the friendly signs we could think of to them, which they answered by menaces; and one of two men, who were advanced before the rest, threw a stone, which struck Mr. Sparrman on the arm. Upon this two muskets were fired, without order, which made them all retire under cover of the woods; and we saw them no more.

After waiting some little time, and till we were satisfied nothing was to be done here, the country being so overrun with bushes that it was hardly possible to come to parley with them, we embarked and proceeded down along shore, in hopes of meeting with better success in another place. After ranging the coast for some miles without seeing a living soul, or any convenient landing-place, we at length came before a small beach, on which lay four canoes. Here we landed by means of a little creek, formed by the flat rocks before it, with a view of just looking at the canoes, and to leave some medals, nails, etc., in them, for not a soul was to be seen. The situation of this place was to us worse than the former. A flat rock lay next the sea; behind it a narrow stone beach; this was bounded by a perpendicular rocky cliff of unequal height, whose top was covered with shrubs; two deep and narrow chasms in the cliff seemed to open a communication into the country. In or before one of these lay the four canoes which we were going to look at; but in the doing of this, I saw we should be exposed to an attack from the natives, if there were any, without being in a situation proper for a defence. To prevent this as much as could be, and to secure a retreat in case of an attack, I ordered the men to be drawn up upon the rock, from whence they had a view of the heights; and only myself and four of the gentlemen went up to the canoes. We had been there but a few minutes, before the natives, I cannot say how many, rushed down the chasm out of the wood upon us. The endeavours we used to bring them to a parley were to no purpose; for they came with the ferocity of wild boars, and threw their darts. Two or three muskets, discharged in the air, did not hinder one of them from advancing still farther, and throwing another dart, or rather a spear, which passed close over my shoulder. His courage would have cost him his life, had not my musket missed fire; for I was not five paces from him when he threw his spear, and had resolved to shoot him to save myself. I was glad afterwards that it happened as it did. At this instant, our men on the rock began to fire at others who appeared on the heights, which abated the ardour of the party we were engaged with, and gave us time to

Second Voyage. 251

join our people, when I caused the firing to cease. The last discharge sent all the islanders to the woods, from whence they did not return so long as we remained. We did not know that any were hurt. It was remarkable, that when I joined our party, I tried my musket in the air, and it went off as well as a piece could do. Seeing no good was to be got with these people, or at the isle, as having no port, we returned on board, and having hoisted in the boats, made sail to W.S.W. I had forgot to mention, in its proper order, that having put ashore a little before we came to this last place, three or four of us went upon the cliffs, where we found the country, as before, nothing but coral rocks, all overrun with bushes; so that it was hardly possible to penetrate into it, and we embarked again with intent to return directly on board, till we saw the canoes; being directed to the place by the opinion of some of us, who thought they heard some people. The conduct and aspect of these islanders occasioned my naming it SAVAGE ISLAND.

CORAL ROCKS.

All the sea-coast, and as far inland as we could see, is wholly covered with trees, shrubs, etc., amongst which were some cocoanut trees; but what the interior parts may produce we know not. To judge of the whole garment by the skirts, it cannot produce much; for so much as we saw of it consisted wholly of coral rocks, all overrun with wood and bushes. Not a bit of soil was to be seen; the rocks alone supplying the trees with humidity. If these coral rocks were first formed in the sea by animals, how came they thrown up to such a height? Has this island been raised by an earthquake? Or has the sea receded from it? Some philosophers have attempted to account for the formation of low isles, such as are in this sea; but I do not know that anything has been said of high islands, or such as I have been speaking of. In this island, not only the loose rocks which cover the surface, but the cliffs which bound the shores, are of coral stone, which the continual beating of the sea has formed into a variety of curious caverns, some of them very large: the roof or rock over them being supported by pillars, which the foaming waves have formed into a multitude of shapes, and made more curious than the caverns themselves.

RECEPTION AT THE FRIENDLY ISLES (ANAMOCKA), JUNE 24. THE SURGEON ROBBED OF HIS GUN.

Anamocka, as it is called by the natives, was first discovered by Tasman, and by him named Rotterdam. It is of a triangular form, each side whereof is about three and a half or four miles. A salt-water lake in the middle of it occupies not a little of its surface, and in a manner cuts off the S.E. angle. Round the island lie scattered a number of small isles, sand-banks, and breakers. We could see no end to their extent to the north; and it is not impossible that they reach as far south as Amsterdam or Tongatabu. These, together with Middleburg, or Eaoowee, and Pylstart, make a group, containing about three degrees of latitude and two of longitude, which I have named the Friendly Isles or Archipelago, as a firm reliance and friendship seem to subsist among their inhabitants, and their courteous behaviour to strangers entitles them to that appellation; under which we might perhaps extend their group much farther, even north to Boscawen and Keppel's Isles, discovered by Captain Wallis, and lying nearly under the same meridian.

I went ashore here, with two boats, to trade with the people, accompanied by several of the officers, and ordered the launch to follow with casks to be filled with water. The natives assisted us to roll them to and from the pond; and a nail or a bead was the expense of their labour. Fruit and roots, especially shaddocks and yams, were brought down in such plenty, that the two boats were laden, sent off, cleared, and laden a second time, before noon; by which time also the launch had got a full supply of water, and the botanical and shooting parties had all come in, except the surgeon, for whom we could not wait, as the tide was ebbing fast out of the cove; consequently he was left behind. As there is no getting into the cove with a boat, from between half ebb to half flood, we could get off no water in the afternoon. However, there is a very good landing-place without it, near the southern point, where boats can get ashore at all times of the tide; here some of the officers landed after dinner, where they found the surgeon, who had been robbed of his gun. Having come down to the shore some time after the boats had put off, he got a canoe to bring him on board; but as he was getting into her, a fellow snatched hold of the gun, and ran off with it. After that no one would carry him to the ship, and they would have stripped him, as he imagined, had he not presented a toothpick case, which they, no doubt, thought was a little gun. As soon as I heard of this, I landed at the place above mentioned, and the few natives who were there fled at my approach. After landing, I went in search of the officers, whom I found in the cove, where we had been in the morning, with a good many of the natives about them. No step had been taken to recover the gun, nor did I think proper to take any; but in this I was wrong. The easy manner of obtaining this gun, which they now, no doubt, thought secure in their possession, encouraged them to proceed in these tricks ; for, on the 28th, when Lieutenant Clerke with the master and fifteen men went again on shore for water, the launch was no sooner landed than the natives gathered about her, behaving in so rude a manner, that the officers were in some doubt if they should land the casks ; and, with difficulty, got them filled, and into the boat again. In the doing of this, Mr. Clerke's gun was snatched from him, and carried off; as were also some of the cooper's tools ; and several of the people were stripped of one thing or another. All this was done, as it were, by stealth ; for they laid hold of nothing by main force. As soon as the natives, who were pretty numerous on the beach, saw me, they fled ; so that I suspected something had happened. I quickly came to a resolution to oblige them to make restitution ; and, for this purpose, ordered all the marines to be armed and sent on shore. I ordered two or three guns to be fired from the ship, in order to alarm Forster and his party, who had gone into the interior ; not knowing how the natives might act on this occasion. I then sent all the boats off but one, with which I stayed, having a good many of the natives about me, who behaved with their usual courtesy. I made them so sensible of my intention, that long before the marines came, the musket was brought, but they used many excuses to divert me from insisting on the other. At length Mr. Edgcumbe, arriving with the marines, alarmed them so much, that some of them fled. The first step I took was to seize on two large double-sailing canoes which were in the cove. One fellow making resistance, I fired some small shot at him, and sent him limping off. The natives being now convinced that I was in earnest, all fled ; but on my calling to them, many returned ; and, presently after, the other musket was brought and laid at my feet. That moment I ordered the canoes to be restored, to show them on what account they were detained.

COOK ACCUSED OF WANT OF GALLANTRY.

On my returning from the pond to the cove, I found a good many people collected together, from whom we understood that the man I had fired at was dead. This story I treated as improbable, and addressed a man, who seemed of some consequence, for the restitution of a cooper's adze we had lost in the morning. He immediately sent away two men, as I thought, for it; but I soon found that we had greatly mistaken each other; for, instead of the adze, they brought the wounded man, stretched out on a board, and laid him down by me, to all appearance dead. I was much moved at the sight; but soon saw my mistake, and that he was only wounded in the hand and thigh. I therefore desired he might be carried out of the sun, and sent for the surgeon to dress his wounds. In the meantime, I addressed several people for the adze; for as I had now nothing else to do, I determined to have it. The one I applied the most to, was an elderly woman, who had always a great deal to say to me, from my first landing; but on this occasion, she gave her tongue full scope. I understood but little of her eloquence; and all I could gather from her arguments was, that it was mean in me to insist on the return of so trifling a thing. But when she found I was determined, she and three or four more women went away; and soon after the adze was brought me, but I saw her no more.

This I was sorry for, as I wanted to make her a present, in return for the part she had taken in all our transactions, private as well as public. For I was no sooner returned from the pond, the first time I landed, than this old lady presented to me a girl, giving me to understand she was at my service. Miss, who probably had received her instructions, wanted, as a preliminary article, a spike-nail, or a shirt, neither of which I had to give her, and soon made them sensible of my poverty. I thought, by that means, to have come off with flying colours; but I was mistaken; for they gave me to understand I might retire with her on credit. On my declining this proposal, the old lady began to argue with me, and then abuse me. Though I comprehended little of what she said, her actions were expressive enough, and shewed that her words were to this effect, sneering in my face, saying, What sort of a man are you, thus to refuse the embraces of so fine a young woman? For the girl certainly did not want beauty; which, however, I could better withstand, than the abuses of this worthy matron, and therefore hastened into the boat. They wanted me to take the young lady aboard; but this could not be done, as I had given strict orders, before I went on shore, to suffer no woman, on any pretence whatever, to come into the ship.

STIRRING ACCIDENT AT MALLICOLLO, JULY 21.

On arriving at this island on our way to the New-Hebrides, a good many came round us, some in canoes, and others swimming. I soon prevailed on one to come on board; which he no sooner did than he was followed by more than I desired; so that not only our deck but rigging was presently filled with them. I took four into the cabin, and gave them various articles, which they showed to those in the canoes, and seemed much pleased with their reception. While I was thus making friends with those in the cabin, an accident happened that threw all into confusion, but in the end, I believe, proved advantageous to us. A fellow in a canoe having been refused admittance into one of our boats that lay alongside, bent his bow to shoot a poisoned arrow at the boat-keeper. Some of his countrymen prevented his doing it at that instant, and gave time to acquaint me with it. I ran instantly on deck, and saw another man struggling with him; one of those who had been in the cabin, and had leaped out of the window for this purpose. The other seemed resolved, shook him off, and directed his bow again to the boat-keeper; but on my calling to him, pointed it at me. Having a musket in my hand, loaded with small-shot, I gave him the contents. This staggered him for a moment, but did not prevent him from holding his bow still in the attitude of shooting. Another discharge of the same nature made him drop it, and the others, who were in the canoe, to paddle off with all speed. At this time, some began to shoot arrows on the other side. A musket discharged in the air had no effect; but a four-pound shot over their heads sent them off in the utmost confusion. Many quitted their canoes and swam on shore: those in the great cabin leaped out of the windows; and those who were on deck, and on different parts of the rigging, all leaped overboard. After this we took no farther notice of them, but suffered them to come off and pick up their canoes; and some even ventured again alongside the ship. Immediately after the great gun was fired, we heard the beating of drums on shore; which was, probably, the signal for the country to assemble in arms. Notwithstanding this untoward event, it was necessary for us to land, to cut wood, of which we were in want, and to try to get some refreshments, nothing of this kind having been seen in any of the canoes.

The next morning accordingly, we put off in two boats, and

landed in the face of four or five hundred people, who were assembled on the shore. Though they were all armed with bows and arrows, clubs and spears, they made not the least opposition. On the contrary, seeing me advance alone, with nothing but a green branch in my hand, one of them, who seemed to be a chief, gave his bow and arrows to another, and met me in the water, bearing also a green branch. This he exchanged for the one I held, and then took me by the hand, and led me up to the crowd. I immediately distributed presents to them, and in the meantime, the marines were drawn up on the beach. I then made signs (for we understood not a word of their language) that we wanted wood; and they made signs to us to cut down the trees. By this time, a small pig was brought down and presented to me, and I gave the bearer a piece of cloth, with which he seemed well pleased. This made us hope that we should soon have some more; but we were mistaken. The pig was not brought to be exchanged for what we had, but on some other account; probably as a peace-offering.

This ape-like people, in general, are the most ugly, ill-proportioned I ever saw, and in every respect different from any we had met with in this sea. They are a very dark-coloured and rather diminutive race; with long heads, flat faces, and monkey countenances. Their hair, mostly black or brown, is short and curly; but not quite so soft and woolly as that of a negro. Their beards are very strong, crisp, and bushy, and generally black and short. But what most adds to their deformity, is a belt, or cord, which they wear round the waist, and tie so tight, that the shape of their bodies is not unlike that of an overgrown ant.

The letter R is used in many of their words; and frequently two or three being joined together, we found it difficult to pronounce. I observed that they could pronounce most of our words with great ease. They express their admiration by hissing like a goose.

ALARMING SCUFFLE AT ERROMANGA,* AUGUST 1774.

On the 3d August at sunrise, we found ourselves abreast a lofty promontory on the S.E. side of the island of Erromanga, and about three leagues from it. Having but little wind, and that from the south, right in our teeth, and being in want of fire-wood, I sent Lieutenant Clerke with two boats to a small islet which lies off the promontory, to endeavour to get some. In the meantime we continued to ply up with the ship; but what we gained by our sails, we lost by the current. At length, towards noon, we got in with the land, under the N.W. side of the head, where we anchored, half a mile from shore. Many people appeared on the shore, and some attempted to swim off to us; but having occasion to send the boat ahead to sound, they retired as she drew near them. This, however gave us a favourable idea of them.

On the 4th, at daybreak, I went with two boats to examine the coast, to look for a proper landing-place, wood, and water. At this time the natives began to assemble on the shore, and by signs invited us to land. I went first to a small beach, which is towards the head, where I found no good landing, on account of some rocks which everywhere lined the coast. I, however, put the boat's bow to the shore, and gave cloth, medals, etc., to some

---

* It was here that Williams, the honoured missionary, lost his life in 1839, in consequence of a misunderstanding with the natives; on which account he has been called the "Martyr of Erromanga." His life and labours have been published under the title of "Missionary Enterprises in the South Sea Islands."

people who were there. For this treatment they offered to haul the boats over the breakers to the sandy beach, which I thought a friendly offer, but had reason afterwards to alter my opinion. When they found I would not do as they desired, they made signs for us to go down into the bay, which we accordingly did, and they ran along shore abreast of us, their number increasing prodigiously. I put into the shore in two or three places, but, not liking the situation, did not land. By this time, I believe, the natives conceived what I wanted, as they directed me round a rocky point, where, on a fine sandy beach, I stepped out of the boat without wetting a foot, in the face of a vast multitude, with only a green branch in my hand, which I had before got from one of them. I took but one man out of the boat with me, and ordered the other boat to lie to a little distance off. They received me with great courtesy and politeness, and would retire back from the boat on my making the least motion with my hand. A man whom I took to be a chief, seeing this, made them form a semicircle round the boat's bow, and beat such as attempted to break through this order. This man I loaded with presents, giving likewise to others, and asked by signs for fresh water, in hopes of seeing where they got it. The chief immediately sent a man for some, who ran to a house, and presently returned with a little in a bamboo ; so that I gained but little information by this. I next asked, by the same means, for something to eat ; and they as readily brought me a yam and some cocoa-nuts. In short, I was charmed with their behaviour ; and the only thing which could give the least suspicion was, that most of them were armed with clubs, spears, darts, and bows and arrows. For this reason I kept my eye continually upon the chief, and watched his looks as well as his actions. He made many signs to me to haul the boat up upon the shore, and at last slipped into the crowd, where I observed him speak to several people, and then return to me, repeating signs to haul the boat up, and hesitating a good deal before he would receive some spike-nails which I then offered him. This made me suspect something was intended, and immediately I stepped into the boat, telling them by signs that I should soon return. But they were not for parting so soon, and now attempted by force what they could not obtain by gentler means. The gang-board happened unluckily to be laid out for me to come into the boat. I say unluckily, for if it had not been out, and if the crew had been a little quicker in getting the boat off, the natives might not have had time to put their design into execution, nor would the following disagreeable scene have happened. As we were putting off the boat, they laid hold of the gang-board, and unhooked it off the boat's stern, but as they did not take it away, I thought this had been done by accident, and ordered the boat in again to take it up. They then themselves hooked it over the boat's stern, and attempted to haul her ashore; others at the same time, snatched the oars out of the people's hands. On my pointing a musket at them, they in some measure desisted, but returned in an instant, seemingly determined to haul the boat ashore. At the head of this party was the chief; the others, who could not come at the boat, stood behind with darts, stones, and bows and arrows in hand, ready to support them. Signs and threats having no effect, our own safety became the only consideration; and yet I was unwilling to fire on the multitude, and resolved to make the chief alone fall a victim to his own treachery; but my musket at this critical moment missed fire. Whatever idea they might have formed of the arms we held in our hands, they must now have looked upon them as childish weapons, and began to let us see how much better theirs were, by throwing stones and darts, and by shooting arrows. This made it absolutely necessary for me to give orders to fire. The first discharge threw them into confusion; but a second was hardly sufficient to drive them off the beach; and, after all, they continued to throw stones from behind the trees and bushes, and, every now and then, to pop out and throw a dart. Four lay, to all appearance dead, on the shore; but two of them afterwards crawled into the bushes. Happy it was for these people, that not half our muskets would go off, otherwise many more must have fallen. We had one man wounded in the cheek with a dart, the point of which was as thick as my finger, and yet it entered above two inches; which shows that it must have come with great force, though indeed we were very near them. An arrow struck Mr. Gilbert's naked breast, who was about thirty yards off; but probably it had struck something before; for it hardly penetrated the skin. The arrows were pointed with hard wood.

As soon as we got on board, I ordered the anchor to be weighed, with a view of anchoring near the landing-place. While this was doing, several people appeared on the low rocky point, displaying two oars we had lost in the scuffle. I looked on this as a sign of submission, and of their wanting to give us the oars. I was, nevertheless, prevailed on to fire a four-pound shot at them, to let them see the effect of our great guns. The ball fell short, but frightened them so much, that none were seen afterwards; and they left the oars standing up against the bushes. It was now calm; but the anchor was hardly at the bow before a breeze sprung up at north, of which we took the advantage, set our sails, and plied out of the bay, as it did not seem capable of supplying our wants, with that conveniency I wished to have. Besides, I always had it in my power to return to this place, in case I should find none more convenient farther south.

These islanders seemed to be a different race from those of Mallicollo, and spoke a different language. They are of the middle size, have a good shape, and tolerable features. Their colour is very dark, and they paint their faces, some with black, and others with red pigment. Their hair is very curly and crisp, and somewhat woolly. I saw a few women, and I thought them ugly. The promontory, or peninsula, I named Traitor's Head, from the treacherous behaviour of its inhabitants.

Arrival at the Volcanic Island of Tanna.

Having found that the light we had seen in the night was occasioned by a volcano, which we observed to throw up vast quantities of fire and smoke, with a rumbling noise heard at a great distance, we now made sail for the island, and, presently after, discovered a small inlet which had the appearance of being a good harbour. In order to be better informed, I sent away two armed boats under the command of Lieutenant Cooper, to sound it;

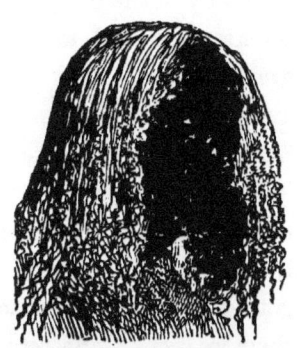

Man of Islands of Tanna.

and, in the meanwhile, we stood on and off with the ship, to be ready to follow, or give them any assistance they might want. On the east point of the entrance, we observed a number of people, and several houses and canoes; and when our boats entered the harbour they launched some, and followed them, but came not near. It was not long before Mr. Cooper made the signal for anchorage; and we stood in with the ship.

While we were employed carrying out anchors to warp in by, many of the natives got together in parties, on several parts of the shore, all armed with bows and spears. Some swam off to us, others came in canoes. At first they were shy, and kept at the distance of a stone's throw; they grew insensibly bolder; and at last, came under our stern, and made some exchanges. The people in one of the first canoes, after coming as near as they durst, threw towards us some cocoa-nuts. I went into a boat and picked them up, giving them in return some cloth and other articles. This induced others to come under the stern, and alongside, where their behaviour was insolent and daring. They wanted to carry off everything within their reach; they got hold of the fly of the ensign, and would have torn it from the staff; others attempted to knock the rings off the rudder; but the greatest trouble they gave us was to look after the buoys of our anchors, which were no sooner thrown out of the boats, or let go from the ship, than they got hold of them. A few muskets fired in the air had no effect; but a four-pounder frightened them so much, that they quitted their canoes that instant, and took to the water. But as soon as they found themselves unhurt, they got again into their canoes; gave us some halloos; flourished their weapons; and returned once more to the buoys. This put us to the expense of a few musketoon shot, which had the desired effect. Although none were hurt, they were afterwards afraid to come near the buoys; very soon all retired on shore; and we were permitted to sit down to dinner undisturbed.

During these transactions, a friendly old man in a small canoe made several trips between us and the shore, bringing off each time a few cocoa-nuts, or a yam, and taking in exchange whatever we gave him. Another was on the gangway, when the great gun was fired, but I could not prevail on him to stay there long. Towards the evening, after the ship was moored, I landed at the head of the harbour, with a strong party of men, without any opposition being made by a great number of the natives who were assembled in two parties, the one on our right, the other on our left, armed with clubs, darts, spears, slings and stones, bows and arrows. After distributing to the old people (for we could distinguish no chief) and some others, presents of cloth, medals, etc., I ordered two casks to be filled with water out of a pond about twenty paces behind the landing-place; giving the natives to understand that this was one of the articles we wanted. Besides water, we got from them a few cocoa-nuts, which seemed to be in plenty on the trees; but they could not be prevailed upon to part with any of their weapons. These they held in constant readiness, and in the proper attitudes of offence and defence; so that little was wanting to make them attack us; at least we thought so, by their pressing so much upon us, and in spite of our endeavours to keep them off. Our early re-embarking probably disconcerted their scheme; and after that they all retired. The friendly old man before mentioned was in one of these parties; and we judged, from his conduct, that his temper was pacific.

As we wanted to take in a large quantity both of wood and water, and as, when I was on shore, I had found it practicable to lay the ship much nearer the landing-place than she now was, which would greatly facilitate that work, as well as overawe the natives, and enable us better to cover and protect the working party on shore; with this view, on the 6th August, we went to work to transport the ship to the place I designed to moor her in. While we were about this, we observed the natives assembling from all parts, and forming themselves into two parties, as they did the preceding evening, one on each side the landing-place, to the amount of some thousands, armed as before. A canoe, sometimes conducted by one, and at other times by two or three men, now and then came off, bringing a few cocoa-nuts or plantains. These they gave us without asking for any return; but I took care that they should always have something. Their chief design seemed to be to invite us on shore. One of those who came off was the old man who had already ingratiated himself into our favour. I made him understand, by signs, that they were to lay aside their weapons, took those which were in the canoe and threw them overboard, and made him a present of a large piece of cloth. There was no doubt that he understood me, and made my request known to his countrymen. For as soon as he landed we observed him to go first to the one party, and then to the other; nor was he ever after seen by us with anything like a weapon in his hand. After this, three fellows came in a canoe under the stern, one of them brandishing a club, with which he struck the ship's side, and committed other acts of defiance, but at last offered to exchange it for a string of beads, and some other trifles. These were sent down to him by a line; but the moment they were in his possession, he and his companions paddled off in all haste, without giving the club, or anything else, in return. This was what I expected, and indeed what I was not sorry for, as I wanted an opportunity to show the multitude on shore the effect of our fire-arms, without materially hurting any of them. I therefore gave the fellow the contents of a fowling-piece loaded with small shot (No. 3); and, when they were above musket-shot off, I ordered some of the musketoons, or wall-pieces, to be fired, which made them leap out of the canoe, keep under her off side, and swim with her ashore. This seemed to make little or no impression. On the contrary, they began to halloo, and to make sport of it.

After mooring the ship, by four anchors, with her broadside to the landing-place, hardly a musket-shot off, and placing our artillery in such a manner as to command the whole harbour, I embarked with the marines, and a party of seamen, in three boats, and rowed in for the shore. It has been already mentioned, that the two divisions of the natives were drawn up on each side the landing-place. They had left a space between them of about thirty or forty yards, in which were laid, to the most advantage, a few small bunches of plantains, a yam, and two or three roots. Between these and the water were stuck upright in the sand, for what purpose I never could learn, four small reeds, about two feet from each other, in a line at right angles to the shore, where they remained for two or three days after. The old man before mentioned, and two more, stood by these things, inviting us by signs to land; but I had not forgot the trap I was so near being caught in at the last island; and this looked something like it. We answered, by making signs for the two divisions to retire farther back, and give us more room. The old man seemed to desire them so to do, but no more regard was paid to him than to us. More were continually joining them, and, except two or three old men, not one unarmed. In short, everything conspired to make us believe they meant to attack us as soon as we should be on shore;

the consequence of which was easily supposed; many of them must have been killed and wounded, and we should hardly have escaped unhurt; two things I equally wished to prevent. Since, therefore, they would not give us the room we required, I thought it was better to frighten them into it, than to oblige them by the deadly effect of our fire-arms. I accordingly ordered a musket to be fired over the party on our right, which was by far the strongest body; but the alarm it gave them was momentary. In an instant they recovered themselves, and began to display their weapons. One fellow showed us his backside, in a manner which plainly conveyed his meaning. After this I ordered three or four muskets to be fired. This was the signal for the ship to fire a few great guns, which presently dispersed them; and then we landed, and marked out the limits, on the right and left, by a line. Our old friend stood his ground, though deserted by his two companions, and I rewarded his confidence with a present. The natives came gradually to us, seemingly in a more friendly manner; some even without their weapons, but by far the greatest part brought them; and when we made signs to lay them down, they gave us to understand that we must lay down ours first. Thus all parties stood armed. The presents I made to the old people, and to such as seemed to be of consequence, had little effect on their conduct. They indeed climbed the cocoa-nut trees, and threw us down the nuts, without requiring anything for them; but I took care they should always have somewhat in return. I observed that many were afraid to touch what belonged to us; and they seemed to have no notion of exchanging one thing for another. I took the old man, whose name we now found to be Paowang, to the woods, and made him understand I wanted to cut down some trees to take on board the ship; cutting some down at the same time, which we put into one of our boats, together with a few small casks of water, with a view of letting the people see what it was we chiefly wanted. Paowang very readily gave his consent to cut wood; nor was there anyone who made the least objection. He only desired the cocoa-nut trees might not be cut down.

Early in the morning of the 7th, the natives began again to assemble near the watering-place, armed as usual, but not in such numbers as at first. After breakfast we landed, in order to cut wood and fill water. I found many of the islanders much inclined to be friends with us, especially the old people; on the other hand, most of the younger were daring and insolent, and obliged us to keep to our arms.

They gave us to understand, in a manner which I thought admitted of no doubt, that they eat human flesh, and that circumcision was practised among them. They began the subject of eating human flesh of their own accord, by asking us if we did; otherwise I should never have thought of asking them such a question. I have heard people argue that no nation could be cannibals, if they had other flesh to eat, or did not want food; thus deriving the custom from necessity. The people of this island can be under no such necessity; they have fine pork and fowls, and plenty of roots and fruits. But since we have not actually seen them eat human flesh, it will admit of doubt with some whether they are cannibals.

THE VOLCANO AT TANNA.

The volcano, which was about four miles to the west of us, vomited up vast quantities of fire and smoke; and the flames were seen during the night to rise above the hill which lay between us and it. At every eruption, it made a long rumbling noise like that of thunder, or the blowing up of large mines. A heavy shower of rain, which fell at this time, seemed to increase it; and the wind blowing from the same quarter, the air was loaded with its ashes, which fell so thick that everything was covered with the dust. It was a kind of fine sand or stone, ground or burnt to powder, and was exceedingly troublesome to the eyes.

During the whole of the 11th, the volcano was exceedingly troublesome, and made a terrible noise, throwing up prodigious columns of fire and smoke at each explosion, which happened every three or four minutes; and at one time great stones were seen high in the air. Forster and his party went up the hill on the west side of the harbour, where he found three places from whence smoke of a sulphureous smell issued, through cracks or fissures in the earth. The ground about these was exceedingly hot, and parched or burnt, and they seemed to keep pace with the volcano, for at every explosion of the latter, the quantity of smoke or steam in these was greatly increased, and forced out so as to rise in small columns, which we saw from the ship, and had taken for common fires made by the natives.

A thermometer placed in a little hole made in one of them, rose from 80, at which it stood in the open air, to 170. Several other parts of the hill emitted smoke or steam all the day, and the volcano was unusually furious, insomuch that the air was loaded with its ashes. The rain which fell at this time was a compound of water, sand, and earth; so that it properly might be called showers of mire. Whichever way the wind was, we were plagued with the ashes; unless it blew very strong indeed from the opposite direction. Notwithstanding the natives seemed well enough satisfied with the few expeditions we had made in the neighbourhood, they were unwilling we should extend them farther. As a proof of this, some undertook to guide us, when we were in the country, to a place where we might see the mouth of the volcano. We very readily embraced the offer, and were conducted down to the harbour before we perceived the cheat, as they did everything to discourage the attempt. After proceeding a considerable way, therefore, I resolved, especially as we could get no one to be our guide, to return; and had but just put this in execution, when we met between twenty and thirty people, who had collected with a design, as we judged, to oppose our advancing into the country; but as they saw us returning, they suffered us to pass unmolested. Some of them put us into the right road, accompanied us down the hill, made us stop by the way to entertain us with cocoa-nuts, plantains, and sugar-cane; and what we did not eat on the spot, they brought down the hill with us.

Thus, we found these people hospitable, civil, and good-natured, when not prompted to a contrary conduct by jealousy; a conduct I cannot tell how to blame them for, especially when I consider the light in which they must view us. It was impossible for them to know our real design; we enter their ports without their daring to oppose; we endeavour to land in their country as friends, and it is well if this succeeds; we land nevertheless, and maintain the footing we have got, by the superiority of our firearms. Under such circumstances, what opinion are they to form of us? Is it not as reasonable for them to think that we come to invade their country, as to pay them a friendly visit? Time, and some acquaintance with us, can only convince them of the latter. These people are yet in a rude state ; and if we may judge from circumstances and appearances, are frequently at war, not only with their neighbours, but among themselves ; consequently must be jealous of every new face. I will allow there are some exceptions to this rule to be found in this sea ; but there are few nations who would willingly suffer visitors like us to advance far into their country.

AN UNFORTUNATE SHOT.

As the wind was unfavourable for sailing, the guard was sent on shore on the 19th, as before, and a party of men to cut up and bring off the remainder of a tree from which we had got a new tiller. Having nothing else to do, I went on shore with them, and finding a good number of the natives collected about the landing-place as usual, I distributed among them all the articles I had with me, and then went on board for more. In less than an hour I returned, just as our people were getting some large logs into the boat. At the same time four or five of the natives stepped forward to see what we were about, and as we did not allow them to come within certain limits, unless to pass along the beach, the sentry ordered them back, which they readily complied with. At this time, having my eyes fixed on them, I observed the sentry present his piece (as I thought at these men), and was just going to reprove him for it, because I had observed that, whenever this was done, some of the natives would hold up their arms, to let us see that they were equally ready. But I was astonished beyond measure when the sentry fired, for I saw not the least cause. At this outrage most of the people fled : it was only a few I could prevail on to remain. As they ran off, I observed one man to fall ; and he was immediately lifted up by two others, who took him into the water, washed his wound, and then led him off. Presently after, some came and described to me the nature of his wound; and, as I found he was not carried far, I sent for the surgeon. As soon as he arrived, I went with him to the man, whom we found expiring. The ball had struck his left arm, which was much shattered, and then entered his body by the short ribs, one of which was broken. The rascal who fired pretended that a man had laid an arrow across his bow, and was going to shoot at him, so that he apprehended himself in danger. But this was no more than they had always done, and with no other view than to show they were armed as well as we; at least I have reason to think so, as they never went farther.

What made this incident the more unfortunate was, it not appearing to be the man who bent the bow that was shot, but one who stood by him. This affair threw the natives into the utmost consternation; and the few that were prevailed on to stay ran to the plantations and brought cocoa-nuts, etc., which they laid down at our feet. So soon were these daring people humbled!

These people are of the middle size, rather slender than otherwise; many are little, but few tall or stout; the most of them have good features, and agreeable countenances; are like all the tropical race, active and nimble; and seem to excel in the use of arms, but not to be fond of labour. They never would put a hand to assist in any work we were carrying on, which the people of the other islands used to delight in. But what I judge most from, is their making the females do the most laborious work, as if they were pack horses. I have seen a woman carrying a large bundle on her back, or a child on her back and a bundle under her arm, and a fellow strutting before her with nothing but a club or spear, or some such thing. We have frequently observed little troops of women pass to and fro, along the beach, laden with fruit and roots, escorted by a party of men under arms; though, now and then, we have seen a man carry a burden at the same time, but not often. I know not on what account this was done, nor that an armed troop was necessary. At first, we thought they were moving out of the neighbourhood with their effects; but we afterwards saw them both carry out and bring in every day.

I cannot say the women are beauties; but I think them handsome enough for the men, and too handsome for the use that is made of them. Both sexes are of a very dark colour, but not black; nor have they the least characteristic of the negro about them. They make themselves blacker than they really are, by painting their faces with a pigment of the colour of black-lead. They also use another sort which is red, and a third sort brown, or a colour between red and black. All these, but especially the first, they lay on with a liberal hand, not only on the face, but on the neck, shoulders, and breast.

Mysterious Noise in the Woods.

During the night the wind had veered round to S.E. As this was favourable for getting out of the harbour, on the morning of the 20th August, we weighed anchor, and put to sea. As soon as we were clear of the land, I brought to, waiting for the launch which was left behind to take up a kedge-anchor and hawser we had out, to cast by. About day-break a noise was heard in the woods, nearly abreast of us, on the east side of the harbour, not unlike singing of psalms. I was told that the like had been heard at the same time every morning, but it never came to my knowledge till now, when it was too late to learn the occasion of it. Some were of opinion that at the east point of the harbour (where we observed, in coming in, some houses, boats, etc.), was something sacred to religion, because some of our people had attempted to go to this point, and were prevented by the natives. I thought, and do still think, it was only owing to a desire they showed, on every occasion, of fixing bounds to our excursions. So far as we had once been, we might go again, but not farther with their consent; but by encroaching a little every time, our country expeditions were insensibly extended without giving the least umbrage. Besides, these morning ceremonies, whether religious or not, were not performed down at that point, but in a part where some of our people had been daily.

DISCOVERY OF NEW CALEDONIA.

At sunrise on the 1st of September 1774, after having stood to S.W. all night, no more land was to be seen. At eight o'clock on the 4th, as we were steering to the south, land was discovered bearing S.S.W., and at noon it extended from S.S.E. to W. by S., distant about six leagues. We continued to steer for it with a light breeze at east, till five in the evening, when we were stopped by a calm. To the S.E. the coast seemed to terminate in a high promontory, which I named Cape Colnett, after one of my midshipmen, who first discovered this land. Breakers were seen about half-way between us and the shore; and, behind them, two or three canoes under sail, standing out to sea, as if their design had been to come off to us.

We now saw that the coast was low land, and that it was all connected, except the western extremity, which was an island, known by the name of Balabea, as we afterwards learnt.

SPEECHMAKING AT BALABEA.

I went on shore with two armed boats, having with us one of the natives who had attached himself to me. We landed on a sandy beach before a vast number of people, who had got together with no other intent than to see us; for many of them had not a stick in their hands; consequently we were received with great courtesy, and with the surprise natural for people to express at seeing men and things so new to them as we must be. I made presents to all those my friend pointed out, who were either old men, or such as seemed to be of some note; but he took not the least notice of some women who stood behind the crowd, holding my hand when I was going to give them some beads and medals. Here we found the same chief who had been seen in one of the canoes in the morning. His name, we now learnt, was Teabooma; and we had not been on shore above ten minutes before he called for silence. Being instantly obeyed by every individual present, he made a short speech; and soon after another chief having called for silence, made a speech also. It was pleasing to see with what attention they were heard. Their speeches were composed of short sentences; to each of which two or three old men answered, by nodding their heads, and giving a kind of grunt, significant, as I thought, of approbation. It was impossible for us to know the purport of these speeches; but we had reason to think they were favourable to us, on whose account they doubtless were made. I kept my eyes fixed on the people all the time, and saw nothing to induce me to think otherwise.

While we were with them, having inquired, by signs, for fresh water, some pointed to the east, and others to the west. My friend undertook to conduct us to it, and embarked with us

for that purpose. We rowed about two miles up the coast to
the east, where the shore was mostly covered with mangrove
trees; and entering amongst them, by a narrow creek or river,
which brought us to a little straggling village above all the
mangroves, there we landed, and were shewn fresh water. The
ground near this village was finely cultivated, being laid out in
plantations of sugar-canes, plantains, yams, and other roots; and
watered by little rills, conducted by art from the main stream,
whose source was in the hills. Here were some cocoa-nut trees,
which did not seem burdened with fruit. We heard the crow-
ing of cocks, but saw none.

A Poisonous Fish.

A fish-being struck by one of the natives near the watering-
place, my clerk purchased it, and sent it to me, after my return
on board. It was of a new species, something like a sun-fish,
with a large, long, ugly head. Having no suspicion of its being
of a poisonous nature, we ordered it to be dressed for supper; but,
very luckily, the operation of drawing and describing took up so
much time, that it was too late, so that only the liver and roe were
dressed, of which the two Mr. Forsters and myself did but taste.
About three o'clock in the morning, we found ourselves seized with
an extraordinary weakness and numbness all over our limbs: I had
almost lost the sense of feeling, nor could I distinguish between
light and heavy bodies, of such as I had strength to move;* a
quart-pot full of water and a feather being the same in my hand.
We each of us took an emetic, and after that a sweat, which gave

* A few years since, several officers and seamen in Captain Sir Everard Home's
ship (the Calliope), were made seriously ill by eating fish of a poisonous nature,
and one or two died. It was long before the others recovered.

us much relief. In the morning, one of the pigs which had eaten the entrails was found dead. When the natives came on board, and saw the fish hang up, they immediately gave us to understand it was not wholesome food, and expressed the utmost abhorrence of it; though no one was observed to do this when the fish was to be sold, or even after it was purchased.

On the 8th, the guard and a party of men were on shore as usual. In the afternoon, I received a message from the officer, acquainting me that Teabooma, the chief, was come with a present, consisting of a few yams and sugar-canes. In return I sent him, amongst other articles, two dogs, both young, but nearly full-grown. The one was red and white, but the other was all red, or the colour of an English fox. I mention this, because they may prove the Adam and Eve of their species in that country. When the officer returned on board in the evening, he informed me that the chief came attended by about twenty men, so that it looked like a visit of ceremony, and it was some time before he would believe the dogs were intended for him; but as soon as he was convinced, he seemed lost in an excess of joy, and sent them away immediately.

From this little excursion, I found that we were to expect nothing from these people but the privilege of visiting their country undisturbed. For it was easy to see they had little else than good-nature to bestow. In this they exceeded all the nations we had yet met with; and although it did not satisfy the demands of nature, it at once pleased and left our minds at ease.

Everything being in readiness to put to sea, at sunrise on the 13th of September we weighed, and with a fine gale at E. by S. stood out for the same channel we came in by.

We continued to ply, with variable light winds, without meeting with anything remarkable, till the 20th at noon, when Cape Colnett bore N. 78° W., distant six leagues. From this cape the land extended round by the south to E.S.E. till it was lost in the horizon; and the country appeared with many hills and valleys. We stood in-shore with a light breeze at east till sunset, when we were between two and three leagues off. Two small islets lay without this last direction, distant from us four or five miles; some others lay between us and the shore, and to the east, where they seemed to be connected by reefs, in which appeared some openings from space to space. The country was mountainous, and had much the same aspect as about Balade. On one of the western small isles was an elevation like a tower; and over a low neck of land within the isle were seen many other elevations resembling the masts of a fleet of ships.

On the 25th, about ten o'clock A.M., having got a fair breeze at E.S.E., we stood to S.S.W., in hopes of getting round the Foreland; but, as we drew near, we perceived more low isles beyond the one already mentioned, which at last appeared to be connected by breakers, extending towards the Foreland, and seeming to join the shore. We stood on till half-past three o'clock, when we saw, from the deck, rocks just peeping above the surface of the sea, on the shoal above mentioned. It was now time to alter the course, as the day was too far spent to look for a passage near the shore, and we could find no bottom to anchor in during the night. We therefore stood to the south, to look for a passage without the small isles.

We gained nothing by this but the prospect of a sea strewed with shoals, which we could not clear but by returning in the track by which we came. We tacked nearly in the same place where we had tacked before, and on sounding found a bottom of fine sand. But anchoring in a strong gale, with a chain of breakers to leeward, being the last resource, I rather chose to spend the night in making short boards over that space we had, in some measure, made ourselves acquainted with in the day. And thus it was spent; but under the terrible apprehension, every moment, of falling on some of the many dangers which surrounded us.

Daylight showed that our fears were not ill-founded, and that we had been in the most imminent danger, having had breakers continually under our lee, and at a very little distance from us. We owed our safety to the interposition of Providence, a good look-out, and the very brisk manner in which the ship was managed; for, as we were standing to the north, the people on the lee gangway and forecastle saw breakers under the lee-bow, which we escaped by quickly tacking the ship. I was now almost tired of a coast which I could no longer explore but at the risk of losing the ship and ruining the whole voyage. I was, however, determined not to leave it till I knew what trees those were which had been the subject of our speculation; especially as they appeared to be of a sort useful to shipping, and had not been seen anywhere but in the southern part of this land. These we found to be a kind of spruce pine, very proper for spars, of which we were in want. After making this discovery, I landed again with two boats, accompanied by several of the officers and men, having with us the carpenter and some of his crew, to cut down such trees as were wanting. To this island I gave the name of

THE ISLE OF PINES.

The purpose for which I anchored under this isle being answered, I was now to consider what was next to be done. We had, from the topmast head, taken a view of the sea around us, and observed the whole, to the west, to be strewed with small islets, sandbanks, and breakers, to the utmost extent of our horizon. They seemed, indeed, not to be all connected, and to be divided by winding channels. But when I considered that the extent of this S.W. coast was already pretty well determined, the great risk attending a more accurate survey, and the time it would require to accomplish it, on account of the many dangers we should have to encounter, I determined not to hazard the ship down to leeward, where we might be so hemmed in as to find it difficult to return, and by that means lose the proper season for getting to the south.

At eight o'clock in the morning, on the 3d, the wind veered to S.W., and blew a strong gale by squalls, attended with rain. I now gave over all thought of returning to the land we had left. Indeed, when I considered the vast ocean we had to explore to the south; the state and condition of the ship, already in want of some necessary stores; that summer was approaching fast; and that any considerable accident might detain us in this sea another year; I did not think it advisable to attempt to regain the land.

Thus I was obliged, as it were by necessity, for the first time, to leave a coast I had discovered, before it was fully explored. I called it

NEW CALEDONIA,

and, if we except New Zealand, it is perhaps the largest island in the South Pacific Ocean.

We continued to stretch to W.S.W. till the 10th, when, at

daybreak, we discovered land bearing S.W., which on a nearer approach we found to be an island of good height, and five leagues in circuit. I named it

NORFOLK ISLE,

in honour of the noble family of Howard. A party of us embarked in two boats, and landed on the island, without any difficulty, behind some large rocks which lined part of the coast on the N.E. side. We found it uninhabited, and were undoubtedly the first that ever set foot on it. We observed many trees and plants common at New Zealand; and in particular, the flax-plant, which is rather more luxuriant here than in any part of that country: but the chief produce is a sort of spruce pine, which grows in great abundance, and to a large size, many of the trees being as thick, breast-high, as two men could fathom, and exceedingly straight and tall. This pine is of a sort between that which grows in New Zealand and that in New Caledonia; the foliage differing something from both; and the wood not so heavy as the former, nor so light and close-grained as the latter. It is a good deal like the Quebec pine.

After leaving Norfolk Isle, I steered for New Zealand, my intention being to touch at Queen Charlotte's Sound, to refresh my crew, and put my ship in a condition to encounter the southern latitudes.

We hauled round Point Jackson, through a sea which looked terrible, occasioned by a rapid tide and a high wind—but as we knew the coast, it did not alarm us—and anchored before Ship Cove; the strong flurries from off the land not permitting us to get in.

I have now done with the Southern Pacific Ocean; and flatter myself that no one will think that I have left it unexplored; or that more could have been done, in one voyage, towards obtaining that end, than has been done in this.

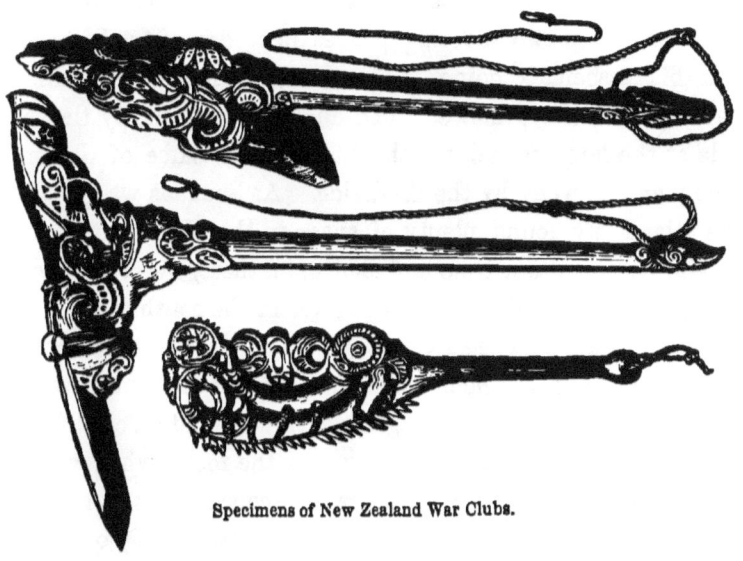

Specimens of New Zealand War Clubs.

PROVIDENTIAL SUPPLY OF GEESE AT CHRISTMAS SOUND.

In proceeding round the south end of Shag Island, we observed the shags (crested cormorant) to breed in vast numbers in the cliffs of the rocks. Some of the old ones we shot, but could not come at the young ones, which are by far the best eating. On the east side of the island we saw some geese; and having with difficulty landed, we killed three, which at this time were a valuable acquisition.

In the evening we got on board, when Mr. Pickersgill, who had just arrived before, informed me that the land opposite to our station was an island, which he had been round; that, on another, more to the north, he found many *terns'* eggs, and that without the great island, between it and the east head, lay a cove in which were many geese; one only of which he got, besides some young goslings. This information of Mr. Pickersgill induced me to make up two shooting parties next day; Mr. Pickersgill and his associates going in the cutter, and myself and the botanists in the pinnace. Mr. Pickersgill went by the N.E. side of the large island, which obtained the name of Goose Island; and I went by the S.W. side. As soon as we got under the island, we found plenty of shags in the cliffs, but, without staying to spend our time and shot upon these, we proceeded on, and presently found sport enough; for in the south of the island were abundance of geese. It happened to be the moulting season, and most of them were on shore for that purpose, and could not fly. There being a great surf, we found much difficulty in landing, and very bad climbing over the rocks when we were landed; so that hundreds of the geese escaped us—some into the sea, and others up into the island. We, however, by one means or other, got sixty-two; with which we returned on board, all heartily tired; but the acquisition we had made overbalanced every other consideration, and we sat down with a good appetite to supper, on part of what the preceding day had produced. Mr. Pickersgill and his associates had got on board some time before us, with fourteen geese; so that I was able to make distribution to the whole crew, which was the more acceptable on account of the approaching festival; for, had not Providence thus singularly provided for us, our Christmas cheer must have been salt beef and pork.

I now learnt that a number of the natives, in nine canoes, had been alongside the ship, and some on board. Little address was required to persuade them to either; for they seemed to be well enough acquainted with Europeans, and had amongst them some of their knives. The next morning, the 25th, they made us another visit. I found them to be of the same nation I had formerly seen in Success Bay; and the same which M. de Bougainville distinguishes by the name of Pecheras, a word which these had on every occasion in their mouths. They are a little, ugly, half-starved, beardless race: I saw not a tall person amongst them. I know not if they resemble the Esquimaux in their love of train oil; but they, and everything they had, smelt most intolerably of it. I ordered them some biscuit, but did not observe them so fond of it as I had been told. They were much better pleased when I gave them some medals, knives, etc.

They all retired before dinner, and did not wait to partake of our Christmas cheer. Indeed, I believe no one invited them, and for good reasons; for their dirty persons, and the stench they carried about them, were enough to spoil the appetite of any European; and that would have been a real disappointment, as we had not experienced such fare for some time.* Roast and boiled geese, goose-pie, etc., was a treat little known to us; and we had yet some Madeira wine left, which was the only article of our provision that was mended by keeping. So that our friends in England did not, perhaps, celebrate Christmas more cheerfully than we did.

The festival which we celebrated at this place occasioned my giving it the name of Christmas Sound.

* The natives, to this day, are in the same degraded state. A full and interesting account of them will be found in Parker Snow's Voyage to the South Seas, in the "Allen Gardener" yacht.

From Christmas Sound, I proceeded round Cape Horn to the Cape of Good Hope, whence I sailed for England, having previously, in pursuance of my instructions, demanded of the officers and petty officers the log-books and journals they had kept; which were delivered to me accordingly, and sealed up for the inspection of the Admiralty.* I also enjoined them, and the

---

* Notwithstanding this injunction, so great was the sensation caused by the voyage, that the publishers of the day were as anxious to obtain the account of it, as recently in the case of M'Clintock's voyage, when his journal was as eagerly sought for by all our leading publishers—the prize falling into the hands of Mr. Murray. The following correspondence is somewhat amusing:—

"*Mile End*, 18*th September* 1775.

"SIR—Last Saturday morning I examined Mr. Anderson, the gunner, about the publication of my late voyage, said to be in the press, and told him that he was suspected of being the author. He affirmed that he had no knowledge or hand in it, and would use his endeavours to find out the author, and yesterday made me the enclosed report.

"To-day Marra called upon me, and confirmed what is therein set forth; and farther added, that Bordel my coxswain, and Reardon the boatswain's mate, each kept a journal, which they had offered to the booksellers, but they were so badly written that no one could read them. I have no reason to suspect this story, but will, however, call upon the printer, and endeavour to get a sight of the manuscript, as I know most of their writings. This Marra was one of the gunner's mates, the same as wanted to remain at Otaheite. If this is the only account of the voyage that is printing, I do not think it worth regarding. I have taken some measures to find out if there are any more, and such information as I may get shall be communicated to you by, Sir, your most obedient humble servant,

." *Philip Stephens, Esq., Admiralty.*   (Signed)   JAMES COOK."

(Enclosure.)

"SIR—According to your direction, I overhauled every bookseller's shop in St. Paul's, till at last I came to Mr. Francis Newbury's. I fairly caught his shopman, who answered me (when I demanded the 'Resolution's' Voyage), that they had not time to print it yet; I then asked him if it was the Captain's Journal they had; on which he looked at me, and said, they had no journal at all yet, but stood as fair a chance to publish the voyage as others. By this time he under-

whole crew, not to divulge where we had been, till they had their Lordships' permission so to do.

On the 29th July 1775, we made the land near Plymouth.
stood I was pumping of him, so went and brought me one of the shop bills, and bid me good day; telling me that before the voyage was published it would be advertised. I then drove to Marra and Peckover's lodging; found the former at home. I told him I had a message from you, Sir, to deliver to Peckover, on which he, Marra, went and found him. I told him that there would be nothing ever done for him or me, unless we could find out who it was that was publishing the voyage. This made all present very sorry; there was some of your late crew. Some told me Reading wrote a journal, which Enell produced. I deposited five guineas if he would let me shew you the account. He consented. Others told me Rollet kept a journal, interlined in his Bible. I wrote down all this information for your satisfaction. At last, Marra pulled the paper from before me (wrote at the Angel, Angel Court, in the borough of Southwark). 'Send that to Captain Cook; if he pleases to send a line for or to me, I'll clear every man that is suspected;' adding, 'I'm the man that is publishing the voyage; I want no preferment, and God forbid I should hinder those whose bread depends on the navy; and, Mr. Anderson, as you have always been my friend, come with me, I'll convince you further that the name of Anderson was never intended to be prefixed to the voyage.' He ordered the coach to drive to Newbury's; carried me into a back parlour; informed Mr. Newbury his friend was kept out of bread, therefore he had discovered all. 'Now,' says he, 'what name is my journal of the voyage to come out in?' 'In no name at all,' says the bookseller. 'Then,' says the other, 'let it come out in the name of John Marra!' At length adding, 'If Captain Cook pleases to call here, Mr. Newbury, give him all the satisfaction in your power.' Mr. Newbury said he would; after which Mr. Newbury invited us both to dinner.

"I should, Sir, have waited on you last night, but I'm so lame I could not come up. If you will be pleased to let me know when you will send for Marra, I'll wait on you at the same time to confront him; but there is too many witnesses for him to retract.

"Honoured Sir, you'll please to observe that this is twice I innocently fell under your displeasure, which God has been pleased to clear me of.—I am, Sir, with the greatest respect, your most obedient and most humble servant,

(Signed) "RT. ANDERSON."

Records of the Admiralty, Whitehall, Captain's Letters, C. vol. 23.

The next morning we anchored at Spithead; and the same day I landed at Portsmouth, and set out for London, in company with Messrs. Wales, Forsters, and Hodges.

Having been absent from England three years and eighteen days, in which time, and under all changes of climate, I lost but four men, and only one of them by sickness, it may not be amiss, at the conclusion of this journal, to enumerate the several causes to which, under the care of Providence, I conceive this uncommon good state of health experienced by my people was owing. Extraordinary attention was paid by the Admiralty in causing such articles to be put on board as, either from experience or suggestion, it was judged would tend to preserve the health of the seamen. I shall not trespass upon the reader's time in mentioning them all, but confine myself to such as were found the most useful. We were furnished with a quantity of malt, of which was made *Sweet Wort*. To such of the men as showed the least symptoms of the scurvy, and also to such as were thought to be threatened with that disorder, this was given from one to two or three pints a day each man; or in such proportion as the surgeon found necessary, which sometimes amounted to three quarts. This is, without doubt, one of the best antiscorbutic sea medicines yet discovered; and, if used in time, will, with proper attention to other things, I am persuaded, prevent the scurvy from making any great progress for a considerable while. But I am not altogether of opinion that it will cure it at sea.

Sour Krout, of which we had a large quantity, is not only a wholesome vegetable food, but, in my judgment, highly antiscorbutic; and it spoils not by keeping. A pound of this was served to each man when at sea, twice a week or oftener, as was thought necessary. *Portable Broth* was another great article, of which we had a large supply. An ounce of this to each man, or such other proportion as circumstances pointed out, was boiled in their pease, three days in the week; and when we were in places where vegetables were to be got, it was boiled with them, and wheat or oatmeal every morning for breakfast; and also with pease and vegetables for dinner. It enabled us to make several nourishing and wholesome messes, and was the means of making the people eat a greater quantity of vegetables than they would otherwise have done. *Rob of Lemon* and *Orange* is an antiscorbutic we were not without. The surgeon made use of it in many cases, with great success. Amongst the articles of victualling we were supplied with *Sugar* in the room of *Oil*, and with *Wheat* for a part of *Oatmeal;* and were certainly gainers by the exchange. Sugar, I apprehend, is a very good antiscorbutic; whereas oil (such as the navy is usually supplied with), I am of opinion, has the contrary effect.

But the introduction of the most salutary articles, either as provisions or medicines, will generally prove unsuccessful, unless supported by certain regulations. On this principle, many years' experience, together with some hints I had from Sir Hugh Palliser, Captains Campbell, Wallis, and other intelligent officers, enabled me to lay a plan whereby all was to be governed. The crew were at three watches, except upon some extraordinary occasions. By this means they were not so much exposed to the weather as if they had been at watch and watch; and had generally dry clothes to shift themselves, when they happened to get wet. Care was also taken to expose them as little wet weather as possible. Proper methods were used to keep their persons, hammocks, bedding, clothes, etc., constantly clean and dry. Equal care was taken to keep the ship clean and dry betwixt decks. Once or twice a week she was aired with fires; and when this could not be done, she was smoked with gunpowder mixed with vinegar or water. I had also frequently a fire made in an iron pot at the bottom of the well, which was of great use in purifying the air in the lower parts of the ship. To this and to cleanliness, as well in the ship as amongst the people, too great attention cannot be paid; the least neglect occasions a putrid and disagreeable smell below, which nothing but fires will remove. Proper attention was paid to the ship's coppers, so that they were kept constantly clean. The fat which boiled out of the salt beef and pork, I never suffered to be given to the people; being of opinion that it promotes the scurvy.

I was careful to take in water wherever it was to be got, even though we did not want it. Because I look upon fresh water from the shore to be more wholesome than that which has been kept some time on board a ship. Of this essential article, we were never at an allowance, but had always plenty for every necessary purpose. Navigators in general cannot, indeed, expect, nor would they wish to meet with, such advantages in this respect, as fell to my lot. The nature of our voyage carried us into very high latitudes. But the hardships and dangers inseparable from that situation were, in some degree, compensated by the singular felicity we enjoyed, of extracting inexhaustible supplies of fresh water from an ocean strewed with ice. We came to few places where either the art of man or the bounty of nature had not provided some sort of refreshment or other, either in the animal or vegetable way. It was my first care to procure whatever of any kind could be met with, by every means in my power; and to oblige our people to make use thereof, both by my example and authority; but the benefits arising from refreshments of any kind soon became so obvious, that I had little occasion to recommend the one or to exert the other.

CONCLUSION.

It does not become me to say how far the principal objects of our voyage have been obtained. Though it has not abounded with remarkable events, nor been diversified by sudden transitions of fortune ; though my relation of it has been more employed in tracing our course by sea, than in recording our operations on shore ; this, perhaps, is a circumstance from which the curious reader may infer, that the purposes for which we were sent into the southern hemisphere were diligently and effectually pursued. Had we found out a continent there, we might have been better enabled to gratify curiosity ; but we hope our not having found it, after all our persevering searches, will leave less room for future speculation about unknown worlds remaining to be explored. But whatever may be the public judgment about other matters, it is with real satisfaction, and without claiming any merit but that of attention to my duty, that I can conclude this account with an observation which facts enable me to make, that our having discovered the possibility of preserving health amongst a numerous ship's company, for such a length of time, in such varieties of climate and amidst such continued hardships and fatigues, will make this voyage remarkable in the opinion of every benevolent person, when the disputes about a southern continent shall have ceased to engage the attention and to divide the judgment of philosophers.

Third Voyage

TO THE

PACIFIC OCEAN, AND FOR EXPLORING THE NORTHERN HEMISPHERE.

IN H.M. SHIPS "RESOLUTION," 462 TONS, AND "DISCOVERY," 300 TONS, IN THE YEARS 1776-7-8-9-80.

IN the preceding voyage, the question respecting the existence of a southern continent was for the time set at rest, but the practicability of a northern passage to the Pacific Ocean was still an object of so vast importance to England as to excite an earnest desire for the most diligent investigation.

It had long been a favourite scheme with the most celebrated navigators, and with the learned men of the day, to discover a shorter and more commodious course to the Oriental regions than by the Cape of Good Hope. This had been attempted in various directions for two centuries and upwards, but the completion of this favourite object was as distant as ever, and the problem of a junction of the two great oceans, the Atlantic and Pacific, by the northern shores of America, was left to be solved in our own time by the several voyages and discoveries of Sir Edward Parry, Ross, Sir John Franklin, Collinson, M'Clure, Sir Leopold M'Clintock, Dease, Simpson, Back, Richardson, and Rae—Franklin being now proved, beyond all doubt, to be the *first* discoverer of a north-west passage.

For the conduct of such an enterprise, it was evident that great skill, perseverance, and abilities, were required; and though, by the universal voice of mankind, Captain Cook was the best qualified, no one could venture to solicit him on the subject. The services he had already rendered to his country, the labours he had sustained, and the dangers he had encountered, were so many and so various, that it was deemed unreasonable to urge him to engage in fresh perils.

As an honourable testimony, however, to his merit and knowledge, it was resolved to ask his advice respecting the most proper person to be intrusted with the conduct of this voyage; and to determine this point, some of the most distinguished naval characters were invited to meet Captain Cook at the house of Lord Sandwich, who then presided over the Board of Admiralty.

While the conversation became animated on the subject, Cook's mind was fired with the magnitude of the design, and the consequences likely to result from it. He suddenly started up, under the impression of a noble enthusiasm, and offered his best services to direct the important objects in view. No proposal could have been more grateful. Captain Cook was immediately invested with the command.*

* The following letter, dated at the Admiralty, 10th Feb. 1776, formally offers his services :—

Admiralty Office, 10*th February* 1776.

SIR,—Having understood that their Lordships have ordered two ships to be fitted out for the purpose of making further discoveries in the Pacific Ocean, I take the liberty, as their Lordships, when they were pleased to appoint me a captain in Greenwich Hospital, were at the same time pleased also to say, it should not be in prejudice to any further offer which I might make of my service, to submit myself to their directions, if they think fit to appoint me to the command on the said intended voyage; relying, if they condescend to accept this offer, they

This preliminary step settled, the exact plan of the undertaking was next taken into serious consideration. All former navigators round the globe had returned by the Cape of Good Hope; but to Captain Cook was assigned the arduous task of attempting the same thing by reaching the high northern latitudes between Asia and America; and it appears that this plan was adopted in consequence of his own suggestions. His instructions were, to proceed to the Pacific Ocean, and through that cluster of islands he had before visited within the southern tropic; and thence, if practicable, to make his way into the Atlantic, along the northern coast of America, in whatever latitude it might be found to lie; for nothing whatever was known at that time respecting it.

To give every stimulus to the prosecution of this great design, motives of interest were superadded to the obligations of duty. An Act of Parliament, which passed in 1745, offering a reward of £20,000 to such as should discover a passage through Hudson's Bay, was enlarged and explained; and it was now enacted, that if any ship belonging to his Majesty, or his subjects, should find and sail through any passage by sea, between the Atlantic and Pacific Oceans, in any direction or parallel of the northern hemisphere, to the northward of the 52d deg. of northern latitude, the sum of £20,000 was to reward such discovery.

The vessels destined for this service were the "Resolution" and the "Discovery." The command of the former was given to

will on my return, either restore me to my appointment in the Hospital, or procure for me such other mark of the royal favour as their Lordships, upon the review of my past services, shall think me deserving of. I am, sir, your most humble servant,   JAMES COOK.

To George Jackson, Esq.

—Admiralty Records.

Captain Cook, and that of the latter to Captain Clerke, who had been second lieutenant on the former voyage. Nearly the same complement of men and officers was assigned to each as before. The following is the list of the principal officers appointed to the two ships :—

"RESOLUTION."

John Gore, James King, John Williamson, lieutenants.
William Bligh, master.
William Anderson, surgeon.
Molesworth Philips, lieutenant, royal marines.

"DISCOVERY."

James Burney, John Rickman, lieutenants.
Thomas Edgar, master.
John Law, surgeon.

Several months were spent in the equipment and preparation of the ships, that the health of the seamen, and the success of the expedition, might have every advantage which a liberal and enlightened attention could bestow. In order that the inhabitants of Otaheite, and other islands in the South Seas where the English had been treated with so much hospitality, might be benefited by the voyage, his Majesty was graciously pleased to order some of the most useful European cattle to be put on board for those countries.

Besides these, Captain Cook was furnished with a quantity of garden seeds, and the Board of Admiralty added such articles of commerce as were most likely to promote a friendly intercourse with the natives and to induce them to open traffic with the English.

Omai, who has been mentioned in the preceding voyage, was likewise to be carried back to his native country.

This voyage, like the previous, is written by Captain Cook, till his lamented death, and afterwards by Captain King, who published the whole. Some of the general descriptions were furnished by Mr. Anderson, the surgeon of the "Resolution;" a man of distinguished abilities, and to whose talents Captain Cook acknowledged himself much indebted for many interesting parts of his voyage. As the important part of this voyage commenced with Cook's departure for the North Seas, we shall relate only cursorily what occurred before that.

Contrary winds, and other circumstances, prevented the ships from clearing the Channel till the 14th of July 1776. On board both vessels were one hundred and ninety-two persons, officers included. On the 1st of August 1776, they arrived off Teneriffe, crossed the Equator on 1st September, and anchored in Table Bay on the 18th of October. Here a violent tempest occurred, the effects of which were felt both on sea and land. It lasted three days, and the "Resolution" was the only ship in the bay that rode out the storm without dragging her anchors. On shore the tents and observatory were destroyed, and the astronomical quadrant narrowly escaped irreparable damage. The "Discovery," which had been some time later in sailing from England, was driven off the coast, and did not arrive till the 10th of November.

While at this place, a disaster happened which threatened the loss of most of the live stock. The bull and two cows had been put ashore to graze among other cattle; but Captain Cook had been advised to keep the sheep, sixteen in number, near the tents, where they were penned in every night. But some dogs having got in amongst them in the night-time, killed four, and dispersed the rest. Six of them were recovered the next day, but the two rams and two of the finest ewes in the flock were missing. Baron Plettenberg, the governor, was applied to, but all his endeavours were unsuccessful, until some of the meanest and lowest of the people were employed, fellows who for a ducatoon would have cut their master's throat, burned the house over his head, and buried him and his whole family in ashes. After all, two of the finest ewes in the flock were missing, and never could be recovered. In order to repair this loss, and to make an addition to the original stock, there were purchased two young bulls, two entire horses, two mares, two heifers, two rams, several ewes and goats, with some rabbits and poultry. Having finished all business, sail was set on the 30th of November, though it was not till the 3d of December that the land was cleared.

Having explored some desolate islands in the southern seas, Captain Cook set sail for New Zealand. During this part of the voyage, so thick a fog prevailed, that, according to the authors of Captain Cook's life, "they sailed three hundred leagues in the dark." The first land afterwards reached was New Holland, where they remained till the 30th of January 1777, when they set sail for New Zealand, and on the 12th of February anchored in Queen Charlotte's Sound. Here the people were shy and timorous, on account of their having formerly destroyed ten of Captain Furneaux's people who had been sent ashore to gather vegetables. The cause of the quarrel could not be known, as none of the party were left alive to tell the news. Lieutenant Burney, who went ashore in quest of them, found only some fragments of their bodies; from which it appeared that they had been killed and devoured by the savages. It was not the intention of Captain Cook, at this distance of time, to resent the injury; he even refused to put to death a chief named Kahoora, who, as he was informed by the natives themselves, had killed Mr. Rowe, the commander of the party. He was, however, particularly careful that no opportunity should now be given the savages of committing such an action with impunity; and with this view a boat was never sent on shore without being well armed, and the men under the command of such officers as could be depended upon. The New Zealanders were no sooner assured of Captain Cook's pacific disposition, than they threw aside their fears and suspicions, and entered into a commercial intercourse with the people. It would have been the less excusable in Captain Cook to have revenged at this time the massacre of Mr. Rowe's party, as he was assured that the quarrel originated from some petty thefts of the savages, which were too hastily resented on the part of the British; and that, had it not been for this, no mischief would have happened.

On the 25th of February New Zealand was left, and at the request of Omai, two boys were taken into the ship, the eldest about eighteen, and the youngest about ten. So much time had now been spent in sailing up and down in the Pacific Ocean, where several new islands were discovered, that Captain Cook judged it impossible to accomplish anything this year in the high northern latitudes; for which reason he determined to bear away for the Friendly Islands, in order to supply himself with those necessaries which he had found it impossible to procure at any of the islands which he had just discovered. In his run thither, several new islands were visited; and in prosecuting these discoveries another narrow escape was made from shipwreck. The danger at this time arose from a low sandy island which the "Resolution" was very near running upon, and from which she was only saved by the circumstance of all the men having been accidentally called upon deck to put the vessel about. Soon after this both ships struck upon some sunk coral rocks, but happily got off without material damage.

After a stay of between two and three months, Captain Cook took leave of the Friendly Islands on the 13th of July 1777, and on the 12th of August reached Otaheite, where he introduced Omai to his countrymen. Here the captain found the people of Otaheite ready to engage in a war with those of Eimeo; but though strongly solicited by the former to assist them in an expedition against their enemies, he refused to take any concern in the affair, alleging, by way of excuse, that the people of Eimeo had never offended him. This seemed to satisfy most of the chiefs; but one, named Towha, was so much displeased that Captain Cook could never regain his favour.

From Otaheite Captain Cook next proceeded to Eimeo, where, on account of some thefts committed by the natives, he was obliged to commence hostilities, by burning a number of their war canoes, and even some houses. These transactions gave him much concern; and the more that he had been so much solicited to make war on these people by his friends at Otaheite, to whose entreaties he had refused to listen. From Eimeo he proceeded to Huaheine, where he saw Omai finally settled, and left with him the two New Zealand youths already mentioned. The youngest of these was so much attached to the English that it was necessary to carry him out of the ship and put him ashore by force. During his stay on this island, it was found necessary to punish a thief with greater severity than had ever been done before, by causing his head and beard to be shaved, and his ears cut off. Some other disagreeable transactions took place, particularly the desertion of two of the crew, who were not recovered without the greatest difficulty. In the course of the exertions that were made for their recovery, it was found necessary to detain the son, daughter, and son-in-law of the chief of an island named Otaha. This had almost produced very serious consequences, the natives having formed a plot for carrying off Captain Cook himself, as well as Captain Clerke and Mr. Gore. As to the commander, they were disappointed by his own caution and vigilance; but Clerke and Gore were in particular danger; and it was only owing to the circumstance of one of them having a pistol in his hand as they walked together on shore, that they were not seized.

CHAPTER VII.

DEPARTURE FOR THE NORTH SEAS, FEBRUARY 1778.

After the "Discovery" had joined us, we stood away to the northward. Notwithstanding our advanced latitude, and its being the winter season, we had only begun, for a few days past, to feel a sensation of cold in the mornings and evenings. This is a sign of the equal and lasting influence of the sun's heat, at all seasons, to 30° on each side the line. The disproportion is known to become very great after that. This must be attributed, almost entirely, to the direction of the rays of the sun, independent of the bare distance, which is by no means equal to the effect. We had on the 25th Feburary reached the latitude of 42° 30', and the longitude of 219°; and then we began to meet with the rock-weed, mentioned by the writer of Lord Anson's voyage, under the name of sea-leek, which the Manilla ships generally fall in with. Now and then a piece of wood also appeared. But if we had not known that the continent of North America was not far distant, we might, from the few signs of the vicinity of land hitherto met with, have concluded that there was none within some thousand leagues of us. We had hardly seen a bird, or any oceanic animal, since we left Sandwich Islands.

NEW ALBION.

On the 6th of March at noon, being in the latitude of 44° 10' N., and the longitude of $234\frac{1}{2}$° E., we saw two seals and several whales; and at daybreak the next morning, the long-looked-for coast of New Albion was seen extending from north-east to south-east, distant ten or twelve leagues. The land appeared to be of a moderate height, diversified with hills and valleys, and almost everywhere covered with wood. There was, however, no very striking object on any part of it, except one hill, whose elevated summit was flat. This bore east from us at noon. At the northern extreme the land formed a point, which I called *Cape Foulweather*, from the very bad weather that we soon after met with. Our difficulties now began to increase, and it was not until after being unprofitably tossed about for a fortnight that we saw land on the morning of the 22d March 1778.

At this time we were in the latitude of 47° 5' north, and in the longitude of 235° 10' east, and about four leagues from the land, which extended from north to south-east half east. A small round hill, which had the appearance of being an island, bore north three quarters east, distant six or seven leagues, as I guessed: it appears to be of a tolerable height, and was but just to be seen from the deck. Between this island or rock, and the northern extreme of the land, there appeared to be a small opening, which flattered us with the hopes of finding a harbour. These hopes lessened as we drew nearer; and, at last, we had some reason to think that the opening was closed by low land. On this account I called the point of land to the north of it *Cape Flattery*. There is a round hill of a moderate height over it; and all the land upon this part of the coast is of a moderate and pretty equal height, well covered with wood, and had a very pleasant and fertile appearance. It is in this very latitude where we now were, that geographers have placed the pretended strait of Juan de Fuca.

We saw nothing like it; nor is there the least probability that ever any such thing existed.

VANCOUVER'S ISLAND, MARCH 1778.

As we drew near the coast, we perceived the appearance of two inlets; one in the north-west, and the other in the north-east corner of the bay. As I could not fetch the former, I bore up to the latter, and passed some breakers, or sunken rocks, that lay a league or more from the shore.

We no sooner drew near the inlet, than we found the coast to be inhabited; and three canoes came off to the ship. In one of these were two men, in another six, and in the third ten. Having come pretty near us, a person in one of the two last stood up, and made a long harangue, inviting us to land, as we guessed by his gestures. At the same time, he kept strewing handfuls of feathers towards us, and some of his companions threw handfuls of red dust or powder in the same manner. The person who played the orator wore the skin of some animal, and held in each hand something which rattled as he kept shaking it. After tiring himself with his repeated exhortations, of which we did not understand a word, he was quiet; and then others took it by turns to say something, though they acted their part neither so long, nor with so much vehemence as the other. We observed that two or three had their hair quite strewed over with small white feathers, and others had large ones stuck into different parts of the head. After the tumultuous noise had ceased, they lay at a little distance from the ship, and conversed with each other in a very easy manner; nor did they seem to show the least surprise or distrust. Some of them now and then got up, and said something after the manner of their first harangues;

and one sang a very agreeable air with a degree of softness and melody which we could not have expected; the word *haela* being often repeated as the burden of the song.

Though our visitors behaved very peaceably, and could not be suspected of any hostile intention, we could not prevail upon any of them to come on board. They showed great readiness, however, to part with anything they had, and took from us whatever we offered them in exchange; but were more desirous of iron than of any other of our articles of commerce, appearing to be perfectly acquainted with the use of that metal. Many of the canoes followed us to our anchoring-place; and a group of about ten or a dozen of them remained alongside the "Resolution" most part of the night. These circumstances gave us a reasonable ground of hope that we should find this a comfortable station to supply all our wants, and to make us forget the hardships and delays experienced during a constant succession of adverse winds and boisterous weather almost ever since our arrival upon the coast of America.

After coming to anchor, I lost no time in finding a commodious harbour, where we stationed ourselves during our continuance in the sound.

A great many canoes, filled with the natives, were about the ships all day; and a trade commenced betwixt us and them, which was carried on with the strictest honesty on both sides. The articles which they offered to sale were skins of various animals, such as bears, wolves, foxes, deer, racoons, polecats, martins; and, in particular, of the sea otters, which are found at the islands east of Kamtschatka. But the most extraordinary of all the articles which they brought for sale were human skulls, and hands not yet quite stripped of the flesh, which they made our people plainly understand they had eaten; and, indeed, some of them had evident marks that they had been upon the fire. We had but too much reason to suspect, from this circumstance, that the horrid practice of feeding on their enemies is as prevalent here as we had found it to be at New Zealand and other South Sea Islands. For the various articles which they brought, they took in exchange knives, chisels, pieces of iron and tin, nails, looking-glasses, buttons, or any kind of metal. Glass beads they were not fond of; and cloth of every sort they rejected.

A considerable number of the natives visited us daily; and every now and then we saw new faces. On their first coming, they generally went through a singular mode of introducing themselves. They would paddle with all their strength quite round both ships, a chief, or other principal person in the canoe, standing up with a spear, or some other weapon, in his hand, and speaking, or rather hallooing all the time. Sometimes the orator of the canoe would have his face covered with a mask, representing either a human visage, or that of some animal; and, instead of a weapon, would hold a rattle in his hand.* After making this circuit round the ships, they would come alongside, and begin to trade without further ceremony. Very often, indeed, they would first give us a song, in which all in the canoe joined with a very pleasing harmony. During these visits they gave us no other trouble than to guard against their thievish tricks.

After a fortnight's bad weather, having now finished most of our heavy work, in refitting the rigging, I set out to take a view of the Sound. I first went to the west point, where I found a large village, and before it a very snug harbour, in which were from nine to four fathoms' water, over a bottom of fine sand.

* The medicine man.

The people of this village, who were numerous, and to most of whom I was well known, received me very courteously, every one pressing me to go into his house, or rather his apartment; for several families live under the same roof. I did not decline the invitation; and my hospitable friends whom I visited spread a mat for me to sit upon, and showed me every other mark of civility. In most of the houses there were women at work, making dresses from the plant or bark before mentioned, which they executed exactly in the same manner that the New Zealanders manufacture their cloth.

CURING SARDINES.

Others were occupied in opening sardines. I had seen a large quantity of them brought on shore from canoes, and divided by measure amongst several people, who carried them up to their houses, where the operation of curing them by smoke-drying is performed. They hang them on small rods, at first about a foot from the fire; afterwards they remove them higher and higher, to make room for others, till the rods on which the fish hang reach the top of the house. When they are completely dried they are taken down and packed close in bales, which they cover with mats. Thus they are kept till wanted; and they are not a disagreeable article of food. Cod and other large fish are also cured in the same manner by them; though they sometimes dry these in the open air, without fire.

From this village I proceeded up the west side of the Sound. For about three miles I found the shore covered with small islands, which are so situated as to form several convenient harbours, having various depths of water, from thirty to seven fathoms, with a good bottom. Two leagues within the Sound, on this west side, there runs in an arm in the direction of north north-west; and two miles farther is another nearly in the same direction, with a pretty large island before it. I had no time to examine either of these arms; but have reason to believe that they do not extend far inland, as the water was no more than brackish at their entrances. A mile above the second arm I found the remains of a village. The logs or framings of the houses were standing; but the boards that had composed their sides and roofs did not exist. Before this village were some large fishing weirs; but I saw nobody attending them. These weirs were composed of pieces of wicker-work made of small rods, some closer than others, according to the size of the fish intended to be caught in them. These pieces of wicker-work (some of whose superficies are at least twenty feet by twelve) are fixed up edgewise in shallow water, by strong poles or pickets that stand firm in the ground. Behind this ruined village is a plain of a few hours' extent, covered with the largest pine-trees that I ever saw. This was the more remarkable, as the elevated ground in most other parts of this west side of the Sound was rather naked.

From this place I crossed over to the other, or east side of the Sound, passing an arm of it that runs in north north-east, to appearance not far. I now found what I had before conjectured, that the land under which the ships lay was an island; and that there were many smaller ones lying scattered in the Sound on the west side of it. Opposite the north end of our large island, upon the mainland, I observed a village, and there I landed. The inhabitants of it were not so polite as those of the other I had just visited. But this cold reception seemed, in a great measure, if not entirely, owing to one surly chief, who would not let me enter their houses, following me wherever I went; and several times, by expressive signs, marking his impatience that I should be gone. I attempted in vain to soothe him by presents, but though he did not refuse them, they did not alter his behaviour. Some of the young women, better pleased with us than their inhospitable chief, dressed themselves expeditiously in their best apparel, and assembling in a body welcomed us to their village, by joining in a song, which was far from harsh or disagreeable. The day being now far spent, I proceeded for the ships round the north end of the large island; meeting in my way with several canoes laden with sardines, which had been just caught somewhere in the east corner of the Sound. When I got on board I was informed, that while I was absent the ships had been visited by some strangers, in two or three large canoes, who by signs made our people understand that they had come from the southeast, beyond the bay. They brought several skins, garments, and other articles, which they bartered. But what was most singular, two silver table-spoons were purchased from them, which, from their peculiar shape, we supposed to be of Spanish manufacture. One of these strangers wore them round his neck by way of ornament. These visitors also appeared to be more plentifully supplied with iron than the inhabitants of the Sound.

On my arrival in this inlet I had honoured it with the name of King George's Sound, but I afterward found that it is called Nootka by the natives. The climate, as far as we had any experience of it, is infinitely milder than that on the east coast of America, under the same parallel of latitude. The mercury in the thermometer never, even in the night, fell lower than 42°; and very often in the day it rose to 60°. No such thing as frost was perceived in any of the low ground; on the contrary, vegetation had made a considerable progress; for I met with grass that was already above a foot long. The trees which chiefly compose the woods are the Canadian pine, white cypress, *Cupressus thyoides*, the wild pine, with two or three other sorts of pine less common. The first two make up almost two-thirds of the whole; and, at a distance, might be mistaken for the same tree, as they both run up into pointed spire-like tops; but they are easily distinguished on coming nearer from their colour, the cypress being of a much paler green, or shade, than the other. The trees, in general, grow with great vigour, and are all of a large size.

The persons of the natives are in general under the common stature, but not slender in proportion, being commonly pretty full or plump, though not muscular. Neither does the soft fleshiness seem ever to swell into corpulence, and many of the older people are rather spare or lean. The visage of most of them is round and full, and sometimes, also, broad, with large prominent cheeks; and above these the face is frequently much depressed, or seems fallen in quite across the temples, the nose also flattening at its base, with pretty wide nostrils, and a rounded point. The forehead rather low, the eyes small, black, and rather languishing than sparkling, the mouth round with large round thickish lips, the teeth tolerably equal and well set, but not remarkably white.

The nastiness and stench of their houses are at least equal to the confusion; for, as they dry their fish within doors, they also gut them there, which, with their bones and fragments thrown down at meals, and the addition of other sorts of filth, lie everywhere in heaps, and are, I believe, never carried away till it becomes troublesome, from their size, to walk over them. In a word, their houses are as filthy as hog-sties, everything in and about them stinking of fish, train-oil, and smoke. But, amidst all the filth and confusion that are found in the houses, many of them are decorated with images. These are nothing more than the trunks of very large trees four or five feet high, set up singly or by pairs at the upper end of the apartment, with the front carved into a human face, the arms and hands cut out upon the sides and variously painted; so that the whole is a truly monstrous figure. The general name of those images is *Klumma*, and the names of two particular ones which stood abreast of each other, three or four feet asunder in one of the houses, were *Natchkoa* and *Matseeta*.

Their manner of eating is exactly consonant to the nastiness of their houses and persons; for the troughs and platters, in which they put their food, appear never to have been washed from the time they were first made, and the dirty remains of a former meal are only swept away by the succeeding one. They also tear everything, solid or tough, to pieces with their hands and teeth; for though they make use of their knives to cut off the larger portions, they have not, as yet, thought of reducing these to smaller pieces and mouthfuls, by the same means, though obviously more convenient and cleanly. But they seem to have no idea of cleanliness; for they eat the roots which they dig from the ground without so much as shaking off the soil that adheres to them. We are uncertain if they have any set time for meals; for we have seen them eat at all hours in their canoes. And yet, from seeing several messes of the porpoise-broth preparing toward noon, when we visited the village, I should suspect that they make a principal meal about that time.

(It is unnecessary to follow minutely Captain Cook's narrative from this point northwards. Suffice it to say that after leaving Nootka Sound he proceeded northwards by *Cross Sound, Hinch-*

inbrook Island, Prince William Sound, Cook's Inlet, the island of Conalashka and Cape Newenham, to Cape Prince of Wales in Behring Straits, and other places which still retain the names he gave them.)

ICY CAPE.

On Monday the 7th August 1778, before noon, we perceived a brightness in the northern horizon like that reflected from ice, commonly called the blink. About an hour after, the sight of a large field of ice left us no longer in doubt about the cause of the brightness of the horizon. At half-past two we tacked close to the edge of the ice, in twenty-two fathoms water, not being able to stand on any further, for the ice was quite impenetrable, and extended from west to south to east by north, as far as the eye could reach. Here were abundance of sea-horses.

On the 18th, at noon, we were near five leagues farther to the eastward. We were at this time close to the edge of the ice, which was as compact as a wall, and seemed to be ten or twelve feet high at least; but farther north it appeared much higher.

We now stood to the southward, and after running six leagues, shoaled the water to seven fathoms, but it soon deepened to nine fathoms. At this time we saw land extending from south to south-east by east, about three or four miles distant. The eastern extreme forms a point which was much encumbered with ice, for which reason it obtained the name of Icy Cape.* The other extreme of the land was lost in the horizon, so that there can be no doubt of its being a continuation of the American continent.

---

* Icy Cape, Captain Cook's farthest, was passed by Captain Beechey in H.M.S. "Blossom" in 1826, on which occasion the late Mr. Elson and Mr. (now Admiral)

Our situation was now more and more critical. We were in shoal water upon a lee shore, and the main body of the ice to windward driving down upon us. I therefore made the signal for the "Discovery" to tack, and tacked myself at the same time.

Next day we had a good deal of drift ice about us, and the main ice was about two leagues to the north. It was too close and in too large pieces to attempt forcing the ships through it. On the ice lay a prodigious number of sea-horses, and as we were in want of fresh provisions the boats from each ship were sent to get some.

By the time that we had got our sea-horses on board, we were in a manner surrounded with the ice, and had no way left to clear it but by standing to the southward, which was done till three o'clock next morning. At two in the afternoon we fell in with the main ice, along the edge of which we kept, being partly directed by the roaring of the sea-horses, for we had a very thick fog. Thus we continued sailing till near midnight, when we got in amongst the loose ice, and heard the surge of the sea upon the main ice.

Next morning, the fog clearing away, we saw the continent of America, extending from south by east to east by south; and at noon from south-west half south to east; the nearest part five leagues distant.

I continued to steer in for it until eight o'clock, in order to

Smyth reached Point Barrow, 126 miles north-east of Icy Cape, in the "Blossom's" barge. The first vessel that ever rounded the Point was the "Nancy Dawson" yacht, —Robert Shedden, Esq.,—in 1849; then Sir Robert M'Clure and Captain Collinson, who pushed their ships boldly on to the eastward, along the northern shore of America, opening the way to all future navigators; neither should we omit the name of Captain Maguire, who passed two winters at Point Barrow in H.M.S. "Plover," and greatly civilized the natives.

get a nearer view of it and to look for a harbour, but seeing nothing like one I stood again to the north.

The ice obliged us to change our course frequently till the 27th, when we tacked and stood to the west, and at seven in the evening we were close in with the edge of the ice, which lay east from north-east, and west south-west, as far each way as the eye could reach. Having but little wind I went with the boats to examine the state of the ice. I found it consisting of loose pieces of various extent, and so close together that I could hardly enter the outer edge with a boat; and it was as impossible for the ships to enter it as if it had been so many rocks.

A thick fog which came on while I was thus employed with the boats, hastened me aboard rather sooner than I could have wished, with one sea-horse to each ship. We had killed more, but could not wait to bring them with us. The number of these animals, on all the ice that we had seen, is almost incredible.* By this time our people began to relish them. We now stretched to the south-west.

On the 29th, the weather, which had been hazy, cleared up. This enabled us to have a pretty good view of the Asiatic coast, which in every respect is like the opposite one of America; that is, low land next the sea with elevated land farther back. It was perfectly destitute of wood and even snow, but was probably covered with a mossy substance that gave it a brownish cast.

---

* Captain Sir Robert M'Clure in the "Investigator" fell in with immense herds of walrusses in the same locality. "A gun was at first loaded with grape and canister for the purpose of shooting some of them; but the order was countermanded by Captain M'Clure, from the kindly feelings awakened by the affection evinced between the mothers and babes of this brute community."—Vide *Captain Sherard Osborn's Narrative.*

In the low ground, lying between the high land and the sea, was a lake extending to the south-east farther than we could see.

RETURN TO THE SOUTHERN SEAS, SEPTEMBER 1778.

The season was now far advanced, and the time when the frost was expected to set in so near at hand, that I did not think it consistent with prudence to make any farther attempts to find a passage into the Atlantic this year in any direction, so little was the prospect of succeeding. My attention was now directed toward finding out some place where we might supply ourselves with wood and water; and the object uppermost in my thoughts was, how I should spend the winter so as to make some improvements in geography and navigation, and at the same time be in a condition to return to the north in farther search of a passage the ensuing summer.

After standing off till we got into eighteen fathoms water, I bore up to the eastward along the coast of Asia. At daybreak on the 30th we made sail, and steered such a course as I thought would bring us in with the land; for the weather was as thick as ever, and it snowed incessantly. At ten we got sight of the coast, bearing south-west, four miles distant.

The inland country hereabout is full of hills, some of which are of a considerable height. The land was covered with snow.

September 2d, we had now fair weather and sunshine; and as we ranged along the coast at the distance of four miles, we saw several of the inhabitants, and some of their habitations, which looked like little hillocks of earth. None of them, however, attempted to come off to us, which seemed a little extraordinary. These people must be the Tschutski, a nation that, at the time Mr. Muller wrote, the Russians had not been able to conquer.

The more I was convinced of my being now upon the coast of Asia, the more I was at a loss to reconcile Mr. Staehlin's map of the New Northern Archipelago with my observations, and I had no way to account for the great difference but by supposing that I had mistaken some part of what he calls the Island of Alaschka for the American continent, and had missed the channel that separates them. Admitting even this, there would still have been a considerable difference. It was with me a matter of some consequence to clear up this point the present season, that I might have but one object in view the next. And as the northern isles are represented by him as abounding with wood, I was in hopes, if I should find them, of getting a supply of that article, which we now began to be in great want of on board.

With these views, I steered over for the American coast, and on the 6th we got sight of it.

Pursuing our course, on the 9th we found ourselves upon a coast covered with wood, an agreeable sight, to which of late we had not been accustomed. Next morning, being about a league from the west shore, I took two boats and landed, attended by Mr. King, to seek wood and water. Here we observed tracks of deer and foxes on the beach, on which also lay a great quantity of drift-wood, and there was no want of fresh water. I returned on board with an intention to bring the ships to an anchor here, but the wind then veering to north-east, I stretched over to the opposite shore, in hopes of finding wood there also, and anchored at eight o'clock in the evening, but next morning we found it to be a peninsula united to the continent by a low neck of land, on each side of which the coast forms a bay, which obtained the name of Cape Denbigh.

Several people were seen upon the peninsula, and one man came off in a small canoe. I gave him a knife and a few beads, with which he seemed well pleased. Having made signs to him to bring us something to eat, he immediately left us and paddled towards the shore, but meeting another man coming off, who happened to have two dried salmon, he got them from him, and, on returning to the ship, would give them to nobody but me. Some of our people thought that he had asked for me under the name of Capitane; but in this they were probably mistaken.

Lieutenant Gore being now sent to the peninsula, reported that there was but little fresh water, and that wood was difficult to be got at, by reason of the boats grounding at some distance from the beach. This being the case I stood back to the other shore, and at eight o'clock the next morning sent all the boats and a party of men, with an officer, to get wood from the place where I had landed two days before.

Next day a family of the natives came near to our wooding party. I know not how many there were at first, but I saw only the husband, the wife, and their child, and a fourth person, who bore the human shape and that was all, for he was the most deformed cripple I had ever seen or heard of. The other man was almost blind; and neither he nor his wife were such good-looking people as we had sometimes seen amongst the natives of this coast. The under lips of both were bored, and they had in their possession some such glass beads as I had met with before amongst their neighbours. But iron was their beloved article. For four knives, which we had made out of an old iron hoop, I got from them near four hundred pounds weight of fish, which they had caught on this or the preceding day. I gave the child, who was a girl, a few beads, on which the mother burst into tears, then the father, then the cripple, and at last, to complete the concert, the girl herself. But this music continued not long. Before night we had got the ships amply supplied with wood, and had carried on board above twelve tuns of water to each.

Some doubts being still entertained whether the coast we were now upon belonged to an island or the American continent, and the shallowness of the water putting it out of our power to determine this with our ships, I sent Lieutenant King with two boats under his command to make such searches as might leave no room for a variety of opinions on the subject.

This officer returned from his expedition on the 16th, and reported that he proceeded with the boats about three or four leagues farther than the ships had been able to go, that he then landed on the west side; that from the heights he could see the two coasts join, and the inlet terminate in a small river or creek, before which were banks of sand or mud, and everywhere shoal water.

From the elevated spot on which Mr. King surveyed the Sound, he could distinguish many extensive valleys with rivers running through them, well wooded, and bounded by hills of a gentle ascent and moderate height.

In honour of Sir Fletcher Norton, speaker of the House of Commons, and Mr. King's near relation, I named this inlet Norton's Sound.

RESOLUTION TO WINTER AT THE SANDWICH ISLANDS.

It was now high time to think of leaving these northern regions, and to retire to some place during the winter, where I might procure refreshments for my people, and a small supply of provisions. No place was so conveniently within our reach where we could expect to have our wants relieved as the Sandwich Islands. To them, therefore, I determined to proceed.

On the 2d of October, at daybreak, we saw the island of Oonalashka, bearing south-east. But as this was to us a new point of view, and the land was obscured by a thick haze, we were not sure of our situation till noon, when the observed latitude determined it. But as all harbours were alike to me, provided they were equally safe and convenient, I hauled into a bay that lies ten miles to the westward of Samganoodha, known by the name of Egoochshac; but we found very deep water, so that we were glad to get out again. The natives, many of whom lived here, visited us at different times, bringing with them dried salmon and other fish, which they exchanged with the seamen for tobacco. But a few days before, every ounce of tobacco that was in the ship had been distributed among them; and the quantity was not half sufficient to answer their demands. Notwithstanding this, so improvident a creature is an English sailor, that they were as profuse in making their bargains as if we had arrived at a port in Virginia.

In the afternoon of the 3d, we anchored in Samganoodha harbour; and the next morning the carpenters of both ships were set to work to overhaul and repair the ships.

There were great quantities of berries found ashore. In order to avail ourselves as much as possible of this useful refreshment, one-third of the people by turns had leave to go and pick them. Considerable quantities of them were also procured from the natives. If there were any seeds of the scurvy in either ship, these berries, and the use of spruce beer which they had to drink every other day, effectually eradicated them.

We also got plenty of fish; at first mostly salmon, both fresh and dried, which the natives brought us. Some of the fresh salmon was in high perfection; we caught a good many salmon trout, and once a halibut that weighed two hundred and fifty-four pounds. The fishery failing, we had recourse to hooks and lines. A boat was sent out every morning, and seldom returned without eight or ten halibut, which were more than sufficient to serve all our people.

On the 8th, I received by the hands of an Oonalashka man, named Derramoushka, a very singular present, considering the place. It was a rye loaf, or rather a pie made in the form of a loaf, for it inclosed some salmon highly seasoned with pepper. This man had the like present for Captain Clerke, and a note for each of us, written in a character which none of us could read. It was natural to suppose that this present was from some Russians now in our neighbourhood, and therefore we sent by the same hand to these, our unknown friends, a few bottles of rum, wine, and porter. I also sent along with Derramoushka, Corporal Lediard of the marines, an intelligent man, in order to gain some farther information, with orders that, if he met with any Russians, he should endeavour to make them understand that we were English, the friends and allies of their nation.

On the 10th, Lediard returned with three Russian seamen, or furriers, who with some others resided at Egoochshac, where they had a dwelling-house, some store-houses, and a sloop of about thirty tons burthen. They were all three well-behaved intelligent men, and very ready to give me all the information I could desire; but for want of an interpreter, we had some difficulty to understand each other.

On the 14th, in the evening, while Mr. Webber and I were

at a village, at a small distance from Samganoodha, a Russian landed there, who I found was the principal person amongst his countrymen in this and the neighbouring islands. His name was Erasim Gregorioff Sin Ismyloff. He arrived in a canoe carrying three persons, attended by twenty or thirty other canoes, each conducted by one man. I took notice that the first thing they did after landing was to make a small tent for Ismyloff, of materials which they brought with them; and then they made others for themselves of their canoes and paddles, which they covered with grass, so that the people of the village were at no trouble to find them lodging. Ismyloff, having invited us into his tent, set before us some dried salmon and berries, which I was satisfied was the best cheer he had. He appeared to be a sensible, intelligent man, and I felt no small mortification in not being able to converse with him unless by signs, assisted by figures and other characters, which, however, were a very great help. I desired to see him on board the next day, and accordingly he came with all his attendants.

I found that he was very well acquainted with the geography of these parts, and with all the discoveries that had been made in them by the Russians. On seeing the modern maps, he at once pointed out their errors.

From what we could gather from Ismyloff and his countrymen, the Russians have made several attempts to get a footing upon that part of the continent that lies contiguous to Oonalashka and the adjoining islands, but have always been repulsed by the natives, whom they describe as a very treacherous people. They mentioned two or three captains or chief men who had been murdered by them, and some of the Russians showed us wounds which they said they had received there.

He would fain have made me a present of a sea-otter skin which he said was worth eighty roubles at Kamtschatka. However, I thought proper to decline it, but I accepted of some dried fish, and several baskets of the lily or saranne root, which is described at large in the History of Kamtschatka. Next day Mr. Ismyloff left us with all his retinue, promising to return in a few days. Accordingly, on the 19th, he made us another visit, and remained with us till the 21st, in the evening, when he took his final leave. To his care I entrusted a letter to the Lords Commissioners of the Admiralty, in which was enclosed a chart of all the northern coasts I had visited.* Mr. Ismyloff seemed

* The following is the letter alluded to, remarkably clear and concise as usual, and of great interest :—

"Resolution, at the Island of Unalaschka, on the coast of America, in the latitude of 53° N., longitude 192° 30′ E. from Greenwich, the 20th October 1778.

"SIR—Having accidentally met with some Russians, who have promised to put this in a way of being sent to Petersburgh, and as I neither have, nor intend to visit Kamtschatka as yet, I take this opportunity to give their Lordships a short account of my proceedings from leaving the Cape of Good Hope to this time.

"After leaving the Cape, I, pursuant to their Lordships' instructions, visited the island lately seen by the French, situated between the latitude of 48° 40′ and 50° S., and in the longitude of 69½° E. These islands abound with good harbours and fresh water, but produceth neither tree nor shrub, and but very little of any kind of vegetation. After spending five days on the coast thereof, I quitted it on the 30th December; just touched at Van Diemen's Land; arrived at Queen Charlotte's Sound in New Zealand, the 13th February 1777; left it again on the 25th, and pushed for Otaheite; but we had not been long at sea before we met with an easterly wind which continued so long, that the season was too far spent to proceed to the north that year. At length the want of water and food for the cattle I had on board obliged me to bear away for the Friendly Islands, so that it was August before I arrived at Otaheite. I found that the Spaniards from Callao had been twice at this island from the time of my leaving it in 1774. The first time they came they left behind them, designedly, four Spaniards, who remained upon the island about ten months, but were all gone some time before my arrival.

to have abilities that might entitle him to a higher station in life than that in which we found him.

They had also brought and left on the island, goats, hogs, and dogs, one bull and a ram, but never a female of either of these species, so that those I carried and put on shore there were highly acceptable. These consisted of a bull and three cows, a ram and five ewes, besides poultry of four sorts, and a horse and a mare with Omai. At the Friendly Isles I left a bull and cow, a horse and mare, and some sheep; in which, I flatter myself that the laudable intention of the King and their Lordships have been fully answered.

"I left Omai at Huaheine; quitted the Society Isles the 9th of December; proceeded to the north, and in the lat. of 22° N., long. 200° E., fell in with a group of islands, inhabited by the same nation as Otaheite, and abounding with hogs and roots. After a short stay at these islands, continued our route for the coast of America, which we made on the 7th of last March; and on the 29th, after enduring several storms, got into a port in the lat. of 49¼° N. At this place, besides taking in wood and water, the Resolution was supplied with a new mizen-mast, fore top-mast, and her fore-mast got out and repaired.

"I put to sea again the 26th of April, and was no sooner out of port than we were attacked by a violent storm, which was the occasion of so much of the coast being passed unseen. In this gale the Resolution sprung a leak, which obliged me to put into a port in the lat. of 61°, long. 213° E. In a few days I was again at sea, and soon found we were on a coast where every step was to be considered, where no information could be had from maps, either modern or ancient; confiding too much in the former, we were frequently misled, to our no small hindrance. On an extensive coast, altogether unknown, it may be thought needless to say that we met with many obstacles before we got through the narrow strait that divides Asia from America, where the coast of the latter takes a N.E. direction. I followed it, flattered with the hopes of having at last overcome all difficulties, when, on the 17th of August, in lat. 70° 45', long. 198° E., we were stopped by an impenetrable body of ice, and had so far advanced between it and the land before we discovered it, that little was wanting to force us on shore.

"Finding I could no longer proceed along the coast, I tried what could be done farther out; but the same obstacles everywhere presented themselves, quite over to the coast of Asia, which we made on the 29th of the same month (August), in the lat. of 68° 55', long. 180½° E. As frost and snow, the forerunners of winter, began to set in, it was thought too late in the season to make a farther attempt

In the morning of the 22d we made an attempt to get to sea, with the wind at south-east, which miscarried. The following afternoon we were visited by one Jacob Ivanovitch Sopos-

for a passage this year in any direction, I therefore steered to the S.E., along the coast of Asia : passed the strait above mentioned, the narrow strait that divides Asia from America, and then stood over for the American coast, to clear up some doubts, and to search, but in vain, for a harbour to complete our wood and water. Wood is a very scarce article in all these northern parts; except in one place, there is none upon the sea coast but what is thrown ashore by the sea, some of which we got on board, and then proceeded to this place, where we had been before, to take in water. From hence I intend to proceed to Sandwich Islands ; that is, those discovered in 22° N. lat. After refreshing there, return to the north by the way of Kamtschatka ; and the ensuing summer, make another and final attempt to find a northern passage; but I must confess, I have little hopes of succeeding. Ice, though an obstacle not easily surmounted, is perhaps not the only one in the way.—The coasts of the two continents are flat for some distance off; and even in the middle, between the two, the depth of water is inconsiderable. This and some other circumstances, all tending to prove that there is more land in the Frozen Sea than as yet we know of, where the ice has its source ; and that the Polar part is far from being an open sea.

"There is another discouraging circumstance attending the navigating these northern parts, and that is the want of harbours, where a ship can occasionally retire to secure herself from the ice, or repair any damage she may have sustained. For a more particular account of the American coast, I beg leave to refer you to the enclosed chart, which is hastily copied from an original of the same scale.

"The reason of my not going to the harbour of St. Peter and St. Paul in Kamtschatka, to spend the winter, is the great dislike I have to lay inactive for six or eight months, while so large a part of the Northern Pacific Ocean remains unexplored, and the state and condition of the ships will allow me to be moving. Sickness has been little felt in the ships, and scurvy not at all. I have, however, had the misfortune to lose Mr. Anderson, my surgeon, who died of a lingering consumption two months ago, and one man some time before, of the dropsy ; and Captain Clerke had one drowned by accident, which are all we have lost since we left the Cape of Good Hope.

"Stores and provisions we have enough for twelve months and longer ; without a supply of both, will hardly be possible for us to remain in those seas ; but

nicoff, a Russian, who commanded a small vessel at Oomanak. This man had a great share of modesty and intelligence.

After we became acquainted with these Russians, some of our gentlemen, at different times, visited their settlement on the island, where they always met with a hearty welcome. This settlement consisted of a dwelling-house and two store-houses. And, besides the Russians, there was a number of the Kamtschadales, and of the natives, as servants or slaves to the former. Some others of the natives, who seemed independent of the Russians, lived at the same place. They all dwell in the same house, the Russians at the upper end, the Kamtschadales in the middle, and the natives at the lower end, where is fixed a large boiler for preparing their food, which consists chiefly of what the sea produces, with the addition of wild roots and berries.

As the island supplies them with food, so it does, in a great measure, with clothing. This consists chiefly of skins, and is perhaps the best they could have. The upper garment is made

whatever time we do remain shall be spent in the improvement of geography and navigation, by, Sir, your most obedient humble servant,
"JAMES COOK."

"Islands discovered in the voyage, not mentioned in this letter,—
Mangiá-nooe-nai-naiws, lat. 21° 57′ S., long. 201° 53′ E.
Wantien, ... ,, 20° 01′ S., ,, 201° 45′ E.
Toobooi, ... ,, 23° 25′ S., ,, 210° 24′ E.

"These three islands are inhabited. There is anchorage and good landing at the last, but not at the others.

"Christmas Island, lat. 1° 55′ N., long. 202° 40′ E., a low, barren, uninhabited island, with anchorage on the west side. It abounds with turtle, but has no fresh water.

"Besides these islands, we visited some not known before, between 19° and 20° S., adjoining to, and making part of, the Friendly Islands."—*Captain's Letters*, C. vol. 25.—*Admiralty Records, Whitehall.*

like our waggoner's frock, and reaches as low as the knee. Besides this, they wear a waistcoat or two, a pair of breeches, a fur cap, and a pair of boots, the soles and upper leathers of which are of Russian leather, but the legs are made of some kind of strong gut.

They make use of no paint, but the women puncture their faces slightly; and both men and women bore the under lip, to which they fix pieces of bone.

Their food consists of fish, sea animals, birds, roots, and berries, and even of sea-weed. They eat almost everything raw. Boiling and broiling were the only methods of cookery that I saw them make use of, and the first was probably learnt from the Russians.

I was once present when the Chief of Oonalashka made his dinner on the raw head of a large halibut, just caught, which he swallowed with as much satisfaction as we should do raw oysters. When he had done, the remains of the head were cut in pieces, and given to the attendants, who tore off the meat with their teeth, and gnawed the bones like so many dogs.

Their method of building is as follows:—They dig in the ground an oblong square pit, the length of which seldom exceeds fifty feet, and the breadth twenty; but in general the dimensions are smaller. Over this excavation they form the roof of wood which the sea throws ashore. This roof is covered first with grass, and then with earth, so that the outward appearance is like a dunghill. In the middle of the roof, towards each end, is left a square opening, by which the light is admitted: one of these openings being for this purpose only, and the other being also used to go in and out by, with the help of a ladder. Round the sides and ends of the huts, the families (for several are lodged together) have their separate apartments, where they sleep and sit at work, not upon benches, but in a kind of concave trench, which is dug all round the inside of the house, and covered with mats, so that this part is kept tolerably decent. But the middle of the house, which is common to all the families, is far otherwise; for, although it be covered with dry grass, it is a receptacle for dirt of every kind.

Their household furniture consists of bowls, spoons, buckets, piggins or cans, matted baskets, and perhaps a Russian kettle or pot. All these utensils are very neatly made, and well formed, and yet we saw no other tools among them but the knife and the hatchet. There are few, if any of them, that do not smoke, chew tobacco, and take snuff; a luxury that bids fair to keep them always poor.

I saw not a fire-place in any one of their houses. They are lighted, as well as heated, by lamps, which are simple, and yet answer the purpose very well. They are made of a flat stone, hollowed on one side like a plate, and about the same size, or rather larger. In the hollow part they put the oil, mixed with a little dry grass, which serves the purpose of a wick.

I have frequently remarked how nearly the natives, on this north-west side of America, resemble the Greenlanders and Esquimaux, in various particulars of person, dress, weapons, canoes, and the like. However, I was much less struck with this than with the affinity which we found subsisting between the dialects of the Greenlanders and Esquimaux, and those of Norton's Sound and Oonalashka. From which there is great reason to believe that all these nations are of the same extraction; and if so, there can be no doubt of there being a northern communication of some sort, by sea, between this west side of America and the east side, through Baffin's Bay; which communication, however, may be effectually shut up against ships by ice and other impediments. Such, at least, was my opinion at this time.

In the morning of Monday, the 26th of October, we put to sea from Samganoodha harbour. My intention was now to proceed to the Sandwich Islands, there to spend a few of the winter months, in case we should meet with the necessary refreshments, and then to direct our course to Kamtschatka, so as to endeavour to be there by the middle of May the ensuing summer. In consequence of this resolution, I gave Captain Clerke orders how to proceed in case of separation; appointing the Sandwich Islands for the first place of rendezvous, and the harbour of Petropaulowska in Kamtschatka for the second.

Nothing remarkable happened during our course. At daybreak on the 26th of November, land was seen extending from south south-east to west. We were now satisfied that the group of the Sandwich Islands had been only imperfectly discovered, as those which we had visited in our progress northward all lie to the leeward of our present station.

I bore up and ranged along the coast to the westward. It was not long before we saw people on several parts of the shore, and some houses and plantations. The country seemed to be both well wooded and watered.

At noon, seeing some canoes coming off to us, I brought to. We got from our visitors a quantity of cuttle-fish for nails and pieces of iron. They brought very little fruit and roots; but told us that they had plenty of them on their island, as also hogs and fowls. Having no doubt that the people would return to the ships next day with the produce of their country, I kept plying off all night, and in the morning stood close in shore. At first only a few of the natives visited us; but toward noon we had the company of a good many, who brought with them bread-fruit, potatoes, taro, or eddy roots, a few plantains, and small pigs; all of which they exchanged for nails and iron tools.

In the afternoon of the 30th, being off the north-east end of the island, several canoes came off to the ships. Most of these belonged to a chief named Terreeoboo, who came in one of them. He made me a present of two or three small pigs; and we got by barter from the other people a little fruit. After a stay of about two hours they all left us, except six or eight of their company, who chose to remain on board. A double sailing canoe came soon after to attend upon them, which we towed astern all night. In the evening we discovered another island to windward, which the natives call Owhyhee.

RETURN TO THE SANDWICH ISLANDS, DECEMBER 1778.

On the 1st of December, at eight in the morning, finding that we could fetch Owhyhee, I stood for it; and our visitors from another island, called Mowee, not chusing to accompany us, embarked in their canoe, and went ashore.

Next morning we were surprised to see the summits of the mountains on Owhyhee covered with snow. As we drew near the shore, some of the natives came off to us. They were a little shy at first, but we soon enticed some of them on board, and at last prevailed upon them to return to the island and bring off what we wanted.

Having procured a quantity of sugar-cane, and finding a strong decoction of it produced a very palatable beer, I ordered some more to be brewed for our general use. But when the cask was now broached, not one of my crew would even so much as taste it. I myself and the officers continued to make use of it whenever we could get materials for brewing it. A few hops, of which we had some on board, improved it much. It has the taste of new malt beer; and I believe no one will doubt of its being very wholesome. Yet my inconsiderate crew alleged that it was injurious to their health.

Every innovation whatever on board a ship, though ever so much to the advantage of seamen, is sure to meet with their highest disapprobation. Both portable soup and sour krout were at first condemned as stuff unfit for human beings. Few commanders have introduced into their ships more novelties, as useful varieties of food and drink, than I have done. It has, however, been in a great measure owing to various little deviations from established practice that I have been able to preserve my people, generally speaking, from that dreadful distemper, the scurvy, which has perhaps destroyed more of our sailors in their peaceful voyages than have fallen by the enemy in military expeditions.

I kept at some distance from the coast till the 13th, when I stood in again; and, after having had some trade with the natives who visited us, returned to sea.

At daybreak a dreadful surf breaking upon the shore, which was not more than half a league distant, made it evident that we had been in the most imminent danger. Nor were we yet in safety, the wind veering more easterly, so that for some time we did but just keep our distance from the coast. In the afternoon of the 20th, some of the natives came off in their canoes, bringing with them a few pigs and plantains. We continued trading with the people till four in the afternoon, when, having got a pretty good supply, we made sail and stretched off to the northward.

I had never met with a behaviour so free from reserve and

suspicion in my intercourse with any tribes of savages, as we experienced in the people of this island. It was very common for them to send up into the ship the several articles they brought off for barter; afterward, they would come in themselves, and make their bargains on the quarter-deck. The people of Otaheite, even after our repeated visits, do not care to put so much confidence in us.

On the 23d we tacked to the southward, and had hopes of weathering the island. We should have succeeded if the wind had not died away, and left us to the mercy of a great swell which carried us fast toward the land, which was not two leagues distant. At length some light puffs of wind which came with showers of rain, put us out of danger. While we lay as it were becalmed, several of the islanders came off with hogs, fowls, fruit, and roots.

At four in the afternoon, after purchasing everything that the natives had brought off, which was full as much as we had occasion for, we made sail and stretched to the north. At midnight we tacked and stood to the south-east. Upon a supposition that the "Discovery" would see us tack, the signal was omitted; but she did not see us, as we afterwards found, and continued standing to the north; for at daylight next morning she was not in sight. At six in the evening the southernmost extreme of the island bore south-west, the nearest shore seven or eight miles distant, so that we had now succeeded in getting to the windward of the island, which we had aimed at with so much perseverance.

The "Discovery," however, was not yet to be seen. But the wind as we had it, being very favourable for her to follow us, I concluded that it would not be long before she joined us.

We began to be in want of fresh provision on the 30th. At ten o'clock next morning we were met by the islanders with fruit and roots; but in all the canoes were only three small pigs.

Before daybreak the atmosphere was again loaded with heavy clouds; and the new year was ushered in with very hard rain, which continued at intervals till past ten o'clock. We lay to, trading with the inhabitants till three o'clock in the afternoon; when, having a tolerable supply, we made sail with a view of proceeding to look for the "Discovery."

The three following days were spent in running down the south-east side of the island.

On the 5th January 1779, in the morning, we passed the south point of the island. On this there stands a pretty large village, the inhabitants of which thronged off to the ship with hogs and women. It was not possible to keep the latter from coming on board. This part of the country, from its appearance, did not seem capable of affording any vegetables. Marks of its having been laid waste by the explosion of a volcano everywhere presented themselves: the devastation that it had made in this neighbourhood was visible to the naked eye.

Between ten and eleven next morning we saw with pleasure the "Discovery" coming round the south point of the island; and at one in the afternoon she joined us. Captain Clerke then coming on board, informed me that he had cruised four or five days where we were separated, and then plied round the east side of the island; but that, meeting with unfavourable winds, he had been carried to some distance from the coast. He had one of the islanders on board all this time, who had remained there from choice, and had refused to quit the ship, though opportunities had offered.

For several days we kept as usual standing off and on with occasional visits from the natives. At daybreak on the 16th, seeing the appearance of a bay, I sent Mr. Bligh with a boat from each ship to examine it, being at this time three leagues off. Canoes now began to arrive from all parts, so that before ten o'clock there were not fewer than a thousand about the two ships, most of them crowded with people, and well laden with hogs and other productions of the island. One of our visitors took out of the ship a boat's rudder. He was discovered, but too late to recover it. I thought this a good opportunity to show these people the use of firearms, and two or three muskets, and as many fourpounders, were fired over the canoe which carried off the rudder. As it was not intended that any of the shot should take effect, the surrounding multitude of natives seemed rather more surprised than frightened. In the evening Mr. Bligh returned, and reported that he had found a bay, in which was good anchorage and fresh water. Here I resolved to carry the ships to refit, and supply ourselves with every refreshment the place could afford. Numbers of our visitors request permission to sleep on board. Curiosity was not the only motive, at least with some; for the next morning several things were missing, which determined me not to entertain so many another night.

At eleven o'clock in the forenoon we anchored in the bay, which is called by the natives Karakakooa. The ships continued to be much crowded with natives, and were surrounded by a multitude of canoes. I had nowhere, in the course of my voyages, seen so numerous a body of people assembled at one place. For besides those in canoes, all the shore was covered with spectators, and many hundreds were swimming round the ships like shoals of fish. We could not but be struck with the singularity of this scene; few now lamented our having failed in our endeavours to find a northern passage homeward last summer. To this disappointment we owed our having it in our power to revisit the Sandwich Islands, and to enrich our voyage with a discovery which, though the last, seemed in many respects to be the most important that had hitherto been made by Europeans throughout the extent of the Pacific Ocean.

Here Captain Cook's Journal ends, January **1779.**

THE SANDWICH ISLANDS
CAPTAIN COOK'S LAST DISCOVERY
Scale of English Miles.

CHAPTER VIII.

The Closing Scene, January, February 1779.

While Captain Cook seems to have enjoyed the idea of this discovery, little did he imagine that his labours were so soon to be terminated at this disastrous place, which will ever derive a disgraceful immortality from his sad fate. Here his journal ends; and as we have recorded the principal events of his useful life, we shall detail the melancholy circumstances that led to his lamented death, preserving as nearly as possible the words of his amiable coadjutor Captain King, whose account of the voyage now commences.

Karakakooa Bay is situated on the west side of the island of Owhyhee, in a district called Akona. It is about a mile in depth, and bounded by two low points of land at the distance of half a league from each other. On the north point, which is flat and barren, stands the village of Kowrowa; and in the bottom of the bay, near a grove of tall cocoa-nut trees, there is another village of a more considerable size called Kakooa. This bay appearing to Captain Cook a proper place to refit the ships, and lay in an additional supply of water and provisions, we moored on the north side.

As soon as the inhabitants perceived our intention of anchoring in the bay, they came off from the shore in astonishing numbers, and expressed their joy by singing and shouting, and exhibiting a variety of wild and extravagant gestures.

Among the chiefs that came on board the "Resolution" was a young man called Pareea, whom we soon perceived to be a person of great authority. On presenting himself to Captain Cook, he told him that he was jakanee to the king of the island, who was at that time engaged on a military expedition at Mowee, and was expected to return within three or four days. A few presents from Captain Cook attached him entirely to our interests, and he became exceedingly useful to us in the management of his countrymen, as we had soon occasion to experience; for we had not been long at anchor, when it was observed that the "Discovery" had such a number of people hanging on one side, as occasioned her to heel considerably; and that the men were unable to keep off the crowds which continued pressing into her. Captain Cook being apprehensive that she might suffer some injury, pointed out the danger to Pareea, who immediately went to their assistance, cleared the ship of its incumbrances, and drove away the canoes that surrounded her.

The authority of the chiefs over the inferior people appeared, from this incident, to be of the most despotic kind. A similar instance of it happened the same day on board the "Resolution," where the crowd being so great as to impede the necessary business of the ship, we were obliged to have recourse to the assistance of Kaneena, another of their chiefs, who had likewise attached himself to Captain Cook. The inconvenience we laboured under being made known, he immediately ordered his countrymen to quit the vessel; and we were not a little surprised to see them jump overboard without a moment's hesitation.

Both these chiefs were men of strong and well-proportioned bodies, and of countenances remarkably pleasing; Kaneena, especially, was one of the finest men I ever saw. He was about six feet high, had regular and expressive features, with lively dark eyes; his carriage was easy, firm, and graceful.

The inhabitants had hitherto behaved with great fairness and honesty, but we now found the case exceedingly altered. The immense crowd of islanders which blocked up every part o the ships not only afforded frequent opportunity of pilfering, without risk of discovery, but our inferiority in number held forth a prospect of escaping with impunity in case of detection. Another circumstance to which we attributed this alteration in their behaviour, was the presence and encouragement of their chiefs; for generally tracing the booty into the possession of some men of consequence, we had the strongest reason to suspect that these depredations were committed at their instigation.

Soon after the "Resolution" had got into her station, our two friends Pareea and Kaneena brought on board a third chief, named Koah, who, we were told, was a priest, and had been in his youth a distinguished warrior. He was a little old man, of an emaciated figure ; his eyes exceedingly sore and red, and his body covered with a white leprous scurf, the effects of an immoderate use of the ava. Being led into the cabin, he approached Captain Cook with great veneration, and threw over his shoulders a piece of red cloth which he had brought along with him. Then stepping a few paces back, he made an offering of a small pig, which he held in his hand, whilst he pronounced a discourse that lasted for a considerable time.

When this ceremony was over, Koah dined with Captain Cook, eating plentifully of what was set before him ; but, like the rest of the inhabitants of the islands in these seas, could scarcely be prevailed on to taste a second time our wine or spirits. In the evening Captain Cook, attended by Mr. Bayly and myself, accompanied him on shore. We landed at the beach, and were received by four men who carried wands tipped with dog's hair, and marched before us, pronouncing with a loud voice a short sentence, in which we could only distinguish the word Orono.* The crowd which had been collected on the shore retired at our approach, and not a person was to be seen except a few lying prostrate on the ground, near the huts of the adjoining village.

* Captain Cook generally went by this name amongst the natives of Owhyhee ; but we could never learn its precise meaning, though it was certainly a title of religious veneration.

Before I proceed to relate the adoration that was paid to Captain Cook, and the peculiar ceremonies with which he was received on this fatal island, it will be necessary to describe a morai, or burying-place, situated at the south side of the beach at Kakooa. It was a square solid pile of stones, about forty yards long, twenty broad, and fourteen in height. The top was flat and well paved, and surrounded by a wooden rail, on which were fixed the skulls of the captives sacrificed on the death of their chiefs. In the centre of the area stood a ruinous old building of wood, connected with the rail on each side by a stone wall, which divided the whole space into two parts. On the side next the country were five poles, upwards of twenty feet high, supporting an irregular kind of scaffold; on the opposite side, toward the sea, stood two small houses, with a covered communication.

We were conducted by Koah to the top of this pile, by an easy ascent. At the entrance we saw two large wooden images, with features violently distorted, and a long piece of carved wood, of a conical form inverted, rising from the top of their heads; the rest was without form, and wrapped round with red cloth. We were here met by a tall young man with a long beard, who presented Captain Cook to the images; and after chanting a kind of hymn, in which he was joined by Koah, they led us to that end of the morai where the five poles were fixed. At the foot of them were twelve images, ranged in a semicircular form, and before the middle figure stood a high stand or table, on which lay a putrid hog, and under it pieces of sugar-cane, cocoa-nuts, bread-fruit, plantains, and sweet potatoes. Koah, having placed the Captain under the stand, took down the hog, and held it toward him; and after having a second time addressed him in a long speech, pronounced with much vehemence and rapidity, he let it fall on the ground, and led him to the scaffolding, which they began to climb together, not without great risk of falling. At this time we saw, coming in solemn procession, at the entrance of the top of the morai, ten men carrying a live hog, and a large piece of red cloth. Being advanced a few paces, they stopped, and prostrated themselves; and Kaireekeea, the young man above mentioned, went to them, and receiving the cloth, carried it to Koah, who wrapped it round the Captain and afterward offered him the hog, which was brought by Kaireekeea with the same ceremony.

Whilst Captain Cook was aloft, in this awkward situation, swathed round with red cloth, and with difficulty keeping his hold amongst the pieces of rotten scaffolding, Kaireekeea and Koah began their office, chanting sometimes in concert, and sometimes alternately. This lasted a considerable time; at length Koah let the hog drop, when he and the Captain descended together. He then led him to the images before mentioned, and having said something to each in a sneering tone, snapped his fingers at them as he passed, he brought him to that in the centre, which, from its being covered with red cloth, appeared to be in greater estimation than the rest. Before this figure he prostrated himself and kissed it, desiring Captain Cook to do the same, who suffered himself to be directed by Koah throughout the whole of this ceremony.

We were now led back into the other division of the morai, where there was a space ten or twelve feet square, sunk about three feet below the level of the area. Into this we descended, and Captain Cook was seated between two wooden idols, Koah supporting one of his arms, while I was desired to support the other. At this time arrived a second procession of natives carrying a baked hog and a pudding, some bread-fruit, cocoa-nuts, and other vegetables which were presented as before.

When this offering was concluded, the natives sat down, fronting us, and began to cut up the baked hog, to peel the vegetables, and break the cocoa-nuts, whilst others employed themselves in brewing the ava, which is done by chewing it in the same manner as at the Friendly Islands. Kaireekeea then took part of the kernel of a cocoa-nut which he chewed, and wrapped it in a piece of cloth, rubbed with it the captain's face, head, hands, arms, and shoulders. The ava was then handed round, and after we had tasted it, Koah and Pareea began to pull the flesh of the hog in pieces, and to put it into our mouths. I had no great objection to be fed by Pareea, who was very cleanly in his person; but Captain Cook, who was served by Koah, recollecting the putrid hog, could not swallow a morsel; and his reluctance, as may be supposed, was not diminished, when the old man, according to his own mode of civility, had chewed it for him.

When this last ceremony was finished, which Captain Cook put an end to as soon as he decently could, we quitted the morai, after distributing amongst the people some pieces of iron and other trifles, with which they seemed highly gratified. The men with wands conducted us to the boats, repeating the same words as before. The people again retired, and the few that remained, prostrated themselves as we passed along the shore. We immediately went on board, our minds full of what we had seen, and extremely well satisfied with the good dispositions of our new friends, whose respect to the person of Captain Cook seemed approaching to adoration.

The next morning I went on shore with a guard of eight marines, including the corporal and lieutenant, having orders to erect the observatory in such a situation as might best enable me to superintend and protect the waterers and the other working parties that were to be on shore. As we were viewing a spot conveniently situated for this purpose in the middle of the village, Pareea offered to pull down some houses that would have obstructed our observations. However, we thought it proper to decline this offer, and fixed on a field of sweet potatoes adjoining to the morai, which was readily granted us; and the priests, to prevent the intrusion of the natives, immediately consecrated the place by fixing their wands round the wall by which it was enclosed.

No canoes ever presumed to land near us; the natives sat on the wall, but none offered to come within the tabooed space, till he had obtained our permission. But though the men at our request would come across the field with provisions, yet not all our endeavours could prevail on the women to approach us. This circumstance afforded no small matter of amusement to our friends on board, where the crowds of people, and particularly of women that continued to flock thither, obliged them almost every hour to clear the vessel, in order to have room to do the necessary duties of the ship.

From the 19th to the 24th, when Pareea and Koah left us to attend Terreeoboo, who had landed on some other part of the island, nothing very material happened on board.

We had not been long settled at the observatory before we discovered in our neighbourhood the habitations of a society of priests, whose regular attendance at the morai had excited our curiosity. Their huts stood round a pond of water, and were surrounded by a grove of cocoa-nut trees, which separated them from the beach and the rest of the village, and gave the place an air of religious retirement. On my acquainting Captain Cook with these circumstances, he resolved to pay them a visit; and, as he expected, was received in the same manner as before.

During the rest of the time we remained in the bay, whenever Captain Cook came on shore he was attended by one of these priests, who went before him, giving notice that the Orono had landed, and ordering the people to prostrate themselves. The same person also constantly accompanied him on the water, standing in the bow of the boat with a wand in his hand, and giving notice of his approach to the natives who were in canoes, on which they immediately left off paddling, and lay down on their faces till he had passed.

The civilities of this society were not, however, confined to mere ceremony and parade. Our party on shore received from them every day a constant supply of hogs and vegetables more than sufficient for our subsistence; and several canoes loaded with provisions were sent to the ships with the same punctuality. No return was ever demanded, or even hinted at in the most distant manner. Their presents were made with a regularity more like the discharge of a religious duty than the effect of mere liberality.

We had not always so much reason to be satisfied with the conduct of the warrior-chiefs, or earees, as with that of our priests. In all our dealings with the former, we found them sufficiently attentive to their own interests; and besides their habit of stealing, which may admit of some excuse from the universality of the practice amongst the islanders of these seas, they make use of other artifices equally dishonourable.

On the 24th we were a good deal surprised to find that no canoes were suffered to put off from the shore, and that the natives kept close to their houses. After several hour's suspense, we learned that the bay was tabooed, and all intercourse with us interdicted, on account of the arrival of Terreeoboo. In the afternoon of next day, Terreeoboo visited the ships in a private manner, attended only by one canoe, in which were his wife and children. He stayed on board till near ten o'clock, when he returned to the village of Kowrowa.

The next day about noon, the king in a large canoe, attended by two others, set out from the village, and paddled toward the ship in great state. Their appearance was grand and magnificent. In the first canoe was Terreeoboo and his chiefs, dressed in their rich feathered cloaks and helmets, and armed with long spears and daggers; in the second came the venerable Kaoo, the chief of the priests and his brethren, with their idols displayed on red cloth. The third canoe was filled with hogs and various sorts of vegetables. As they went along, the priests in the centre canoe sung their hymns with great solemnity; and, after paddling round the ships, instead of going on board as we expected, they made toward the shore at the beach where we were stationed.

As soon as I saw them approaching, I ordered out our little guard to receive the king; and Captain Cook perceiving that he was going on shore, followed him, and arrived nearly at the same time. We conducted them into the tent, where they had scarcely been seated when the king rose up, and in a very graceful manner threw over the captain's shoulders the cloak he himself wore, put a feathered helmet upon his head, and a curious fan into his hand. He also spread at his feet five or six other cloaks, all exceedingly beautiful, and of the greatest value. His attendants then brought four very large hogs, with sugar-canes, cocoa-nuts, and bread-fruit; and this part of the ceremony was concluded by the king's exchanging names with Captain Cook, which, amongst all the islanders of the Pacific Ocean, is esteemed the strongest pledge of friendship. A procession of priests with a venerable old personage at their head, now appeared, followed by a long train of men leading large hogs, and others carrying plantains, sweet potatoes, etc. By the looks and gestures of Kaireekeea, I immediately knew the old man to be the chief of the priests on whose bounty we had so long subsisted. He had a piece of red cloth in his hands which he wrapped round Captain Cook's shoulders, and afterward presented him with a small pig in the usual form.

As soon as the formalities of the meeting were over, Captain Cook carried Terreeoboo, and as many chiefs as the pinnace could hold, on board the "Resolution." They were received with every mark of respect that could be shown them; and Captain Cook, in return for the feathered cloak, put a linen shirt on the king, and girt his own hanger round him. The ancient Kaoo, and about half a dozen more old chiefs remained on shore, and took up their abode at the priests' houses. During all this time not a canoe was seen in the bay, and the natives either kept within their huts, or lay prostrate on the ground.

The quiet and inoffensive behaviour of the natives having taken away every apprehension of danger, we did not hesitate to trust ourselves amongst them at all times, and in all situations. The officers of both ships went daily up the country in small parties, or even singly, and frequently remained out the whole night. It would be endless to recount all the instances of kindness and civility which we received upon those occasions.

Wherever we went, the people flocked about us, eager to offer every assistance in their power, and highly gratified if their services were accepted.

The satisfaction we derived from their gentleness and hospitality was, however, frequently interrupted by that propensity to stealing which they have in common with all the other islanders of these seas. This circumstance was the more distressing, as it sometimes obliged us to have recourse to acts of severity, which we should willingly have avoided, if the necessity of the case had not absolutely called for them.

On the 28th January, Captain Clerke, whose ill health confined him for the most part on board, paid Terreeoboo his first visit at his hut on shore. He was received with the same formalities as were observed with Captain Cook; and on his coming away, though the visit was quite unexpected, he received a present of thirty large hogs, and as much fruit and roots as his crew could consume in a week.

As we had not yet seen anything of their sports or athletic exercises, the natives, at the request of some of our officers, entertained us this evening with a boxing-match. Though these games were much inferior, as well in point of solemnity and magnificence, as in the skill and power of the combatants, to what we had seen exhibited at the Friendly Islands, yet, as they differed in some particulars, it may not be improper to give a short account of them. We found a vast concourse of people assembled on a level spot of ground, at a little distance from our tents. A long space was left vacant in the midst of them, at the upper end of which sat the judges, under three standards, from which hung slips of cloth of various colours, the skins of two wild geese, a few small birds, and bunches of feathers. When the sports were ready to begin, the signal was given by the judges, and immediately two combatants appeared. They came forward slowly, lifting up their feet very high behind and drawing their hands along the soles. As they approached, they frequently eyed each other from head to foot in a contemptuous manner, casting several arch looks at the spectators, straining their muscles, and using a variety of affected gestures. Being advanced within reach of each other, they stood with both arms held out strait before their faces, at which part all their blows were aimed. They struck in what appeared to our eyes an awkward manner, with a full swing of the arm, made no attempt to parry, but eluded their adversary's attack by an inclination of the body, or by retreating. The battle was quickly decided, for if either of them was knocked down, or even fell by accident, he was considered as vanquished, and the victor expressed his triumph by a variety of gestures, which usually excited, as was intended, a loud laugh among the spectators. As these games were given at our desire, we found it was universally expected that we should have borne our part in them; but our people, though much pressed by the natives, turned a deaf ear to their challenge, remembering full well the blows they got at the Friendly Islands.

This day died William Watman, a seaman of the gunner's crew, who, with the sincerest attachment, had followed Captain Cook's fortunes for a number of years.

At the request of the king of the island, he was buried on the morai, and the ceremony was performed with as much solemnity as our situation permitted.* Old Kaoo and his brethren

---

* May not this public display of the mortality of their visitors have tended to lessen the exalted ideas which the natives at first seemed to entertain ?

were spectators, and preserved the most profound silence and attention whilst the service was reading. When we began to fill up the grave, they approached it with great reverence, threw in a dead pig, some cocoa-nuts and plantains, and for three nights afterwards they surrounded it, sacrificing hogs, and performing their usual ceremonies of hymns and prayers, which continued till daybreak.

The ships being in great want of fuel, the Captain desired me, on the 2d of February, to treat with the priests for the purchase of the rail that surrounded the top of the morai. I must confess I had at first some doubt about the decency of this proposal, and was apprehensive that even the bare mention of it might be considered by them as a piece of shocking impiety. In this, however, I found myself mistaken. Not the smallest surprise was expressed at the application, and the wood was readily given, even without stipulating for anything in return.

Terreeoboo and his chiefs had, for some days past, been very inquisitive about the time of our departure. This circumstance had excited in me a great curiosity to know what opinion this people had formed of us, and what were their ideas respecting the cause and objects of our voyage. I took some pains to satisfy myself on these points, but could never learn anything farther than that they imagined we came from some country where provisions had failed, and that our visit to them was merely for the purpose of filling our bellies. Indeed, the meagre appearance of some of our crew, the hearty appetites with which we sat down to their fresh provisions, and our great anxiety to purchase and carry off as much as we were able, led them naturally enough to such a conclusion. It was ridiculous enough to see them stroking the sides and patting the bellies of the sailors (who were certainly much improved in the sleekness of their looks during our short stay in the island), and telling them, partly by signs and partly by words, that it was time for them to go, but if they should come again the next bread-fruit season, they should be better able to supply their wants. On our telling Terreeoboo we should leave the island the next day but one, we observed that a sort of proclamation was immediately made through the villages, to require the people to bring in their hogs and vegetables for the king to present to the Orono on his departure.

The next day being fixed for our departure, Terréeoboo invited Captain Cook and myself to attend him on the 3d, to the place where Kaoo resided. On our arrival, we found the ground covered with parcels of cloth, a vast quantity of red and yellow feathers tied to the fibres of cocoa-nut husks, and a great number of hatchets and other pieces of ironware that had been got in barter from us. At a little distance from these lay an immense quantity of vegetables of every kind, and near them was a very large herd of hogs. At first we imagined the whole to be intended as a present for us, till Kaireekeea informed me that it was a gift, or tribute from the people of that district to the king; and accordingly, as soon as we were seated, they brought all the bundles, and laid them severally at Terreeoboo's feet, who gave all the hogs and vegetables, and two-thirds of the cloth, to Captain Cook and myself. We were astonished at the value and magnitude of this present, which far exceeded everything of the kind we had seen, either at the Friendly or Society Islands.

The same day we quitted the morai, and got the tents and astronomical instruments on board. The charm of the taboo was now removed; and here I hope I may be permitted to relate a trifling occurrence, in which I was principally concerned. Having had the command of the party on shore, during the whole time we were in the bay, I had an opportunity of becoming well acquainted with the natives.

I spared no endeavours to conciliate their affections and gain their esteem; and had the good fortune to succeed so far, that, when the time of our departure was made known, I was strongly solicited to remain behind, not without offers of the most flattering kind. When I excused myself by saying that Captain Cook would not give his consent, they proposed that I should retire into the mountains, where they said they would conceal me, till after the departure of the ships; and on my farther assuring them that the Captain would not leave the bay without me, Terreeoboo and Kaoo waited upon Captain Cook, whose son they supposed I was, with a formal request that I might be left behind. The Captain, to avoid giving a positive refusal to an offer so kindly intended, told them that he could not part with me at that time, but that he should return to the island next year, and would then endeavour to settle the matter to their satisfaction.

Early in the morning of the 4th of February, we unmoored and sailed out of the bay, and were followed by a great number of canoes. Captain Cook's design was to finish the survey of Owhyhee before he visited the other islands, in hopes of meeting with a road better sheltered than the bay we had just left.

We had calm weather this and the following day, which made our progress to the northward very slow. In the morning of the 6th, having passed the westermost point of the island, we found ourselves abreast of a deep bay, called by the natives Toe-yah-yah. We had great hopes that this bay would furnish us with a safe and commodious harbour, as we saw to the northeast several fine streams of water. On examination, however, it was found unfit for our purpose.

After encountering some gales of wind with immaterial damage, on the 8th, at daybreak, we found that the foremast had given way. This accident induced Captain Cook to return to Karakakooa Bay. On the 10th, the weather became moderate, and a few canoes came off to us, from which we learnt that the late storm had done much mischief, and that several large canoes had been lost. During the remainder of the day we kept beating to windward, and before night we were within a mile of the bay; but not choosing to run on while it was dark, we stood off and on till daylight next morning, when we dropt anchor nearly in the same place as before.

We were employed the whole of the 11th, and part of the 12th, in getting out the foremast, and sending it, with the carpenters, on shore. As these repairs were likely to take up several days, Mr. Bayley and myself got the astronomical apparatus on shore on the 12th, and pitched our tents on the morai, having with us a guard of a corporal and six marines. We renewed our friendly correspondence with the priests, who, for the greater security of the workmen and their tools, tabooed the place where the mast lay, sticking their wands round it as before. The sailmakers were also sent on shore, to repair the damages which had taken place in their department during the late gales.

Upon coming to anchor, we were surprised to find our reception very different from what it had been on our first arrival; no shouts, no bustle, no confusion; but a solitary bay, with only here and there a canoe stealing close along the shore. The impulse of curiosity, which had before operated to so great a degree, might now, indeed, be supposed to have ceased; but the hospitable treatment we had invariably met with, and the friendly footing on which we parted, gave us some reason to expect that they would again have flocked about us with great joy on our return.

We were forming various conjectures upon the occasion of this extraordinary appearance, when our anxiety was at length relieved by the return of a boat which had been sent on shore, and brought us word that Terreeoboo was absent, and had left the bay under the taboo. Though this account appeared very satisfactory to most of us, yet others were of opinion that the interdiction of all intercourse with us, on pretence of the king's absence, was only to give him time to consult the chiefs in what manner it might be proper to treat us. Whether these suspicions were well founded, or the account given by the natives was the truth, we were never able to ascertain. For though it is not improbable that our sudden return, for which they could see no apparent cause, and the necessity of which we afterwards found it very difficult to make them comprehend, might occasion some alarm; yet the unsuspicious conduct of Terreeoboo, who, on his supposed arrival the next morning, came immediately to visit Captain Cook, and the consequent return of the natives to their former friendly intercourse with us, are strong proofs that they neither meant nor apprehended any change of conduct.

Toward the evening of the 13th, however the officer who commanded the watering party of the "Discovery" came to inform me that several chiefs had assembled at the well near the beach, driving away the natives, whom we had hired to assist the sailors in rolling down the casks to the shore. He told me at the same time that he thought their behaviour extremely suspicious, and that they meant to give him some farther disturbance. At his request, therefore, I sent a marine along with him, but suffered him to take only his side-arms. In a short time the officer returned, and on his acquainting me that the islanders had armed themselves with stones, and were grown very tumultuous, I went myself to the spot, attended by a marine, with his musket. Seeing us approach, they threw away their stones, and on my speaking to some of the chiefs, the mob were driven away, and those who chose it were suffered to assist in filling the casks.

Soon after our return to the tents, we were alarmed by a continued fire of muskets from the "Discovery," which we observed to be directed at a canoe that we saw paddling toward the shore in great haste, pursued by one of our small boats. We immediately concluded that the firing was in consequence of some theft, and Captain Cook ordered me to follow him with a marine armed, and to endeavour to seize the people as they came on shore. Accordingly we ran toward the place where we supposed the canoe would land, but were too late; the people having quitted it, and made their escape into the country before our arrival; but the goods stolen had been recovered.

During our absence a difference of a more serious and unpleasant nature had happened. The officer who had been sent in the small boat, and was returning on board with the goods which had been restored, observing Captain Cook and me engaged in the pursuit of the offenders, thought it his duty to seize the canoe, which was left drawn up on the shore. Unfortunately this canoe belonged to Pareea, who arriving at the same moment from on board the "Discovery," claimed his property with many protestations of his innocence. The officer refusing to give it up, and being joined by the crew of the pinnace, a scuffle ensued, in which Pareea was knocked down by a violent blow upon his head with an oar. The natives, who were collected about the spot, and had hitherto been peaceable spectators, immediately attacked our people with such a shower of stones as forced them to retreat with great precipitation, and swim off to a rock at some distance from the shore. The pinnace was immediately ransacked by the islanders; and but for the timely interposition of Pareea, who seemed to have recovered from the blow, and forgot it at the same instant, would soon have been entirely demolished. Having driven away the crowd, he made signs to our people that they might come and take possession of the pinnace, and that he would endeavour to get back the things which had been taken out of it. After their departure he followed them in his canoe with a midshipman's cap and some other trifling articles of the plunder, and with much apparent concern at what had happened, asked if the Orono would kill him, and whether he would permit him to come on board next day? On being assured that he should be well received, he joined noses (as their custom is) with the officers, in token of friendship, and paddled over to the village of Kowrowa.

When Captain Cook was informed of what had passed, he expressed much uneasiness at it, and, as we were returning on board, "I am afraid," said he, "that these people will oblige me to use some violent measures; for (he added) they must not be left to imagine that they have gained an advantage over us."

Next morning, the 14th, at daylight, I went on board the "Resolution" for the time-keeper, and in my way was hailed by the "Discovery," and informed that their cutter had been stolen during the night from the buoy where it was moored.

Third Voyage.

When I arrived on board I found the marines arming, and Captain Cook loading his double-barrelled gun. It had been his usual practice whenever anything of consequence was lost at any of the islands in this ocean, to get the king or some of the principal earees on board, and to keep them as hostages till it was restored. This method, which had been always attended with success, he meant to pursue on the present occasion.

It was between seven and eight o'clock when we quitted the ship together; Captain Cook in the pinnace, having Mr. Phillips and nine marines with him, and myself in the small boat. The last orders I received from him were, to quiet the minds of the natives on our side of the bay, by assuring them they should not be hurt; to keep my people together, and to be on my guard. We then parted; the Captain went toward Kowrowa, where the king resided, and I proceeded to the beach. My first care on going ashore was to give strict orders to the marines to remain within the tent, to load their pieces with ball, and not to quit their arms. Afterwards I took a walk to the huts of old Kaoo and the priests, and explained to them as well as I could the object of the hostile preparations, which had exceedingly alarmed them. I found that they had already heard of the cutter's being stolen, and I assured them, that though Captain Cook was resolved to recover it, and to punish the authors of the theft, yet that they, and the people of the village on our side, need not be under the smallest apprehension of suffering any evil from us. Kaoo asked me with great earnestness if Terreeoboo was to be hurt? I assured him he was not; and both he and the rest of his brethren seemed much satisfied with this assurance.

In the meantime Captain Cook having called off the launch, which was stationed at the north point of the bay, and taken it along with him, proceeded to Kowrowa, and landed with the lieutenant and nine marines. He immediately marched to the village, where he was received with the usual marks of respect, the people prostrating themselves before him, and bringing their accustomed offerings of small hogs. Finding that there was no suspicion of his design, his next step was to inquire for Terreeoboo, and the two boys, his sons, who had been his constant guests on board the "Resolution." In a short time the boys returned along with the natives, who had been sent in search of them, and immediately led Captain Cook to the house where the king had slept. They found the old man just awoke from sleep; and after a short conversation about the loss of the cutter, from which Captain Cook was convinced that he was in nowise privy to it, he invited him to return in the boat, and spend the day on board the "Resolution." To this proposal the king readily consented, and immediately got up to accompany him.

Things were in this prosperous train; the two boys being already in the pinnace, and the rest of the party having advanced near the waterside, when an elderly woman, called Kanee-kaba-reea, the mother of the boys, and one of the king's favourite wives, came after him, and with many tears and entreaties, besought him not to go on board. At the same time two chiefs, who came along with her, laid hold of him, and insisting that he should go no farther, forced him to sit down. The natives, who were collecting in prodigious numbers along the shore, and had probably been alarmed by the firing of the great guns, and the appearances of hostility in the bay, began to throng round Captain Cook and their king. In this situation, the lieutenant of marines observing that his men were huddled close together in the crowd, and thus incapable of using their arms, if any occasion should require it, proposed to the Captain to draw them up along the rocks close to the water's edge; and the crowd readily making way for them to pass, they were drawn up in a line at the distance of about thirty yards from the place where the king was sitting.

All this time the old king remained on the ground with the strongest marks of terror and dejection in his countenance; Captain Cook, not willing to abandon the object for which he had come on shore, continuing to urge him in the most pressing manner to proceed; whilst on the other hand, whenever the king appeared inclined to follow him, the chiefs, who stood round him, interposed, at first with prayers and entreaties, but afterwards having recourse to force and violence, insisted on his staying where he was. Captain Cook, therefore, finding that the alarm had spread too generally, and that it was in vain to think any longer of getting him off without bloodshed, at last gave up the point, observing to Mr. Phillips, that it would be impossible to compel him to go on board without running the risk of killing a great number of the inhabitants.

Though the enterprise which had carried Captain Cook on shore had now failed and was abandoned, yet his person did not appear to have been in the least danger, till an accident happened which gave a fatal turn to the affair. The boats, which had been stationed across the bay, having fired at some canoes that were attempting to get out, unfortunately had killed a chief of the first rank. The news of his death arrived at the village where Captain Cook was, just as he had left the king and was walking slowly toward the shore. The ferment it occasioned was very conspicuous; the women and children were immediately sent off, and the men put on their war mats, and armed themselves with spears and stones. One of the natives, having in his hands a stone and a long iron spike (which they called a pahooa), came up to the Captain, flourishing his weapon by way of defiance, and threatening to throw the stone. The Captain desired him to desist, but the man persisting in his insolence, he was at length provoked to fire a load of small shot. The man having his mat on, which the shot was not able to penetrate, this had no other effect than to irritate and encourage them. Several stones were thrown at the marines, and one of the earees attempted to stab Mr. Phillips with his pahooa, but failed in the attempt, and received from him a blow with the but-end of his musket. Captain Cook now fired his second barrel loaded with ball, and killed one of the foremost of the natives. A general attack with stones immediately followed, which was answered by a discharge of musketry from the marines and the people in the boats. The islanders, contrary to the expectations of every one, stood the fire with great firmness ; and before the marines had time to reload, they broke in upon them with dreadful shouts and yells. What followed was a scene of the utmost horror and confusion.

Four of the marines were cut off amongst the rocks in their retreat, and fell a sacrifice to the fury of the enemy ; three more were dangerously wounded, and the lieutenant, who had received a stab between the shoulders with a pahooa, having fortunately reserved his fire, shot the man who had wounded him just as he was going to repeat his blow. Our unfortunate commander, the last time he was seen distinctly, was standing at the water's edge, and calling out to the boats to cease firing and to pull in. Whilst he faced the natives none of them had offered him any violence, but having turned about to give his orders to the boats, he was stabbed in the back and fell with his face into the water. On seeing him fall, the islanders set up a great shout, and his body

Before the mariners had time to reload, the Islanders broke in upon them with dreadful shouts and yells, p. 358.

was immediately dragged on shore, and surrounded by the enemy, who, snatching the dagger out of each other's hands, showed a savage eagerness to have a share in his destruction.

Thus fell our great and excellent commander!

After a life of so much distinguished and successful enterprise, his death, as far as regards himself, cannot be reckoned premature, since he lived to finish the great work for which he seems to have been designed, and was rather removed from the enjoyment, than cut off from the acquisition of glory.* How sincerely his loss was felt and lamented by those who had so long found their general security in his skill and conduct, and every consolation under their hardships in his tenderness and humanity, it is neither necessary nor possible for me to describe, much less shall I attempt to paint the horror with which we were struck, and the universal dejection and dismay which followed so dreadful and unexpected a calamity.

It has been already related that four of the marines who attended Captain Cook were killed by the islanders on the spot. The rest, with Mr. Phillips their lieutenant, threw themselves into the water and escaped, under cover of a smart fire from the boats. On this occasion a remarkable instance of gallant behaviour, and of affection for his men, was shown by that officer. For he had scarcely got into the boat, when seeing one of the marines, who was a bad swimmer, struggling in the water, and in danger of being taken by the enemy, he immediately jumped into the sea to his assistance, though much wounded himself,

---

* So too may with truth be asserted of Sir John Franklin; he had finished the great work for which he seems to have been designed, and was the first to discover a north-west passage.

and after receiving a blow on the head from a stone, which had nearly sent him to the bottom, he caught the man by the hair and brought him safe off.

As soon as the general consternation which the news of this calamity occasioned throughout both crews had a little subsided, their attention was called to our party at the morai, where the mast and sails were on shore, with a guard of only six marines. It is impossible for me to describe the emotions of my own mind, during the time these transactions had been carrying on at the other side of the bay. Being at the distance only of a short mile from the village of Kowrowa, we could see distinctly an immense crowd collected on the spot where Captain Cook had just before landed. We heard the firing of the musketry, and could perceive some extraordinary bustle and agitation in the multitude. We afterwards saw the natives flying, the boats retire from the shore, and passing and repassing, in great stillness, between the ships. I must confess that my heart soon misgave me. Where a life so dear and valuable was concerned, it was impossible not to be alarmed by appearances both new and threatening.

My first care, on hearing the muskets fired, was to assure the people, who were assembled in considerable numbers round the wall of our consecrated field, and seemed equally at a loss with ourselves how to account for what they had seen and heard, that they should not be molested; and that, at all events, I was desirous of continuing on peaceable terms with them. We remained in this posture till the boats had returned on board, when Captain Clerke, observing through his telescope that we were surrounded by the natives, and apprehending they meant to attack us, ordered two four pounders to be fired at them. Fortunately these guns, though well aimed, did no mischief, and yet gave the natives a convincing proof of their power. One of the balls broke a cocoa-nut tree in the middle, under which a party of them were sitting; and the other shivered a rock that stood in an exact line with them. As I had just before given them the strongest assurances of their safety, I was exceedingly mortified at this act of hostility, and, to prevent a repetition of it, immediately despatched a boat to acquaint Captain Clerke that at present I was on the most friendly terms with the natives, and that, if occasion should hereafter arise for altering my conduct toward them I would hoist a jack as a signal for him to afford us all the assistance in his power.

We expected the return of the boat with the utmost impatience, and after remaining a quarter of an hour under the most torturing anxiety and suspense, our fears were at length confirmed by the arrival of Mr. Bligh with orders to strike the tents as quickly as possible, and to send the sails that were repairing on board. Just at the same moment, our friend Kaireekeea, having also received intelligence of the death of Captain Cook from a native who had arrived from the other side of the bay, came to me with great sorrow and dejection in his countenance to inquire if it was true.

Our situation was at this time extremely critical and important. Not only our own lives, but the event of the expedition, and the return of at least one of the ships, being involved in the same common danger. We had the mast of the "Resolution" and the greatest part of our sails on shore, under the protection of only six marines—their loss would have been irreparable; and though the natives had not as yet shown the smallest disposition to molest us, yet it was impossible to answer for the alteration which the news of the transaction at Kowrowa might produce. I therefore thought it prudent to dissemble my belief of the death of Captain Cook, and to desire Kaireekeea to discourage the report, lest either the fear of our resentment, or the successful example of their countrymen, might lead them to seize the favourable opportunity which at this time offered itself of giving us a second blow.

Having placed the marines on the top of the morai, which formed a strong and advantageous post, and left the command with Mr. Bligh, giving him the most positive directions to act entirely on the defensive, I went on board the "Discovery," in order to represent to Captain Clerke the dangerous situation of our affairs. As soon as I quitted the spot the natives began to annoy our people with stones, and I had scarcely reached the ship before I heard the firing of the marines. I therefore returned instantly on shore, where I found things growing every moment more alarming. The natives were arming and putting on their mats, and their numbers increased very fast. I could also perceive several large bodies marching towards us along the cliff which separates the village of Kakooa from the north side of the bay, where the village of Kowrowa is situated.

They began at first to attack us with stones from behind the walls of their inclosures, and finding no resistance on our part, they soon grew more daring. A few resolute fellows having crept along the beach under cover of the rocks, suddenly made their appearance at the foot of the morai, with a design, as it seemed, of storming it on the side next the sea, which was its only accessible part, and were not dislodged till after they had stood a considerable number of shot, and seen one of their party fall.

About this time, a strong reinforcement from both ships having landed, the natives retreated behind their walls; which giving me easy access to our friendly priests, I sent one of them to endeavour to bring their countrymen to some terms, and to propose to them that if they would desist from throwing stones I would not permit our men to fire. This truce was agreed to, and we were suffered to launch the mast and carry off the sails and our astronomical apparatus unmolested. As soon as we had quitted the morai they took possession of it, and some of them threw a few stones, but without doing us any mischief.

It was half an hour past eleven o'clock when I got on board the "Discovery," where I found no decisive plan had been adopted for our future proceedings. The restitution of the boat, and the recovery of the body of Captain Cook, were the objects which, on all hands, we agreed to insist on; and it was my opinion that some vigorous steps should be taken, in case the demand of them was not immediately complied with. However, after mature deliberation, it was determined to accomplish these points by conciliatory measures if possible.

In pursuance of this plan, it was determined that I should proceed toward the shore with the boats of both ships, well manned and armed, with a view to bring the natives to a parley, and, if possible, to obtain a conference with some of the chiefs.

I left the ships about four o'clock in the afternoon, and as we approached the shore I perceived every indication of a hostile reception. The whole crowd of natives was in motion, the women and children retiring, the men putting on their war-mats, and arming themselves with long spears and daggers. Concluding, therefore, that all attempts to bring them to a parley would be in vain unless I first gave them some ground for mutual confidence, I ordered the armed boats to stop, and went on in the small boat alone, with a white flag in my hand, which, by a general cry of joy from the natives, I had the satisfaction to find was instantly understood. The women immediately returned from the side of the hill whither they had retired, the men threw off their mats, and all sat down together by the water-side, extending their arms, and inviting me to come on shore.

Though this behaviour was very expressive of a friendly disposition, yet I could not help entertaining some suspicions of its sincerity. But when I saw Koah with a boldness and assurance altogether unaccountable, swimming off toward the boat with a white flag in his hand, I thought it necessary to return this mark of confidence, and therefore received him into the boat, though armed; a circumstance which did not tend to lessen my suspicions. I must confess I had long harboured an unfavourable opinion of this man. I told him that I had come to demand the body of Captain Cook, and to declare war against them unless it was instantly restored. He assured me that this should be done as soon as possible, and that he would go himself for that purpose; and after begging of me a piece of iron, with as much assurance as if nothing extraordinary had happened, he leaped into the sea and swam ashore, calling out to his countrymen that we were all friends again.

We waited near an hour with great anxiety for his return; during which time the rest of the boats had approached so near the shore as to enter into conversation with a party of the natives at some distance from us; by whom they were plainly given to understand that the body had been cut to pieces, and carried up the country; but of this circumstance I was not informed till our return to the ships.

After various delays, negotiations, and hostile preparations, about eight o'clock, it being very dark, a canoe was heard pad-

Third Voyage. 365

dling toward the ship; and as soon as it was seen, both the sentinels on deck fired into it. There were two persons in the canoe, and they immediately roared out "Tinnee" (which was the way in which they pronounced my name), and said they were friends, and had something for me belonging to Captain Cook. When they came on board, they threw themselves at our feet, and appeared exceedingly frightened. Luckily neither of them was hurt, notwithstanding the balls of both pieces had gone through the canoe. One of them was the person who constantly attended Captain Cook with the circumstances of ceremony already described; and who, though a man of rank in the island, could scarcely be hindered from performing for him the lowest offices of a menial servant. After lamenting with abundance of tears the loss of the Orono, he told us that he had brought us a part of his body. He then presented to us a small bundle wrapped up in cloth, which he brought under his arm; and it is impossible to describe the horror which seized us on finding in it a piece of human flesh about nine or ten pounds weight. This, he said, was all that remained of the body; that the rest was cut to pieces and burnt; but that the head and all the bones, except what belonged to the trunk, were in the possession of Terreeoboo. and the other earees; that what we saw had been allotted to Kaoo, the chief of the priests, to be made use of in some religious ceremony, and that he had sent it as a proof of his innocence and attachment to us.

This afforded an opportunity of informing ourselves whether they were cannibals, and we did not neglect it. They immediately showed as much horror at the idea as any European would have done, and asked, very naturally, if that was the custom amongst us. They afterwards asked us, with great earnestness and apparent apprehension, " When the Orono would come again, and what he would do to them on his return ?" The same inquiry was frequently made afterwards by others ; and this idea agrees with the general tenor of their conduct towards him, which showed that they considered him as a being of a superior nature.

We pressed our two friendly visitors to remain on board till morning, but in vain. They told us that if this transaction should come to the knowledge of the king or chiefs it might be attended with the most fatal consequences to their whole society; in order to prevent which, they had been obliged to come off to us in the dark, and the same precaution would be necessary in returning on shore. They informed us farther that the chiefs were eager to revenge the deaths of their countrymen, and particularly cautioned us against trusting Koah, who, they said, was our mortal and implacable enemy, and desired nothing more ardently than an opportunity of fighting us.

We learned from these men that seventeen of their countrymen were killed in the first action at Kowrowa, of whom five were chiefs ; and that Kaneena and his brother, our very particular friends, were unfortunately of that number. Eight, they said, were killed at the observatory, three of whom were also of the first rank.

During the remainder of this night, we heard loud howling and lamentations. Early in the morning we received another visit from Koah. I must confess I was a little piqued to find that, notwithstanding the most evident marks of treachery in his conduct, and the positive testimony of our friends the priests, he should still be permitted to carry on the same farce, and to make us appear to be the dupes of his hypocrisy. Indeed our situation was become extremely awkward and unpromising; none of the purposes for which this pacific course of proceeding had been adopted having hitherto been in the least forwarded by it.

This day a man had the audacity to come within musket-shot ahead of the ship, and after flinging some stones at us, he waved Captain Cook's hat over his head, whilst his countrymen on shore were exulting and encouraging his boldness. Our people were all in a flame at this insult, and coming in a body on the quarter-deck, begged they might no longer be obliged to put up with these repeated provocations, and requested me to obtain permission for them from Captain Clerke to avail themselves of the first fair occasion of revenging the death of their commander. On my acquainting him with what was passing, he gave orders for some great guns to be fired at the natives on shore, and promised the crew, that if they should meet with any molestation at the watering-place the next day, they should then be left at liberty to chastise them.

It is somewhat remarkable, that before we could bring our guns to bear, the islanders had suspected our intentions from the stir they saw in the ship, and had retired behind their houses and walls. We were therefore obliged to fire in some measure at random; notwithstanding which, our shots produced all the effects that could have been desired; for soon after, we saw Koah paddling toward us with extreme haste, and on his arrival we learned that some people had been killed, and amongst the rest Maiha-maiha, a principal chief, and a near relation to the king.

At night the usual precautions were taken for the security of the ships; and as soon as it was dark, our two friends, who had visited us the night before, came off again. They assured us, that though the effect of our great guns this afternoon had terrified the chiefs exceedingly, they had by no means laid aside their hostile intentions, and advised us to be on our guard.

The next morning the boats of both ships were sent ashore for water; and the "Discovery" was warped close to the beach, in order to cover that service. We soon found that the intelligence which the priests had sent us was not without foundation, and that the natives were resolved to take every opportunity of annoying us, when it could be done without much risk.

Throughout all this group of islands, the villages, for the most part, are situated near the sea, and the adjacent ground is enclosed with stone walls, about three feet high. They consist of loose stones, and the inhabitants are very dexterous in shifting them with great quickness to such situations as the direction of the attack may require. In the sides of the mountain which hangs over the bay, they have also little holes or caves, of considerable depth, the entrance of which is secured by a fence of the same kind. From behind both these defences the natives kept perpetually harassing our waterers with stones; nor could the small force we had on shore, with the advantage of muskets, compel them to retreat.

In this exposed situation our people were so taken up in attending to their own safety, that they employed the whole forenoon in filling only one ton of water. As it was therefore impossible to perform this service till their assailants were driven to a greater distance, the "Discovery" was ordered to dislodge them with her great guns; which being effected by a few discharges, the men landed without molestation. However, the natives soon after made their appearance again in their usual mode of attack; and it was now found absolutely necessary to burn down some straggling houses near the wall, behind which they had taken shelter. In executing these orders, I am sorry to add, that our people were hurried into acts of unnecessary cruelty and devastation.

Their orders were only to burn a few straggling huts which afforded shelter to the natives. We were therefore a good deal surprised to see the whole village on fire; before a boat, that was sent to stop the progress of the mischief, could reach the shore, the houses of our old and constant friends, the priests, were all in flames. I cannot enough lament the illness that confined me on board this day. The priests had always been under my protection.

Several of the natives were shot in making their escape from the flames; and our people cut off the heads of two of them and brought them on board. The fate of one poor islander was much lamented by us all. As he was coming to the well for water, he was shot at by one of the marines. The ball struck his calibash, which he immediately threw from him and fled. He was pursued into one of the caves I have before described, and no lion could have defended his den with greater courage and fierceness, till at last, after having kept two of our people at bay for a considerable time, he expired covered with wounds.

Soon after the village was destroyed, we saw, coming down the hill, a man, attended by fifteen or twenty boys, holding pieces of white cloth, green boughs, plantains, etc., in their hands. As they approached nearer, it was found to be our much esteemed friend Kaireekeea, who had fled on our first setting fire to the village, and had now returned, and desired to be sent on board the "Resolution."

When he arrived we found him exceedingly grave and

thoughtful. We endeavoured to make him understand the necessity we were under of setting fire to the village, by which his house, and those of his brethren, were unintentionally consumed. He expostulated a little with us on our want of friendship, and on our ingratitude. And, indeed, it was not till now that we learnt the whole extent of the injury we had done them. He told us that, relying on the promises I had made them, and the assurances they had afterwards received from the men who had brought us the remains of Captain Cook, they had not removed their effects back into the country, with the rest of the inhabitants, but had put everything that was valuable of their own, as well as what they had collected from us, into a house close to the morai, where they had the mortification to see it all set on fire by ourselves.

On coming on board he had seen the heads of his countrymen lying on the deck, at which he was exceedingly shocked, and desired with great earnestness that they might be thrown overboard. This request Captain Clerke instantly ordered to be complied with.

In the evening the watering party returned on board, having met with no further interruption. We passed a gloomy night, the cries and lamentations we heard on shore being far more dreadful than ever. Our only consolation was, the hope that we should have no occasion in future for a repetition of such severities.

The natives being at last convinced that it was not the want of ability to punish them which had hitherto made us tolerate their provocations, desisted from giving us any farther molestation; and in the evening, a chief called Eappo, who had seldom visited us, but whom we knew to be a man of the very first consequence, came with presents from Terreeoboo to sue for peace. These presents were received, and he was dismissed with the same answer which had before been given, that until the remains of Captain Cook should be restored, no peace would be granted. We learned from this person, that the flesh of all the bodies of our people, together with the bones of the trunks, had been burnt; that the limb bones of the marines had been divided amongst the inferior chiefs; and that those of Captain Cook had been disposed of in the following manner:—The head to a great chief called Kahoo-opeon, the hair to Maiha-maiha, and the legs, thighs, and arms to Terreeoboo.

Between ten and eleven o'clock on the 20th, we saw a great number of people descending the hill which is over the beach, in a kind of procession, each man carrying a sugar-cane or two on his shoulders, and bread-fruit, taro, and plantains in his hand. They were preceded by two drummers, who, when they came to the waterside, sat down by a white flag, and began to beat their drums, while those who had followed them advanced one by one; and having deposited the presents they had brought, retired in the same order. Soon after, Eappo came in sight, in his long feathered cloak, bearing something with great solemnity in his hands; and having placed himself on a rock, he made signs for a boat to be sent him.

Captain Clerke, conjecturing that he had brought the bones of Captain Cook, which proved to be the fact, went himself in the pinnace to receive them; and ordered me to attend him in the cutter. When we arrived at the beach, Eappo came into the pinnace, and delivered to the Captain the bones wrapped up in a large quantity of fine new cloth, and covered with a spotted cloak of black and white feathers. He afterwards attended us to the "Resolution," but could not be prevailed upon to go on board; probably not choosing, from a sense of decency, to be present at the opening of the bundle. We found in it both the hands of Captain Cook entire, which were well known from a remarkable scar on one of them, that divided the thumb from the forefinger, the whole length of the metacarpal bone; the skull, but with the scalp separated from it, and the bones that form the face wanting; the scalp with the hair upon it cut short, and the ears adhering to it; the bones of both arms, with the skin of the forearms hanging to them; the thigh and leg bones joined together, but without the feet. The ligaments of the joints were entire; and the whole bore evident marks of having been in the fire, except the hands, which had the flesh left upon them, and were cut in several places, and crammed with salt, apparently with an intention of preserving them. The scalp had a cut in the back part of it, but the skull was free from any fracture. The lower jaw and feet, which were wanting, Eappo told us had been seized by different chiefs, and that Terreeoboo was using every means to recover them.

The next morning Eappo and the king's son came on board, and brought with them the remaining bones of Captain Cook; the barrels of his gun, his shoes, and some other trifles that belonged to him. Eappo took great pains to convince us that Terreeoboo, Maiha-maiha, and himself, were most heartily desirous of peace; that they had given us the most convincing proof of it in their power; and that they had been prevented from giving it sooner by the other chiefs, many of whom were still our enemies. We found the cutter had been broken up.

Nothing now remained but to perform the last offices to our great and unfortunate commander. Eappo was dismissed with orders to taboo all the bay; and in the afternoon, the bones having been put into a coffin, and the service read over them, they were committed to the deep with the usual military honours. What our feelings were on this occasion, I leave the world to conceive; those who were present know that it is not in my power to express them.

During the forenoon of the 22d, not a canoe was seen paddling in the bay; the taboo, which Eappo had laid on it the day before, at our request, not being yet taken off. At length Eappo came off to us. We assured him that we were now entirely satisfied; and that as the Orono was buried, all remembrance of what had passed was buried with him. We afterwards desired him to take off the taboo, and to make it known that the people might bring their provisions as usual. The ships were soon surrounded with canoes, and many of the chiefs came on board, expressing great sorrow at what had happened, and their satisfaction at our reconciliation. Several of our friends, who did not visit us, sent presents of large hogs and other provisions. Amongst the rest came the old treacherous Koah, but was refused admittance.

As we had now everything ready for sea, about 'eight o'clock this evening we dismissed all the natives; Eappo, and the friendly Kaireekeea, took an affectionate leave of us. We immediately weighed and stood out of the bay. The natives were collected on the shore in great numbers; and as we passed along, received our last farewells with every mark of affection and good-will.

As every minute particular regarding the death of Captain Cook, and of the events which led to it, is of the deepest interest, the Editor, at the risk of repetition, subjoins an extract from the remarks of Captain Clerke, who succeeded to the command of the expedition, written at the time on board the "Resolution," and obtained from the Records of the Admiralty. They will be found to corroborate the account given of this lamentable transaction by Captain King.

"REMARKS ON BOARD HIS MAJESTY'S SLOOP THE 'RESOLUTION' AT OIOHY'HE.

"*Sunday,* 14*th February* 1779.

"Ever since our arrival here, upon this our second visit, we have observed in the natives a stronger propensity to theft than we had reason to complain of during our former stay; every day produced more numerous and more audacious depredations. To-day they behaved so ill on board the 'Discovery,' that I was obliged to order them all out of the ship, which I find was likewise the case on board the 'Resolution.' None but the principal people were suffered on board. However, we let them lay alongside in their canoes, and amuse themselves as they thought proper. In the afternoon, I had a present of a cloak and a hog from Terri'aboo, who, with his retinue, made me a visit. In the evening they left the ship, and soon after a principal aree, whose name was Per'rare, called on board. During my stay in the cabin with them, a rascal by some means got up the ship's side, ran across the deck in the face of everybody there, snatched the armourer's tongs, together with a chisel, and jumped overboard. This was done so instantaneously, that the fellow was in the water before our people well saw what the fellow was about. A canoe immediately took him in, and made for shore. I heard the alarm, ran upon deck, and, being made acquainted with the business, ordered the people to fire at them. At the same time, Mr. Edgar, the Master, put off in the small cutter, in chase of the canoe, which was presently out of the reach of our muskets. However, as I saw the 'Resolution's' pinnace join the chase, and Captain Cook run along shore to intercept the fellow's landing, I concluded it impossible for him to escape all; and the closing of the evening preventing a farther prospect of the business, I was very easy, expecting soon to have the boat back, with the tongs, etc.; but it was near eight before Mr. Edgar returned, and then with such a story as I was a good deal hurt at. In the first place, Captain Cook was led altogether out of the way by those who undertook to be his guides. The pinnace and cutter pursued and ran the canoe where the culprit had taken refuge on shore, when the stolen goods were brought off and returned them; but Mr. Edgar, thinking some punishment ought to be inflicted for such infamous conduct, he seized the canoe which brought off the thief. The boat happened to be that of Per'rare's that had brought him on board, and was waiting his pleasure whilst he was with me in the cabin. This looks very suspicious in Mr.

Per'rare ; but if he did give countenance to these thefts, he added shameful ingratitude to his perfidy, for I had at various times been very attentive and liberal to him. However, he left me soon after the theft had been committed, with a promise of a speedy return with the plunder, which, to do him justice, he had frequently in these cases retrieved for me. He reached the shore as soon as our boat, when, finding his own canoe in danger, he strenuously opposed the seizure, and soon raised too numerous a mob for our boat's crew to deal with ; who not readily giving up their capture, were warmly attacked by Per'rare and his gang he had mustered, with stones, clubs, etc. It unfortunately happened that both the boats were destitute of fire-arms (our friendly connections having lulled us into too great security), and of course had nothing more than equal weapons to repel this attack, the consequence of which was a defeat, being overpowered by numbers ; and after receiving many hard thumps, were glad to get their own boats off, with half their oars broke, lost, etc. This was an unfortunate stroke as matters now stood, as it increased the confidence of these people, which before was too much bordering upon insolence.

"In the morning, at daybreak, Lieutenant Burney, who was the officer of the watch, acquainted me that the large cutter was taken from the buoy where we had moored and sunk her, to prevent the heat of the sun, which is very powerful, from renting the plank. Upon examining part of her moorings that was left upon the buoy, and was a four inch rope, I found plainly that it had been cut by some instrument or other, which clearly evinced she must have been taken away by the Indians, with which circumstance I directly waited upon Captain Cook, and made him acquainted ; and, after some conversation on the subject, he proposed that his boats should go to the N. W. point of the bay, and mine to the S. E. point, to prevent any canoe going away, and if any attempted it, to drive them on shore ; for he said he would seize them all, and made no doubt but to redeem them they would very readily return the boat again. It was now between six and seven o'clock in the morning. I returned on board to put these orders into execution, and sent Lieutenant Rickman with the launch and small cutter, with their crews and some marines, well armed, to the station Captain Cook had assigned them. I soon after took the jolly boat (which now was the only boat I had left), and came to the 'Resolution,' with an intention of having some more discourse with Captain Cook upon this business ; but when I came near the ship, Lieutenant Gore told me that Captain Cook was gone with his pinnace, launch, and small cutter, to a town situated just within the N. W. point, where King Terre'boo and the major part of the people of consequence then resided, upon which I returned to my ship, concluding, as Captain Cook was gone to the king, matters would soon be settled, for we were as yet by no means on bad terms either with arees or anybody else. There were at this time many small canoes trading about the ships. Soon after I got on board, I observed some muskets discharged from my launch and small cutter, upon which I sent the jolly boat to know how matters went, and orders to Lieutenant Rickman, if he had made any seizures of canoes, to send them to the ship by the jolly boat.

"It was now just eight o'clock, when we were alarmed by the discharge of a volley of small arms from Captain Cook's people, and a violent shout of the Indians. With my glass I clearly saw that our people were drove off to their boats, but I could not distinguish persons in that confused crowd. The pinnace and launch, however, continued the fire, and the 'Resolution,' who was near enough to throw her shot on shore, fired her cannon among them. Thus circumstanced, without any boat to go to their assistance, and, consequently, destitute of all means of rendering them any kind of service, I was obliged to wait the return of these engaged boats to hear the event of these unhappy differences. The crews having fired away their ammunition, returned to the 'Resolution,' and Lieutenant Williamson, who commanded them upon this duty, soon after came on board the 'Discovery' with the melancholy account that Captain Cook and four marines had fallen in this confounded fray, and that the rest of the marines who were on shore were with difficulty saved, three of whom were much wounded, particularly Mr. Phillips, the lieutenant, who was a good deal bruised by blows of stones, and had received a deep stab with an iron pike in his shoulder. I immediately went on board the 'Resolution,' sent a strong party of people to protect the astronomers at their tents, and carpenters who were at work upon the mast on the eastern side of the bay, and received from Lieutenant Phillips, who, with his marines, was on shore and present throughout the whole with Captain Cook, the following account:—

"'Captain Cook landed at the town situated within the N. W. point with his pinnace and launch, leaving the small cutter off the point to prevent the escape of any canoes that might be disposed to get off. At his landing, he ordered nine marines, which he had in the boats, and myself on shore to attend him, and immediately marched into the town, where he inquired for Terre'aboo and the two boys (his sons, who had lived principally with Captain Cook on board the 'Resolution' since Terre'aboo's first arrival among us). Messengers were immediately dispatched, and the two boys soon came, and conducted us to their father's house. After waiting some time on the outside, Captain Cook doubted the old gentleman being there, and sent me in that I might inform him. I found our old acquaintance just awoke from sleep; when, upon my acquainting him that Captain Cook was at the door, he very readily went with me to him.

Captain Cook, after some little conversation, observed that Terre'aboo was quite innocent of what had happened, and proposed to the old gentleman to go on board with him, which he readily agreed to, and we accordingly proceeded toward the boats, but having advanced near to the water side, an elderly woman, whose name was Kar'na'cub'ra, one of his wives, came to him, and with many tears and entreaties, begged he would not go on board; at the same time, two chiefs laid hold of him, and insisting that he should not, made him sit down: the old man now appeared dejected and frightened. It was at this period we first began to suspect that they were not very well disposed towards us, and the marines being huddled together in the midst of an immense mob, composed of at least two or three thousand people, I proposed to Captain Cook that they might be arranged in order along the rocks by the water side, which he approving of, the crowd readily made way for them, and they were drawn up accordingly. We now clearly saw they were collecting their spears, etc.; but an awful rascal of a priest was singing and making a ceremonious offering to the Captain and Terre'aboo, to divert their attention from the manœuvres of the surrounding multitude. Captain Cook now gave up all thoughts of taking Terre'aboo on board, with the following observations to me—' We can never think of compelling him to go on board without killing a number of these people,' and I believe was just going to give orders to embark, when he was interrupted by a fellow armed with a long iron spike, which they call a pah'hoo'ah, and a stone. This man made a flourish with his pah'hoo'ah, and threatened to throw his stone, upon which Captain Cook discharged a load of small shot at him; but he having his mat on, the small shot did not penetrate it, and had no other effect than farther to provoke and encourage them. I could not observe the least fright it occasioned. Immediately upon this an aree, armed with a pah'hoo'ah, attempted to stab me, but I foiled his attempt by giving him a severe blow with the but end of my musket. Just at this time they began to throw stones, and one of the marines was knocked down. The Captain then fired a ball and killed a man. They now made a general attack, and the Captain gave orders to the marines to fire, and afterwards called out, 'Take to the boats.' I fired just after the Captain, and loaded again whilst the marines fired. Almost instantaneously upon my repeating the orders to take to the boats, I was knocked down by a stone, and in rising received a stab with a pah'hoo'ah in the shoulder; my antagonist was upon the point of seconding his blow, when I shot him dead. The business now was a most miserable scene of confusion. The shouts and yells of the Indians far exceeded all the noise I ever came in the way of. These fellows, instead of retiring upon being fired upon, as Captain Cook and I believe most people concluded they would, acted so very contrary a part, that they never gave the soldiers time to re-load their pieces, but immediately broke in upon and would have killed every man of them, had not the boats by a smart fire kept them a little off, and picked up those who were not too much wounded to reach them. After being knocked down I saw no more of Captain Cook. All my people I observed were totally vanquished, and endeavouring to save their lives by getting to the boats. I therefore scrambled as well as I could into the water, and made for the pinnace, which I fortunately got hold of, but not before I received another blow from a stone just above the temple, which, had not the pinnace been very near, would have sent me to the bottom.' This is the substance of Lieutenant Phillips' relation of this most unfortunate event, to which I must add one circumstance more in justice to his gallantry and attention. He had not been many minutes in the boat, and of course scarcely recovered from the disagreeable sensations occasioned by the pah'hoo'ah and stones, when he saw one of his marines, who was but a very poor swimmer, and now farther disabled by wounds, just upon the point of sinking. He immediately jumped overboard again, caught the man by his hair, and brought him to the boat. Far the major part of these pah'hoo'ahs, with which many of the arees are now armed, and is their most deadly weapon, were furnished them by ourselves. The arees always seemed very desirous of them, and we troubled ourselves very little about the use they proposed them for. Old Terre'aboo got two from Captain Cook, and one from me, no longer than yesterday evening. Some time before the attack was made, intelligence was brought from the other side of the bay that the boats there, under the command of Lieutenant Rickman, had killed a man who was somewhat of an aree, which our people observed in some degree to disconcert them, but this was some time before they proceeded to violent measures. How the unhappy business was brought about is very hard to determine; to all appearance it was by no means a premeditated plan. On the part of Terre'aboo, if we consider his conduct throughout, we must acquit him of any bad intentions. His son, the young prince Ka'oo'ah, was sitting in the pinnace with Mr. Roberts, one of the mates (who then commanded her), with intention of coming off to the ship, at the time the first gun was fired by Captain Cook. The poor boy said he was frightened, and begged to be put on shore, which was immediately complied with. As to their being armed with their pah'hoo'ahs it was always the case; those who had them were so proud of the acquisition, that they never went anywhere without them; and as to their stones, nature has furnished them most abundantly in every part of their country. Upon the whole, I firmly believe matters would not have been carried to the extremities they were, had not Captain Cook attempted to chastise a man in the midst of this multitude, firmly believing, as his last resource in case of necessity, that the fire of his marines would undoubtedly disperse them. This idea was certainly founded upon great experience among various nations of Indians, in different parts of the world, but the unhappy event of to-day proved it in this case, however, fallacious. One very strong argument that they would not have proceeded thus had not Captain Cook first unfortunately fired, is, that but a very few minutes before the fray began, they readily cleared a way for the marines to march down to the water side, just by where the boats lay (as I have observed), had Captain Cook then been disposed to go off. Mr. Phillips is of opinion, from all appearance at that time, they would have given him no interruption. Now, had they been previously determined upon the ensuing business, the attack upon the marines would have been made with more safety to themselves, and efficacy to their cause, when in the midst of the mob than when they were properly drawn up; this was too obvious an advantage to escape their sagacity. As to their collecting their spears, etc., as Mr. Phillips observed, some time previous to the attack, he is of opinion, and I think very justly, that this arose from an apprehension that some force might be used in getting Terre'aboo to the ship, which I believe they were determined to oppose to the last extremity. However, be these matters as they may, the unfortunate business was now done, and it behoved me to take the most effectual method I could suggest to prevent more. As I before observed, I sent a strong party of people, which were commanded by Lieutenant King, to the eastern side of the bay to defend the astronomers and the carpenters at work upon the fore-mast. I soon observed a vast concourse of the natives assembling near them, when by a spring upon the 'Discovery's' cable, I was enabled to throw her four-pounders about their quarters, being well within distance, which in a great measure dispersed the association; but I could not do it effectually, they had such retreats behind a number of stone walls with which their villages and all parts adjacent abound, and which I now suppose are purposed as a place of retirement when annoyed by the enemy. The vast numbers of people I observed collecting in various parts of the bay, and the resolution they had displayed in the attack, as represented by the Lieutenants Williamson and Phillips, rendered them, I thought, rather a formidable enemy, and that the safest and best method we could take would be to get everything from the shore to the ships, where we could work at our leisure, and they could not possibly annoy us without inevitable destruction to themselves. I therefore ordered the observatories and fore-mast to be got off with all expedition. I make no doubt but we might have protected these matters on shore with a good stout party, but they would have been continually harassed, and the work impeded; and had any unlucky accident gained them the possession of the fore-mast, though only for a few minutes, we should have been totally ruined in respect to another Northern campaign, which is certainly now my principal object to forward. Our party on shore, under Lieutenant King, were arranged on an eminence that the natives had thrown up for a morai, which gave them great advantages, as they commanded every thing around them ; the Indians, however, made two or three attacks with stones thrown from slings, but they were immediately repulsed with the loss, in the whole, of ten or twelve men ; indeed they could not collect themselves to a formidable body for the fire of the 'Discovery.' By noon we had got all our men and other matters on board and the fore-mast alongside : with our glasses we could clearly see the Indians busied in conveying the dead bodies over a hill up the country, I cannot here help lamenting my own unhappy state of health, which is sometimes so bad as hardly to suffer me to keep the deck, and, of course, farther incapacitates me for the succeeding so able a navigator as my honoured friend and predecessor ; however, here are very able officers, and I trust, with a firm dependence upon Providence, that with their assistance I may be able to prosecute the remaining part of their Lordships' instructions with that zeal and alacrity as may procure me the honour of their approbation. The marines who fell with Captain Cook were Corporal Thomas, Theophilus Hinks, John Allan, and Thomas Flabchett ; the lieutenant, serjeant, and two others wounded."

"*Monday*, 15*th February* 1779.

" As there was still a vast concourse of people where this unfortunate fray happened, I had some notion of taking a stout party on shore, make what destruction I could among them, then burn the town, canoes, etc., for I have no doubt but firearms must drive every thing before them when you take room for action ; but the officers who had been present at the fray observed, that though our musquets must in the end prove effectual, such were their numbers, resolution, and advantageous retreats behind these walls, that the attempt would doubtless cost us some, and probably many men ; that we laboured under great disadvantages in landing, which we were there obliged to do upon slippery rocks, where our people with shoes could hardly stand, and they having the fair use of the foot, were perfectly masters of themselves ; upon these considerations, as the loss of a very few men would now be most severely felt by us, I thought it would be improper and probably injurious to the expedition to risk farther loss of the people, I therefore determined to turn all endeavours towards forwarding the equipment of the 'Resolution' as we were now nearly in a tattered condition, and as soon as we were in any tolerable order, if they did not conduct themselves with some degree of propriety, to warp her within a proper distance of the town, and by landing under our own guns, thoroughly convince them that it was to our lenity, not our imbecility, that they owed their safety, so we got our fore-mast into the ship, placed it fore and aft upon the forecastle and quarter deck, and set the carpenters of both ships

to work upon it. In the evening I sent the boats of the two ships, well
manned and armed, under the command of Lieutenants King and Burney,
with a flag of truce, with orders by no means whatever to land, but advance
near enough to hold conversation and demand the bodies of our people,
particularly Captain Cook's. Upon Mr. King's arrival near the shore, and
making known his demands, they appeared quite elate with joy at the
prospect of a reconciliation, threw away their slings and mats which were
their weapons and armour, extended their arms, and in short seemed happy
in suggesting every mode of demonstrating their satisfaction. An old
fellow, whose name is Co'ah'ah, with whom we had all along been acquainted, with a white flag in his hand, swam off to the small cutter where
our flag was, and promised we should have the body of Captain Cook to-
morrow, but that it was carried too far up the country to be brought down
to-night. These assurances Mr. King likewise received from many other
people with whom he conversed by the water side.

"Mr. Burney was some little distance from Mr. King and talked with
different people. He says he clearly understood from some of them that
the body was cut up; however, from their fair promises, I hoped the
morrow would produce it in some state or the other. That we might be
as safe as possible from the machinations of these people, I ordered guard
boats to row round the ships during the darkness of the night, being under
some apprehensions of attempts upon our cables.

"*Tuesday*, 16*th February* 1779.

"In the morning old Co'ah'ah made several trips to us in a small canoe
with his white flag flying, assisted by only one man, and made many fair
promises of the bodies being returned; he brought off two or three little
pigs at different times, which, as he professed so much friendship, and
seemed to confide so much in us, I accepted.

"This evening, just after dark, a priest, whose name was Car'na'care,
a friend of Mr. King's, came on board and brought with him a large piece
of flesh, which we soon saw to be human, and which he gave us to understand was part of the corpse of our late unfortunate Captain; it was clearly
a part of the thigh, about six or eight pounds, without any bone at all.
The poor fellow told us that all the rest of the flesh had been burnt at
different places with some peculiar kind of ceremony, that this had been
delivered to him for that purpose, but as we appeared anxious to recover
the body, he had brought us all that he could get of it; he likewise added,
that the bones, which was all that now remained, were in the possession of
King Terre'aboo. The extraordinary friendship and attention of these
priests, since our first arrival amongst them, has been such as we never before met with nor could expect from any Indians, or indeed I believe I may

say from any nation of people in the world. They abound in the riches of the country, which they deal out with a most liberal hand. Our astronomers and people on shore were fairly kept by them, and they were continually sending presents of hogs, fish, fruit, etc., to both Captain Cook and myself, at the same time were so perfectly disinterested, that it was with difficulty we got them to accept of any return at all adequate to their donations. The latter end of January a party was sent up the country to look a little about them. They set out in the evening, and where they halted for the night were overtaken and joined by a man from old Ca'ha'ha's, who was the chief-priest, or as we termed him, the bishop. This good old gentleman hearing that some people were gone upon an expedition about the isle, sent this man after them with a general order that they should be supplied with whatever they wanted, wherever they thought proper to travel. This honest fellow, Car'na'care, who I believe is son to the bishop; certainly brought off this flesh with a most friendly intention ; he begs we we will put no kind of trust in the social aspects and promises of his countrymen, for that they do mean and are determined to do us farther mischief if they possibly can. Old Co'ah'ah, he says, they make use of as a spy to examine our condition of defence, etc., having some notion of attacking the ships. Here are clearly party matters subsisting between the laity and the clergy, and in these cases a strict attention to the representation of either, I believe, is generally wide of the truth ; however, we must take care not to lay ourselves so open as to render it possible for any plan of treachery to reach us ; and as to their attack upon the ships, I should imagine it must turn out to them the most unhappy expedition they ever experienced. After staying on board about two hours, Car'na'care returned to the shore, observing that regard to his safety obliged him to make his visit in the dark, for should it be publicly known they would immediately destroy him. As the command of course now devolved to me, I appointed myself to the 'Resolution ;' Mr. Gore, the first lieutenant of that ship, to the command of the 'Discovery;' Mr. King the first, Mr. Williamson the second, and Mr. William Harvey, who is now upon his third trip with Captain Cook, to be the third lieutenant of the 'Resolution.' I know nothing of any particular commands of their Lordships in case of vacancies, but have often heard Captain Cook, in private conversation, declare his intention of making Mr. Harvey a lieutenant ; and as I am perfectly ignorant of their Lordships' pleasure upon that head, I hope they will approve of my attention and respect to the memory of that great navigator, in acting consistently with his avowed purposes.

" *Wednesday, 17th February* 1779.

" Early this afternoon an impudent rascal came off from the town, on the north-west point, and having advanced to within 200 yards of the ship, waved a hat to us, which I could clearly distinguish to have been it of Captain Cook's. He then put it upon his head and flung some stones from a sling towards the ship, whilst the vast concourse of people upon the shore were shouting and laughing. This was too gross an insult to bear with any degree of patience. The rascal in his canoe, being right ahead of the ship, soon perceived the people getting into the boat, and made for the shore with too much celerity for us to come near him. I did not fire at him, as it's great odds but he was missed, which would farther show them the fallibility of our arms. However, as he was undoubtedly set on by the people on shore, who were still upon the rocks by the water side, though the ship was too far off to throw the shot with the exactitude I could wish, still we were not quite out of reach, and this multitude being a fine large mark, I fired several of the four-pounders at them, when they dispersed in a great hurry. In the evening two arees came off, and begged we would fire at them no more, and expressed their wishes for peace. I found the great shot had frightened them confoundedly, some having fell among the crowd and wounded a nephew of Terre'aboo's, whose name was Ky'mare'-mare (an old friend of mine), and three or four others, by scattering the splinters of stones among them. We now learnt there were four arees with thirteen men killed, and many others badly wounded in the fray with Captain Cook. In the morning, as I wanted some water, I ordered the 'Discovery' as near as convenient to the shore to cover the watering party, and sent the boats of the two ships properly equipped upon that duty, under the commands of the Lieutenants Rickman and Harvey, with orders not to let any of the natives come near them, but by no means to molest them if they did not first give provocation by acting offensively. Very soon after their landing, such was the strange infatuation of these people, notwithstanding they saw everything was clearly against them, they began to throw stones at the party. They, however, had the discretion in general to get behind some houses of a town that was built all along the head of the beach, or upon a high hill under which the well was situate, and from thence roll them down. Some were daring enough to come upon the open beach for the greater convenience of discharging their stones, but five or six of these being killed, put an end to this beach fighting, and they all retired behind the houses, from whence they continued to throw without ceasing, but to very little effect, for there was such a distance that, by a good look-out, they were easily avoided. At noon the boats returned.

"*Thursday*, 18*th February* 1779.

"In the afternoon the boats returned to the watering business, and, as the natives continued troublesome, we burnt down the town that was at the head of the beach, which deprived them of their principal shelter. The rogues upon the hill continued to roll down stones, and their situation was so elevated we could not possibly annoy them. However, they did us no other harm than somewhat to retard the business, as the people were under a necessity of keeping some look out to avoid the stones. In the evening they were tired of the business; many of them came to the watering party with green boughs and white flags (emblems of peace), and begged we would be friends, promising to give us no farther molestation. They were socially received, and assured of our good offices, if they would conduct themselves properly. In the morning the parties returned to the watering duty, the natives were civil and attentive, supplying them with fruits, etc.

"*Friday*, 19*th February* 1779.

"Our good friends the priests still continue their extraordinary attention and benevolence. They send us many presents of hogs, fruits, etc. By the assistance of these good people, and some poor fellows who came off in the dark and traded, being, as they say, afraid to be seen to hold connection with us, we have all along, except one day, been able to collect roots enough for our own necessary consumption. As to pork, we have abundance.

"*Saturday*, 20*th February* 1779.

"An aree of distinction came off with two hogs and a large quantity of roots, which he said was a present from Terre'aboo, who, he gave me to understand, was very desirous of peace. I told him I had very little objection to peace, but insisted they should first return the remains of Captain Cook, which he promised heartily to do. He took his leave and returned to the shore. About noon E'ar'po came to the beach with abundance of attendants, laden with roots and some hogs. I went in the pinnace, and took Mr. King in the cutter, near enough to the shore to hold conversation, and demanded the remains of Captain Cook, which he delivered to me very decently wrapped up. I then took him on board, and treated him, with three arees, his friends, socially. I asked him for the remains of the other four people; but he told me that Captain Cook, being the principal man, he of course became the property of king Terre'aboo; that the others were taken by various arees, who were now dispersed in different parts of the isle, and that it would be impossible to collect them. I thought this so probable an account, that I said no more upon the subject.

Sunday, 21*st February* 1779.

"In the evening E'ar'po and his friends returned to the shore, apparently very happy. They gave me an account of their loss of men in our various skirmishes, which amounts to four arees killed and six wounded; of their people, twenty-five killed and fifteen wounded. This is the same as I have before heard; and as it is corroborated, I suppose it is the fact. Upon examining the remains of my late honoured and much-lamented friend, I found all his bones, excepting those of the back, jaw, and feet—the two latter articles E'ar'po brought me in the morning—the former, he declared, had been reduced to ashes with the trunk of the body. As Car'na'-care had told us, the flesh was taken from all the bones, excepting those of the hands, the skin of which they had cut through in many places, and salted, with an intention, no doubt, of preserving them. E'ar'po likewise brought with him the two barrels of Captain Cook's gun—the one beat flat, with intention of making a cutting instrument of it; the other a good deal bent and bruised, together with a present of thirteen hogs from Terre'aboo. The day before it on which this miserable business happened, during the old gentleman's visit, I made him a present of a red cloth cloak, which he desired might be edged with green cloth, and left it on board with me for that purpose, proposing to come for it the next morning; but these unhappy circumstances falling out, it still remained in my possession, and he now desired E'ar'po to ask me for it, which of course I sent him, with a proper return for his present. I mention this circumstance among many others, to evince how little idea there was of this miserable breach that has happened between us. During the forenoon, I had a visit from the young prince Ka'oo'ah, who, as I have before observed, is a son of Terre'aboo's, and of course paid great attention and respect to here by all ranks of people."

Monday, 22d February 1779.

"This afternoon we have an abundant market for hogs and fruit. Both arees and people now put themselves in our power, without any kind of apprehension. They appear exceedingly desirous of resuming our former confidence and intercourse, and that with so much appearance of sincerity, that had I any point to carry, I think I might put some degree of confidence in them with great safety; but my business is now to get to sea, and quit this group of islands as soon as circumstances will admit me.

"In the evening I had the remains of Captain Cook committed to the deep, with all the attention and honour we could possibly pay in this part of the world.

We now continue the narrative of Captain King:—

On the 22d we got clear of the land about ten o'clock, and hoisting in the boats, stood to the northward.

After touching at Woahoo, where it was found watering would have been inconvenient, Captain Clerke determined, without farther loss of time, to proceed to Atooi. On the 28th we bore away for that island, which we were in sight of by noon; and about sunset, were off its eastern extremity.

We had no sooner anchored in our old station, than several canoes came alongside of us; but we could observe that they did not welcome us with the same cordiality in their manner, and satisfaction in their countenances, as when we were here before.

Our principal object here was to water the ships with the utmost expedition; and I was sent on shore early in the afternoon. We found a considerable number of people collected on the beach, who received us at first with great kindness; but as soon as we had got the casks on shore, began to be exceedingly troublesome. It was with great difficulty I was able to form a circle, according to our usual practice, for the convenience of our trading party, and had no sooner done it, than I saw a man laying hold of the bayonet of one of the soldier's muskets, and endeavouring with all his force to wrench it out of his hand. This fray was occasioned by the latter's having given the man a slight prick with his bayonet, in order to make him keep without the line.

I now perceived that our situation required great circumspection and management, and accordingly gave the strictest orders that no one should fire, nor have recourse to any other act of violence, without positive commands. As soon as I had given these directions, I was called to the assistance of the watering party, where I found the natives equally inclined to mischief. They had demanded from our people a large hatchet for every cask of water, and this not being complied with, they would not suffer the sailors to roll them down to the boats.

I had no sooner joined them, than one of the natives advanced up to me with great insolence, and made the same claim. I told him that as a friend, I was very willing to present him with a hatchet, but that I should certainly carry off the water without paying anything for it ; and I immediately ordered the pinnace men to proceed in their business, and called three marines from the traders to protect them.

Though the natives continued for the most part to pay great deference and respect to me, yet they did not suffer me to escape without contributing my share to their stock of plunder. One of them came up to me with a familiar air, and with great management diverted my attention, whilst another, wrenching the hanger, which I held carelessly in my hand, from me, ran off with it like lightning.

It was in vain to think of repelling this insolence by force ; guarding therefore against its effects in the best manner we were able, we had nothing to do but to submit patiently to it. My apprehensions were, however, a little alarmed, by the information I soon after received from the serjeant of marines, who told me that, turning suddenly round, he saw a man behind me holding a dagger in the position of striking. In case of a real attack, our whole force, however advantageously disposed, could have made but a poor resistance. On the other hand, I thought it of some consequence to show the natives we were under no fears.

At last we got every thing into the boats, and only the gunner, a seaman of the boat's crew. and myself, remained on shore.

As the pinnace lay beyond the surf, through which we were obliged to swim, I told them to make the best of their way to it, and that I should follow them.

With this order I was surprised to find them both refuse to comply, and the consequence was a contest amongst us who should be the last on shore. It seems that some hasty words I had just before used to the sailor, which he thought reflected on his courage, was the cause of this odd fancy in him; and the old gunner finding a point of honour started, thought he could not well avoid taking a part in it. In this ridiculous situation we might have remained some time, had not our dispute been soon settled by the stones that began to fly about us, and by the cries of the people from the boats to make haste, as the natives were following us into the water with clubs and spears. I reached the side of the pinnace first, and finding the gunner was at some distance behind, and not entirely out of danger, I called out to the marines to fire one musket. In the hurry of executing my orders they fired two, and when I got into the boat I saw the natives running away, and one man with a woman sitting by him, left behind on the beach. The man made several attempts to rise without being able, and it was with much regret I perceived him to be wounded in the groin.

During our absence Captain Clerke had been under the greatest anxiety for our safety. And these apprehensions were considerably increased from his having entirely mistaken the drift of the conversation he had held with some natives who had been on board. The frequent mention of the name of Captain Cook, with other strong and circumstantial descriptions of death and destruction, made him conclude that the knowledge of the unfortunate events at Owhyhee had reached them, and that these were what they alluded to, whereas, all they had in view was to make known to him the wars that had arisen in consequence of the goats that Captain Cook had left at Oneeheow, and the slaughter of the poor goats themselves, during the struggle for the property of them.

The next morning, March 2, I was again ordered on shore with the watering party. The risk we had run the preceding day determined Captain Clerke to send a considerable force from both ships for our guard, amounting in all to forty men under arms. This precaution, however, was now unnecessary, for we found the beach left entirely to ourselves, and the ground between the landing place and the lake tabooed with small white flags. We concluded from this appearance, that some of the chiefs had certainly visited this quarter, and that, not being able to stay, they had kindly and considerately taken this step for our greater security and convenience.

The next day we completed our watering without meeting with any material difficulty. On our return to the ships, we found that several chiefs had been on board, and had made excuses for the behaviour of their countrymen, attributing their riotous conduct to the quarrels which subsisted at that time amongst the principal people of the island. The quarrel had arisen about the goats we had left at Oneeheow the last year, the right of property in which was claimed by Toneoneo, on the pretence of that island's being a dependency of his.

On the 7th we were surprised with a visit from Toneoneo. When he heard the dowager princess was in the ship, it was with great difficulty we could prevail on him to come on board, not from any apprehension that he appeared to entertain of his safety, but from an unwillingness to see her. Their meeting was with sulky and lowering looks on both sides. He stayed but a short time, and seemed much dejected; but we remarked, with some surprise, that the women, both at his coming and going away, prostrated themselves before him; and that he was treated by all the natives on board with the respect usually paid to those of his rank. Indeed it must appear somewhat extraordinary that a person who was at this time in a state of actual hostility with the opposite party, and was even prepared for another battle, should trust himself almost alone within the power of his enemies.

On the 8th, at nine in the morning, we weighed and sailed toward Oneeheow, and at three in the afternoon, anchored in twenty fathoms water, nearly on the same spot as in the year 1778.

On the 12th, the weather being moderate, the master was sent to the north-west side of the island to look for a more convenient place for anchoring. He returned in the evening, having found a fine bay with good anchorage; also to the eastward were four small wells of good water, the road to them level, and fit for rolling casks.

Being now about to leave the Sandwich Islands it may be proper to make a few remarks. This group consists of eleven islands. They are called by the natives—1. Owhyhee; 2. Mowee; 3. Ranai, or Ornai; 4. Morotinnee, Morokinne; 5. Kahowrowee, or Tahoorowa; 6. Morotoi, or Morokoi; 7. Woahoo or Oahoo; 8. Atooi, Atowi, or Towi, and sometimes Kowi; 9. Neeheehow, or Oneeheow; 10. Oreehoua, or Reehoua; and, 11. Tahoora—and all are inhabited excepting Morotinnee and Tahoora. Besides the islands above enumerated, we were told by the Indians that there is another called Modoopapapa, or

Komodoopapapa, which is low and sandy, and visited only for the purpose of catching turtle and sea-fowl.

They were named by Captain Cook the Sandwich Islands, in honour of the Earl of Sandwich, under whose administration he had enriched geography with so many splendid and important discoveries.

The inhabitants of the Sandwich Islands are undoubtedly of the same race with those of New Zealand, the Society and Friendly Islands, Easter Island, and the Marquesas. This fact, which, extraordinary as it is, might be thought sufficiently proved by the striking similarity in their manners and customs, and the general resemblance of their persons, is established beyond all controversy by the absolute identity of their language.

From what continent they originally emigrated, and by what steps they have spread through so vast a space, those who are curious in disquisitions of this nature may perhaps not find it very difficult to conjecture. It has been already observed, that they bear strong marks of affinity to some of the Indian tribes that inhabit the Ladrones and Caroline Islands; and the same affinity may again be traced amongst the Battas and the Malays. When these events happened is not so easy to ascertain; it was probably not very lately, as they are extremely populous, and have no tradition of their own origin but what is perfectly fabulous.

They are in general above the middle size, and well made. Their complexion is rather darker than that of the Otaheiteans, and they are not altogether so handsome a people. However, many of both sexes had fine open countenances, and the women in particular had good eyes and teeth, and a sweetness and sensibility of look, which rendered them very engaging. Their hair is of a brownish black, and neither uniformly straight, like that of the Indians of America, nor uniformly curling, as amongst the African negroes, but varying in this respect like the hair of Europeans.

The same superiority that is observable in the persons of the earees, through all the other islands, is found also here. Those whom we saw were, without exception, perfectly well formed; whereas the lower sort, besides their general inferiority are subject to all the variety of make and figure that is seen in the populace of other countries.

They seem to have few native diseases among them, but many of the earees suffer dreadfully from the immoderate use of the ava. There is something very singular in the history of this pernicious drug. When Captain Cook first visited the Society Islands, it was very little known among them. On his second voyage, he found the use of it very prevalent at Ulietea, but it had still gained very little ground at Otaheite. When we were last there, the dreadful havoc it had made was beyond belief, insomuch that the Captain scarcely knew many of his old acquaintances. At the Friendly Islands it is also constantly drunk by the chiefs, but so much diluted with water that it does not appear to produce any bad effects. At Atooi also it is used with great moderation, and the chiefs are, in consequence a much finer set of men there than in any of the neighbouring islands. Our good friends, Kaireekeea and old Kaoo, were persuaded by us to refrain from it; and they recovered amazingly during the short time we afterward remained in the island.

Notwithstanding the irreparable loss we suffered from the sudden resentment and violence of these people, yet, in justice to their general conduct, it must be acknowledged that they are of the most mild and affectionate disposition, equally remote from the extreme levity and fickleness of the Otaheiteans, and the distant gravity and reserve of the inhabitants of the Friendly Islands. They appear to live in the utmost harmony and friendship with one another. The women who had children were remarkable for their tender and constant attention to them; and the men would often lend their assistance in those domestic offices with a willingness that does credit to their feelings.

The inhabitants of these islands differ from those of the Friendly Isles, in suffering, almost universally, their beards to grow. There were indeed a few, amongst whom was the old king, that cut it off entirely, and others that wore it only upon the upper lip. The same variety in the manner of wearing the hair is also observable here as among the other islanders of the South Sea; besides which they have a fashion, as far as we know, peculiar to themselves. They cut it close on each side of the head down to the ears.

Both sexes wear necklaces made of strings of small variegated shells, and an ornament, in the form of the handle of a cup, about two inches long, and half an inch broad, made of wood, stone, or ivory, finely polished, which is hung about the neck by fine threads of twisted hair, doubled sometimes a hundred fold. Instead of this ornament, some of them wear on their breast a small human figure made of bone, suspended in the same manner.

The custom of tatooing the body they have in common with the rest of the natives of the South Sea islands, but it is only at New Zealand and the Sandwich Islands that they tatoo the face. They have a singular custom amongst them, the meaning of which we could never learn—that of tatooing the tip of the tongues of the females.

The dress of the men generally consists only of a piece of thick cloth, called the maro, about ten or twelve inches broad, which they pass between the legs, and tie round the waist. This is the common dress of all ranks of people. Their mats, some of which are beautifully manufactured, are of various sizes, but mostly about five feet long and four broad. These they throw over their shoulders, and bring forward before; but they are seldom used, except in time of war, for which purpose they seem better adapted than for ordinary use, and capable of breaking the blow of a stone, or any blunt weapon.

The common dress of the women bears a close resemblance to that of the men. They wrap round the waist a piece of cloth that reaches half way down the thighs, and sometimes in the cool of the evening they appear with loose pieces of fine cloth thrown over their shoulders, like the women of Otaheite. The pau is another dress very frequently worn by the younger part of the sex. It is made of the thinnest and finest sort of cloth, wrapt several times round the waist, and descending to the leg, so as to have the appearance of a full short petticoat.

The way of spending their time appears to be very simple, and to admit of little variety. They rise with the sun, and after enjoying the cool of the evening, retire to rest a few hours after sunset. The making of canoes and mats forms the occupation of the earees; the women are employed in manufacturing cloth, and the towtows are principally engaged in the plantations and fishing.

Their music is of a rude kind, having neither flutes nor reeds, nor instruments of any other sort that we saw, except drums of various sizes. But their songs, which they sung in parts, and accompany with a gentle motion of the arms, in the same manner as the Friendly Islanders, had a very pleasing effect.

They are manifestly divided into three classes. The first are the earees, or chiefs of each district, one of whom is superior to the rest, and is called at Owhyhee earee-taboo and earee-moee. By the first of these words they express his absolute authority; and by the latter all are obliged to prostrate themselves (or put themselves to sleep, as the word signifies) in his presence. The second class are those who appear to enjoy a right of property without authority. The third are the towtows, or servants, who have neither rank nor property.

The chiefs exercise their power over one another in the most haughty and oppressive manner. Of this I shall give two instances. A chief of the lower order had behaved with great civility to one of our officers, and in return I carried him on board and introduced him to Captain Cook, who invited him to dine with us. While we were at table, Pareea, who was chief of a superior order, entered, whose face but too plainly manifested his indignation at seeing our guest in so honourable a situation. He immediately seized him by the hair of the head, and was proceeding to drag him out of the cabin when the Captain interfered, and, after a deal of altercation, all the indulgence we could obtain, without coming to a quarrel with Pareea, was, that our guest should be suffered to remain, being seated upon the floor, whilst Pareea filled his place at the table. At another time, when Terreeoboo first came on board the "Resolution," Maiha-maiha, who attended him, finding Pareea on deck, turned him out of the ship in the most ignominious manner.

Their religion resembles, in most of its principal features, that of the Society and Friendly Islands. Their morais, their whattas, their idols, their sacrifices, and their sacred songs, all of which they have in common with each other, are convincing proofs that their religious notions are derived from the same source.

It has been mentioned that the title of Orona, with all its honours, was given to Captain Cook; and it is also certain that they regarded us generally as a race of people superior to themselves, and used often to say that the great Eatooa dwelt in our country.

Human sacrifices are more frequent here, according to the account of the natives themselves, than in any other islands we visited. These horrid rites are not only had recourse to upon the commencement of war, and preceding great battles, and other signal enterprises, but the death of any considerable chief calls for a sacrifice of one or more towtows, according to his rank; and we were told that men were destined to suffer on the death of Terreeoboo.

To this class of their customs may also be referred that of knocking out their fore-teeth, as a propitiatory sacrifice to the Eatooa to avert any danger or mischief to which they might be exposed.

Return to England, March 1779.

On the 15th of March 1779, at seven in the morning, we weighed anchor, and passing to the north of Tahoora, stood on to the south-west.

[But it is unnecessary to follow minutely the remainder of Captain King's Journal.] After visiting the coast of Kamtschatka and receiving great kindness from the Russian officials, we continued, he says, to steer northward, with a moderate southerly breeze and fair weather, till the 13th July at ten in the forenoon, when we again found ourselves close in with a solid field of ice, to which we could see no limits from the masthead. This at once dashed all our hopes of penetrating farther.

Captain Clerke now resolved to make one more and final attempt on the American coast for Baffin's or Hudson's Bay, since we had been able to advance the furthest on this side last year.

On the 16th, in the forenoon, we found ourselves embayed, the ice having taken a sudden turn to the south-east, and in one compact body surrounding us on all sides, except on the south quarter. We therefore hauled our wind to the southward, being at this time in twenty-six fathoms water, and, as we supposed, about twenty-five leagues from the coast of America.

At eight in the morning of the 21st, the wind freshening and the fog clearing away, we saw the American coast to the south-east, at the distance of eight or ten leagues, and hauled in for it, but were again stopped by the ice, and obliged to bear away to the westward along the edge of it. Thus a connected solid field of ice, rendering every effort we could make to a nearer approach to the land fruitless, and joining, as we judged, to it, we took a farewell of a north-east passage to Old England.*

I shall beg leave to give, in Captain Clerke's own words, the reasons of this his final determination, as well as of his future plans; and this the rather, as it is the last transaction his death permitted him to write down.

"It is now impossible to proceed the least farther to the northward upon this coast (America); and it is equally as improbable that this amazing mass of ice should be dissolved by the few re-

* This was first accomplished three quarters of a century afterwards by Sir Robert M'Clure. The highest latitude attained by Captain Clerke appears to have been 71° 56' N., which is to the northward of Icy Cape.

maining summer weeks which will terminate this season; but it will continue, it is to be believed, as it now is, an insurmountable barrier to every attempt we can possibly make. I therefore think it the best step that can be taken for the good of the service, to trace the sea over to the Asiatic coast, and to try if I can find any opening that will admit me farther north; if not, to see what more is to be done upon that coast, where I hope, yet cannot much flatter myself, to meet with better success, for the sea is now so choked with ice, that a passage, I fear, is totally out of the question."

Captain Clerke therefore determined, for the reasons just assigned, to give up all further attempts on the coast of America, and to make his last efforts in search of a passage on the coast of the opposite continent. In this also he was disappointed.

As he found a farther advance to the northward, as well as a nearer approach to either continent, obstructed by a sea blocked up with ice, this, added to the representations of Captain Gore, determined Captain Clerke to sail for Awatska Bay, to repair our damages there; and, before the winter should set in, to explore the coast of Japan.

I will not endeavour to conceal the joy that brightened the countenances of every individual, as soon as Captain Clerke's resolutions were made known. We were all heartily sick of a navigation full of danger, and in which the utmost perseverance had not been repaid with the smallest probability of success. We therefore turned our faces home, after an absence of three years, with a delight and satisfaction which, notwithstanding the tedious voyage we had still to make, and the immense distance we had to run, were as freely entertained, and perhaps as fully enjoyed, as if we had been already in sight of the Land's End.

Third Voyage. 399

Captain Clerke was now no longer able to get out of his bed; and on the 22d of August 1779, at nine o'clock in the morning, he departed this life, in the thirty-eighth year of his age. He died of a consumption which had evidently commenced before he left England, and of which he had lingered during the whole voyage. His very gradual decay had long made him a melancholy object to his friends; yet the equanimity with which he bore it, the constant flow of good spirits, which continued to the last hour, and a cheerful resignation to his fate, afforded them some consolation. It was impossible not to feel a more than common degree of compassion for a person whose whole life had been a continued scene of those difficulties and hardships to which a seaman's occupation is subject, and under which he at last sunk. He was brought up to the navy from his earliest youth, and had been in several actions during the war which began in 1756; particularly in that between the "Bellona" and "Courageux," where being stationed in the mizen top, he was carried overboard with the mast, but was taken up without having received any hurt. He was midshipman in the "Dolphin," commanded by Commodore Byron, on her first voyage round the world, and afterwards served on the American station. In 1768, he made his second voyage round the world in the "Endeavour," as master's mate, and, by the promotion which took place during the expedition, he returned a lieutenant. His third voyage round the world was in the "Resolution," of which he was appointed the second lieutenant; and soon after his return in 1775, he was promoted to the rank of master and commander. When the present expedition was ordered to be fitted out, he was appointed to the "Discovery," to accompany Captain Cook, and by the death of the latter, succeeded, as has been already mentioned, to the chief command.

It would be doing his memory extreme injustice not to say, that during the short time the expedition was under his direction, he was most zealous and anxious for its success. His health, about the time the principal command devolved upon him, began to decline very rapidly, and was every way unequal to encounter the rigours of a high northern climate. But the vigour and activity of his mind had in no shape suffered by the decay of his body; and though he knew that, by delaying his return to a warmer climate, he was giving up the only chance that remained for his recovery, yet careful and jealous to the last degree, that a regard to his own situation should never bias his judgment to the prejudice of the service, he persevered in the search of a passage till it was the opinion of every officer in both ships that it was impracticable, and that any farther attempts would not only be fruitless but dangerous.

Next day we anchored in the harbour of St. Peter and St. Paul, when our old friend the serjeant, who was still the commander of the place, came on board with a present of berries, intended for our poor deceased captain. He was exceedingly affected when we told him of his death, and showed him the coffin that contained his body. He signified his intention of sending off an express to the commander of Bolcheretsk, to acquaint him with our arrival, and Captain Gore availed himself of that occasion of writing him a letter, in which he requested that sixteen head of black cattle might be sent with all possible expedition.

In the morning of the 25th, Captain Gore made out the new commissions, in consequence of Captain Clerke's death; appointing himself to the command of the "Resolution," and me to the command of the "Discovery," and Mr. Lanyan, master's mate of the "Resolution," who had served in that capacity on board the "Adventure" in the former voyage, was promoted to the vacant lieutenancy. These promotions produced several other arrangements of course. On Sunday afternoon, August the 29th, we paid the last offices to Captain Clerke. The officers and men of both ships walked in procession to the grave, whilst the ships fired minute guns; and the service being ended, the marines fired three volleys. He was interred under a tree, which stands on a rising ground in a valley to the north side of the harbour, where the hospital and store-houses are situated. All the Russians in the garrison were assembled, and attended with great respect and solemnity.*

* The following is the Monumental Inscription at Kamtschatka, to the Memory of Captain Clerke :—

"At the foot of this tree lies the body of Captain Charles Clerke, Esq., who succeeded to the command of His Britannic Majesty's ships, the "Resolution" and "Discovery," on the death of Captain James Cook, Esq. (who was unfortunately killed by the natives at an island in the South Sea, on the 14th of February, in the year 1779). He died at sea of a lingering consumption on the 22d of August in the same year, aged 38."

Underneath his escutcheon in the church of Paratoolka, is the following Inscription :

"The above is the escutcheon of Captain Charles Clerke, Esq. He succeeded to the command of His Britannic Majesty's ships, the "Resolution" and "Discovery," on the death of Captain James Cook, Esq. (who was unfortunately killed by the natives at an island in the South Sea, on the 14th of February 1779, after having explored the coast of America from 42° 30', to 70° 44' latitude, in search of a passage from Asia to Europe). Captain Clerke died of a lingering consumption at sea, on the 22d of August 1779, aged 38 years, and lies buried at the foot of a tree near the Ostrog of St. Peter and St. Paul. He had made the second attempt in search of a passage from Asia to Europe, and penetrated as far to the north, within a few miles, as Captain Cook, but found any further progress that way impracticable."

Extract from Captain Gore's Log, 1779-80.—*Records, Admiralty, Whitehall.*

Our instructions from the Board of Admiralty having left a discretionary power with the commanding officer of the expedition, in case of failure in the search of a passage from the Pacific into the Atlantic Ocean, to return to England by whatever route he should think best for the farther improvement of geography, Captain Gore demanded of the principal officers their sentiments in writing respecting the manner in which these orders might most effectually be obeyed. The result of our opinions, which he had the satisfaction to find unanimous, and entirely coinciding with his own, that the condition of the ships, of the sails and cordage, made it unsafe to attempt, at so advanced a season of the year, to navigate the sea between Japan and Asia, which would otherwise have afforded the largest field for discovery; that it was therefore advisable to keep to the eastward of that island, and in our way thither to run along the Kuriles, and examine more particularly the islands that lie nearest the northern coast of Japan, which are represented as of a considerable size, and independent of the Russian and Japanese governments. Should we be so fortunate as to find in these any safe and commodious harbours, we conceived they might be of importance, either as places of shelter for any future navigators who may be employed in exploring these seas, or as the means of opening a commercial intercourse among the neighbouring dominions of the two empires. Our next object was to survey the coast of the Japanese Islands, and afterwards to make the coast of China, as far to the northward as we were able, and run along it to Macao.

This plan being adopted, I received orders from Captain Gore, in case of separation, to proceed immediately to Macao; and, at six o'clock in the evening of the 9th of October, having cleared the entrance of Awatska Bay, we steered to the south-east.

After experiencing very blowing weather and adverse winds, which put us out of the course originally intended, at day-break of the 26th we had the pleasure of descrying high land to the westward, which proved to be Japan.

From the 29th of October to the 5th of November, we continued our course to the south-east, having very unsettled weather, attended with much lightning and rain. On both days we passed great quantities of pumice stone, several pieces of which we took up and found to weigh from one ounce to three pounds. We conjectured that these stones had been thrown into the sea by eruptions of various dates, as many of them were covered with barnacles, and others quite bare.

Captain Gore now directed his course to the west south-west for the Bashee Islands, hoping to procure at them such a supply of refreshments as would help to shorten his stay at Macao; but unfortunately he overshot them, from an inaccuracy in the chart to which he trusted.

In the forenoon of the 29th we passed several Chinese fishing boats, who eyed us with great indifference. Being now nearly in the latitude of the Lema Islands, we bore away west by north, and, after running twenty-two miles, saw one of them nine or ten leagues to the westward.

In the morning of the 30th we ran along the Lema Isles. At nine o'clock a Chinese boat, which had been before with the "Resolution," came alongside, and wanted to put on board us a pilot, which, however, we declined, as it was our business to follow our consort.

We rejoiced to see the "Resolution" soon after fire a gun, and hoist her colours as a signal for a pilot. On repeating the signal we saw an excellent race between four Chinese boats;

and Captain Gore, having engaged with the man who arrived first to carry the ship to the Typa for thirty dollars, sent me word that as we could easily follow, that expense might be saved to us. Soon after a second pilot, getting on board the "Resolution," insisted on conducting the ship, and, without farther ceremony, laid hold of the wheel, and began to order the sails to be trimmed. This occasioned a violent dispute, which at last was compromised by agreeing to go shares in the money.

In obedience to the instructions given to Captain Cook by the Board of Admiralty, it now became necessary to demand of the officers and men their journals, and what other papers they might have in their possession, relating to the history of our voyage. The execution of these orders seemed to require some delicacy as well as firmness. As soon, therefore, as I had assembled the ship's company on deck, I acquainted them with the orders we had received, and the reasons which I thought ought to induce them to yield a ready obedience. At the same time I told them that any papers which they were desirous not to have sent to the Admiralty should be sealed up in their presence, and kept in my own custody, till the intentions of the Board, with regard to the publication of the history of the voyage, were fulfilled, after which they should faithfully be restored back to them.

It is with the greatest satisfaction I can relate that my proposals met with the approbation and the cheerful compliance both of the officers and men; and I am persuaded that every scrap of paper containing any transactions relating to the voyage were given up. Indeed, it is doing bare justice to the seamen of this ship to declare, that they were the most obedient and the best disposed men I ever knew, though almost all of them were very young, and had never before served in a ship of war.

We kept working to windward till six in the evening, when we came to anchor on the 1st of December.

In the evening of the 2d, Captain Gore sent me on shore to visit the Portuguese governor, and to request his assistance in procuring refreshments for our crews. At the same time I took a list of the naval stores, of which both vessels were greatly in want, with an intention of proceeding immediately to Canton and applying to the servants of the East India Company, who were at that time resident there. On my arrival at the citadel, the fort-major informed me that the governor was sick, and not able to see company. On my acquainting the major with my desire of proceeding immediately to Canton, he told me that they could not venture to furnish me with a boat till leave was obtained from the hoppo or officer of the customs, and that the application for this purpose must be made to the Chinese government at Canton.

The mortification I felt at meeting with this unexpected delay could only be equalled by the extreme impatience with which we had so long waited for an opportunity of receiving intelligence from Europe. It often happens that, in the eager pursuit of an object, we overlook the easiest and most obvious means of attaining it. This was actually my case at present, for I was returning under great dejection to the ship, when the Portuguese officer who attended me, asked me if I did not mean to visit the English gentlemen at Macao. I need not add with what transport I received the information this question conveyed to me; nor the anxious hopes and fears, the conflict between curiosity and apprehension, which passed in my mind, as we walked toward the house of one of our countrymen.

In this state of agitation, it is not surprising that our reception, though no way deficient in civility or kindness, should appear cold and formal. In our inquiries, as far as they related to objects of private concern, we met, as was indeed to be expected, with little or no satisfaction; but the events of a public nature, which had happened since our departure, now, for the first time, burst all at once upon us, overwhelmed every other feeling, and left us for some time almost without the power of reflection.

On the 9th, Captain Gore received an answer from the Committee of the English supercargoes at Canton, in which they assured him that their best endeavours should be used to procure the supplies we stood in need of as expeditiously as possible, and that a passport should be sent for one of his officers.

The following day an English merchant, from one of our settlements in the East Indies, applied to Captain Gore for the assistance of a few hands to navigate a vessel he had purchased at Macao up to Canton. Captain Gore judging this a good opportunity for me to proceed to that place, gave orders that I should take along with me my second lieutenant, the lieutenant of marines, and ten seamen. Though this was not precisely the mode in which I could have wished to visit Canton, yet, as it was very uncertain when the passport might arrive, and my presence might contribute materially to the expediting of our supplies, I did not hesitate to put myself on board.

I reached Canton on the 18th a little after it was dark, and landed at the English factory, where, though my arrival was very unexpected, I was received with every mark of attention and civility. Wishing to make my stay as short as possible, I requested the gentlemen to procure boats for me the next day to convey the stores; but I was soon informed that a business of that kind was not to be transacted so rapidly in this country, that many forms were to be complied with, and, in short, that patience was an indispensable virtue in China.

I waited several days for the event of our application, without understanding that the matter was at all advanced toward a conclusion. Whilst I was doubting what measures to pursue, the commander of a country ship brought me a letter from Captain Gore, in which he acquainted me that he had engaged him to bring us down from Canton, and to deliver the stores we had procured at his own risk in the Typa.

In the evening of the 26th I took my leave of the supercargoes, having thanked them for their many obliging favours, amongst which I must not forget to mention a handsome present of tea for the use of the ship's companies, and a large collection of English periodical publications. The latter we found a valuable acquisition, as they both served to amuse our impatience during our tedious voyage home, and enabled us to return not total strangers to what had been transacting in our native country. At one o'clock the next morning we left Canton, and arrived at Macao about the same hour the day following, having passed down a channel which lies to the westward of that by which we had come up.

During our absence a brisk trade had been carrying on with the Chinese for the sea-otter skins, which had every day been rising in their value. One of our seamen sold his stock alone for eight hundred dollars; and a few prime skins, which were clean and had been well preserved, were sold for one hundred and twenty each. The whole amount of the value in specie and goods that was got for the furs in both ships, I am confident did not fall short of £2000 sterling; and it was generally supposed that at least two-thirds of the quantity we had originally got from the

Americans were spoiled and worn out, or had been given away and otherwise disposed of in Kamtschatka.

The rage with which our seamen were possessed to return to Cook's River, and buy another cargo of skins to make their fortunes at one time was not far short of mutiny.

The barter which had been carrying on with the Chinese for our sea-otter skins had produced a very whimsical change in the dress of all our crew. On our arrival here nothing could exceed the ragged appearance both of the younger officers and seamen, for as our voyage had already exceeded, by near a twelvemonth, the time it was at first imagined we should remain at sea, almost the whole of our original stock of European clothes had been long worn out, or patched up with skins, and the various manufactures we had met with in the course of our discoveries. These were now again mixed and eked out with the gaudiest silks and cottons of China.

On the 12th of January 1780, at noon, we unmoored and scaled the guns, which on board my ship now amounted to ten ; so that, by means of four additional ports, we could, if occasion required, fight seven on a side.

We thought it our duty to provide ourselves with these means of defence, though we had some reasons to believe, from the public prints last received at Canton, that the generosity of our enemies had in a great measure rendered them superfluous. As this intelligence was farther confirmed by the private letters of several of the supercargoes, Captain Gore thought himself bound, in return for the liberal exceptions made in our favour, to refrain from availing himself of any opportunities of capture which these might afford, and to preserve throughout his voyage the strictest neutrality.

Third Voyage.   409

At two in the afternoon on the 13th, having got under sail, the "Resolution" saluted the fort of Macao with eleven guns, which was returned with the same number.

In the morning of the 20th we steered for Pulo Condore; and at half-past twelve we got sight of the island. As soon as we were come to anchor, Captain Gore fired a gun with a view of apprizing the natives of our arrival, and drawing them towards the shore, but without effect. Early in the morning of the 21st, parties were sent to cut wood, which was Captain Gore's principal motive for coming hither.

We were now conducted to the town, which consists of between twenty and thirty houses, built close together.

By means of my money, and pointing at different objects in sight, I had no difficulty in making a man who seemed to be the principal person of the company to which we were introduced, comprehend the main business of our errand, and I as readily understood from him that the chief or captain was absent, but would soon return; and that, without his consent, no purchases of any kind could be made.

Having at last procured a supply of buffaloes and some fat hogs, on the 28th of January 1780 we unmoored; and, as soon as we were clear of the harbour, steered south south-west.

On the 5th February we approached the coast of Sumatra. The country is covered with wood down to the water's edge, and the shores are so low, that the sea overflows the land, and washes the trunks of the trees. To this flat and marshy situation of the shore, we may attribute those thick fogs and vapours which we perceived every morning, not without dread and horror, hanging over the island, till they were dispersed by the rays of the sun. The shores of Banca, which are opposite, are much bolder; and the country inland rises to a moderate height, and appears to be well wooded throughout.

In the morning of the 9th, I received orders from Captain Gore to make sail towards a Dutch ship which now hove in sight to the southward, and which we supposed to be from Europe; and, according to the nature of the intelligence we could procure from her, either to join him at Cracatoa, where he intended to stop for the purpose of supplying the ships with arrack, or to proceed to the south-east end of Prince's Island, and there take in our water and wait for him.

I accordingly bore down towards the Dutch ship, which soon after came to an anchor to the eastward; and having got as near her as the tide would permit, we also dropt anchor.

Next morning Mr. Williamson got on board the ship, and learnt that she had been seven months from Europe, and three from the Cape of Good Hope; that, before she sailed, France and Spain had declared war against Great Britain; and that she left Sir Edward Hughes with a squadron of men of war and a fleet of East India ships at the Cape. I immediately sent a boat to acquaint Captain Gore with the intelligence we had received.

At three o'clock in the morning of the 12th we stood over for Prince's Island, and came to an anchor within half a mile of the shore. Lieutenant Lanyan, who had been here before with Captain Cook, in the year 1770, was sent along with the master to look for the watering-place.

The natives, who came to us soon after we anchored, brought a plentiful supply of large fowls and some turtles; but the last, for the most part, were very small.

On the 19th, being favoured by a breeze from the north-west, we broke ground, and the next day had entirely lost sight of this place.

Of this island I shall only observe, that we were exceedingly struck with the great general resemblance of the natives, both in figure, colour, manners, and even language, to the nations we had been so much conversant with in the South Seas.

From the time of our entering these Straits, we began to experience the powerful effects of this pestilential climate. Two of our people fell dangerously ill of malignant putrid fevers, which, however, we prevented from spreading, by putting the patients apart from the rest in the most airy berths; and we had the singular satisfaction of escaping from these fatal seas without the loss of a single life; probably owing to the vigorous health of the crews, and the strict attention now become habitual in our men, to the salutary regulations introduced amongst us by Captain Cook.

It had hitherto been Captain Gore's intention to proceed directly to St. Helena, without stopping at the Cape, but the rudder of the "Resolution" having been reported to be in a dangerous state, he resolved to steer immediately for the Cape, as the most eligible place both for the recovery of the sick and for the repair of the rudder.

In the forenoon of the 10th of April, a ship was seen bearing down to us, which proved to be an English East-India Packet, that had left Table Bay three days before, and was cruising with orders for the China fleet and other India ships.

The next morning we stood into Simon's Bay. We found lying here the "Nassau" and "Southampton" East Indiamen, waiting for convoy for Europe. The "Resolution" saluted the fort with eleven guns, and the same number was returned.

Mr. Brandt, the governor of this place, came to visit us as soon as we had anchored. He appeared much surprised to see our crew in so healthy a condition, as the Dutch ship that had left Macao on our arrival there, and had touched at the Cape some time before, reported that we were in a most wretched state, having only fourteen hands left on board the "Resolution," and seven on board the "Discovery." It is not easy to conceive the motive these people could have had for propagating so wanton and malicious a falsehood.

On the 15th I accompanied Captain Gore to Cape Town, and the next morning we waited on Baron Pletenberg, the governor, by whom we were received with every possible attention and civility. Both he and Mr. Brandt had conceived a great personal affection for Captain Cook, as well as the highest admiration of his character, and heard the recital of his misfortune with many expressions of unaffected sorrow.

During our stay at the Cape we met with every proof of the most friendly disposition towards us, both in the governor and principal persons of the place, as well Africans as Europeans.

Having completed our victualling, and furnished ourselves with the necessary supply of naval stores, we sailed out of the bay on the 9th of May.

On the 12th of June we passed the equator for the fourth time during this voyage.

On the 12th of August we made the western coast of Ireland; and, after a fruitless attempt to get into Port Galway, from whence it was Captain Gore's intention to have sent the journals and maps of our voyage to London, we were obliged, by strong southerly winds, to steer to the northward. Our next object was to put into Lough Swilly; but the wind continuing in the same quarter, we stood on to the northward of Lewis Island; and on the 22d of August, at eleven in the morning, both ships came to an anchor at Stromness. From hence I was dispatched by Captain

Third Voyage. 413

Gore to acquaint the Board of Admiralty with our arrival; and on the 4th day of October the ships arrived safe at the Nore, after an absence of four years two months and twenty-two days.

On quitting the "Discovery" at Stromness, I had the satisfaction of leaving the whole crew in perfect health, and, at the same time, the number of convalescents on board the "Resolution" did not exceed two or three, of whom only one was incapable of service. In the course of our voyage the "Resolution" lost but five men by sickness, three of whom were in a precarious state of health at our departure from England; the "Discovery" did not lose a man. An unremitting attention to the regulations established by Captain Cook, with which the world is already acquainted, may be justly considered as the principal cause, under the blessing of Divine Providence, of this singular success. But the baneful effects of salt provisions might, perhaps, in the end have been felt, notwithstanding these salutary precautions, if we had not assisted them, by availing ourselves of every substitute our situation at various times afforded. These frequently consisting of articles which our people had not been used to consider as food for men, and being sometimes exceedingly nauseous, it required the joint aid of persuasion, authority, and example, to conquer their prejudices and disgust.

The preventives we principally relied on were sour krout and portable soup. As to the anti-scorbutic remedies, with which we were amply supplied, we had no opportunity of trying their effects, as there did not appear the slightest symptoms of the scurvy in either ship during the whole voyage. Our malt and hops had also been kept as a resource in case of actual sickness; and on examination at the Cape of Good Hope were found entirely spoiled.

About the same time were opened some casks of biscuit,

flour, pease, oatmeal, and groats, which, by way of experiment, had been put up in small casks, lined with tin-foil, and found all, except the pease, in a much better state than could have been expected in the usual manner of package.

I cannot neglect this opportunity of recommending to the consideration of government the necessity of allowing a sufficient quantity of Peruvian bark to such of His Majesty's ships as may be exposed to the influence of unwholesome climates. It happened very fortunately in the "Discovery," that only one of the men, who had fevers in the Straits of Sunda, stood in need of this medicine, as he alone consumed the whole quantity usually carried out by surgeons in such vessels as ours. Had more been affected in the same manner, they would probably all have perished from the want of the only remedy capable of affording them effectual relief.

Another circumstance attending this voyage, which, if we consider its duration and the nature of the service in which we were engaged, will appear scarcely less singular than the extraordinary healthiness of the crews, was, that the two ships never lost sight of each other for a day together, except twice, which was owing, the first time, to an accident that happened to the "Discovery" off the coast of Owhyhee, and the second, to the fogs we met with at the entrance of Awatska Bay. A stronger proof cannot be given of the skill and vigilance of our subaltern officers, to whom this share of merit almost entirely belongs.

Thus ended a voyage distinguished by the extent and importance of its discoveries. Besides other inferior islands, it added that fine group called the Sandwich Islands to the former known limits of the terraqueous globe, and ascertained the proximity of the two great continents of Asia and America.

Third Voyage.

This enterprise proved fatal to its principal conductors—Captains Cook and Clerke, as we have seen, never returned. Captain King, with a constitution broken by climate and fatigue, lived indeed to publish the voyage which will immortalize his name; but he soon after fell a martyr to what he had undergone in the service of his country. He died at Nice, whither he had retired for the mild salubrity of the air, in the autumn of 1784; and though cut off in the bloom of life, left a name covered with honour and remembered with regret. He was the fourth son of the Dean of Raphoe in Ireland, but of an English family.

Having come to a conclusion of the voyages in which the genius and talents of that great navigator Captain Cook are so pre-eminently displayed, we cannot omit the opportunity of gratifying a propensity which our readers must naturally feel of being made acquainted with what family he left behind him, and how the dispensations of Providence may have disposed of them; but in doing this, sorry are we to say, that we impose on ourselves a very painful duty, for we are unfortunately compelled to relate a tale of woe, melancholy and distressing in the extreme.

When he set out on his last voyage, Captain Cook's family consisted of his wife and three sons, the second of whom was lost on board the "Thunderer" man of war, about six months after the unfortunate death of his father. The eldest son, who was appointed master and commander of the "Spitfire" sloop of war, while she lay off Poole waiting for hands, in attempting to get on board, was driven to sea in a boat during the night in a heavy gale of wind, and he and every person in the boat perished. But what considerably aggravates this misfortune is, as was afterwards disclosed by one of the sailors on board the vessel, that in their distress they were met by a revenue cutter, the hands of which threw them a rope, and lay to till they could bale their boat, or the fury of the wind should cease. But the master of the cutter, who was then in bed, was no sooner made acquainted with these circumstances, and that it was a king's boat, than, with an oath, he ordered his men immediately to set them adrift, and in that situation they were left to be overwhelmed by a tempestuous sea.

His body was afterwards found, and conveyed to Spithead on board his own vessel, whence it was conveyed to Cambridge, and buried by the side of the youngest brother, who had suddenly died of a fever, and whose funeral he had attended only about six weeks before.

Thus was a tender mother prematurely deprived of her husband and children, and left to mourn their untimely fates, which had so powerful an effect upon her mind as to reduce Mrs. Cook to a mere shadow of what she was formerly.

One thing yet remains to be done,—a public monument to Captain Cook, and one worthy of his great achievements, the benefits he has rendered to mankind, and the lustre shed by his name on the navy of England,—some noble lighthouse in the pathway of ships of all nations, which may lead them safely to their respective havens; or, if this cannot be, at least a statue in Trafalgar Square, where Dr. Jenner and Sir Charles Napier are most grievously out of place, occupying, as they do, the site of statues of Collingwood, Hardy, St. Vincent, Howe, Duncan, etc.

The only memorial to Cook at present is at Cambridge, and is as follows :—

Inscription on the Tablet near the Communion Table in the church of St. Andrew's the Great, Cambridge—

IN MEMORY OF
CAPTAIN JAMES COOK, OF THE ROYAL NAVY.

One of the most celebrated Navigators that this or former ages can boast, Who was killed by the natives of *Owyhee*, In the *Pacific Ocean*, on the 14th day of February 1779, In the 51st year of his age.

Of Mr. NATHANIEL COOK, who was lost with the *Thunderer* man-of-war, *Captain Boyle Walsingham*, in a most dreadful hurricane in October 1780, aged 16 years.

Of Mr. HUGH COOK, of *Christ's College, Cambridge*, who died on the 21st December 1793; aged 17 years.

Of JAMES COOK, Esq., Commander in the Royal Navy, who lost his life on the 25th January 1794, in going from *Poole* to the *Spitfire* sloop-of-war; which he commanded; in the 31st year of his age.

Of ELIZABETH COOK, who died April 9th, 1771; aged 4 years.

JOSEPH COOK, who died September 13th, 1768; aged 1 month.

GEORGE COOK, who died October 1st, 1772; aged 4 months.

All children of the first-mentioned Captain James Cook, by Elizabeth Cook, who survived her husband 56 years, and departed this life 13th May 1835, at her residence, Clapham, Surrey, in the 94th year of her age. Her remains are deposited with those of her sons, James and Hugh, in the middle aisle of this church.

Inscription on the Slab in the floor of the middle aisle of the same church —

Mr. HUGH COOK,
Died 21st December 1793;
Aged 17 years.
JAMES COOK, Esq.,
Died 25th January 1794;
Aged 31 years.
Also,
ELIZABETH COOK, their Mother,
Obit. 13th May 1835;
ÆTAT. 93.

www.ingramcontent.com/pod-product-compliance
Lightning Source LLC
Chambersburg PA
CBHW020533300426
44111CB00008B/652